When Did Southern Segregation Begin?

HISTORIANS AT WORK

Advisory Editor
Edward Countryman, Southern Methodist University

How Did American Slavery Begin?
Edward Countryman, Southern Methodist University

What Caused the Pueblo Revolt of 1680?
David J. Weber, Southern Methodist University

What Did the Declaration Declare?
Joseph J. Ellis, Mount Holyoke College

What Did the Constitution Mean to Early Americans?
Edward Countryman, Southern Methodist University

*Whose Right to Bear Arms Did the Second
Amendment Protect?*
Saul Cornell, The Ohio State University

Does the Frontier Experience Make America Exceptional?
Richard W. Etulain, University of New Mexico

What Were the Causes of the Civil War?
Bruce Levine, University of California, Santa Cruz
(forthcoming)

When Did Southern Segregation Begin?
John David Smith, North Carolina State University

Who Were the Progressives?
Glenda Elizabeth Gilmore, Yale University

What Did the Internment of Japanese Americans Mean?
Alice Yang Murray, University of California,
Santa Cruz

HISTORIANS AT WORK

When Did Southern Segregation Begin?

Readings Selected and Introduced by

John David Smith

North Carolina State University

Selections by

C. Vann Woodward

Joel Williamson

Edward L. Ayers

Howard N. Rabinowitz

Barbara Y. Welke

Leon F. Litwack

Bedford / St. Martin's   *Boston* ♦ *New York*

For Randall M. Miller — a friend and teacher over many years

For Bedford / St. Martin's
Publisher for History: Patricia A. Rossi
Developmental Editors: Sarah Barrash and Chip Turner
Editorial Assistant: Maria Teresa Burwell
Senior Production Supervisor: Joe Ford
Production Assistant: Christie Gross
Marketing Manager: Jenna Bookin Barry
Project Management: Books By Design, Inc.
Text Design: Claire Seng-Niemoeller
Cover Design: Donna Dennison
Composition: Stratford Publishing Services, Inc.
Printing and Binding: Haddon Craftsmen, an RR Donnelley & Sons Company

President: Charles H. Christensen
Editorial Director: Joan E. Feinberg
Director of Marketing: Karen R. Melton
Director of Editing, Design, and Production: Marcia Cohen
Manager, Publishing Services: Emily Berleth

Library of Congress Control Number: 2001087442

For information, write: Bedford/St. Martin's, 75 Arlington Street, Boston, MA 02116 (617-399-4000)

ISBN: 0-312-25738-4 (paperback)
       0-312-23705-7 (hardcover)

Acknowledgments

Acknowledgments and copyrights appear at the back of the book on page 177, which constitutes an extension of the copyright page.

Foreword

The short, inexpensive, and tightly focused books in the Historians at Work series set out to show students what historians do by turning closed specialist debate into an open discussion about important and interesting historical problems. These volumes invite students to confront the issues historians grapple with while providing enough support so that students can form their own opinions and join the debate. The books convey the intellectual excitement of "doing history" that should be at the core of any undergraduate study of the discipline. Each volume starts with a contemporary historical question that is posed in the book's title. The question focuses on either an important historical document (the Declaration of Independence, the Emancipation Proclamation) or a major problem or event (the beginnings of American slavery, the Pueblo Revolt of 1680) in American history. An introduction supplies the basic historical context students need and then traces the ongoing debate among historians, showing both how old questions have yielded new answers and how new questions have arisen. Following this two-part introduction are four to six interpretive selections by top scholars, many reprinted in their entirety from journals and books, including endnotes. Each selection is either a very recent piece or a classic argument that is still in play and is headed by a question that relates it to the book's core problem. Volumes that focus on a document reprint it in the opening materials so that students can read arguments alongside the evidence and reasoning on which they rest.

One purpose of these books is to show students that they *can* engage with sophisticated writing and arguments. To help them do so, each selection includes apparatus that provides context for engaged reading and critical thinking. An informative headnote introduces the angle of inquiry that the reading explores and closes with Questions for a Closer Reading, which invite students to probe the selection's assumptions, evidence, and argument. At the end of the book, Making Connections questions offer students ways to read the essays against one another, showing how interesting problems emerge from the debate. Suggestions for Further Reading

conclude each book, pointing interested students toward relevant materials for extended study.

Historical discourse is rarely a matter of simple opposition. These volumes show how ideas develop and how answers change, as minor themes
turn into major considerations. The Historians at Work volumes bring
together thoughtful statements in an ongoing conversation about topics
that continue to engender debate, drawing students into the historical discussion with enough context and support to participate themselves. These
books aim to show how serious scholars have made sense of the past and
why what they do is both enjoyable and worthwhile.

EDWARD COUNTRYMAN

Preface

Americans are quick to boast of their heterogeneity, their melting-pot society, their freedoms, and their inclusiveness, yet the United States has a long and painful history of racial and ethnic intolerance, oppression, and violence. In 1944 the Swedish social economist Gunnar Myrdal analyzed the omnipresent tension between America's high ideals of equality, liberty, and opportunity on the one hand, and the reality of the country's heritage of inequality, limited freedom, and exploitation on the other. He described it as "an American dilemma."

Slavery, which thrived in the American South for almost 250 years, lay at the root of the country's history of racial discord. In 1861, as white southerners seceded from the Union to protect slavery and their way of life, the United States stood as one of the last and one of the largest slaveholding republics in the world. Four years later the Confederacy lay in ruins, and the South's labor and social systems were in shambles. Unlike slaveholders in slave societies who freed their bondsmen gradually and provided bridges to freedom, emancipation came to white southerners suddenly, unwillingly, and completely, by defeat in a bloody and terribly costly civil war. Slavery also left indelible scars on the South's four million freedmen and women who had been forced to live degraded and inferior lives under the "peculiar institution." How would the ex-slaves and their former masters live together in the post–Civil War South? To what extent would the freedpeople be integrated into southern white society?

Though they agree that racial segregation, not integration, ultimately ruled in the postwar South, for half a century scholars have debated segregation's timing, its causation, and its meaning. Historian C. Vann Woodward's *The Strange Career of Jim Crow* (1955) sparked the discussion by arguing that legalized segregation was not inevitable and appeared only in the 1890s. Woodward's influential book invited challenges from a host of historians, most notably Joel Williamson, whose *After Slavery* (1965) positioned segregation's emergence immediately following the Civil War. Responding to Woodward's and Williamson's writings, many scholars have viewed slavery's emergence through varied lenses, emphasizing questions of race, class, law, and gender. The selections included in this book appear in chronological order to reflect both the ongoing importance of the Woodward-Williamson debate and the changing perspectives that historians have brought to the discussion.

Though this book focuses on the debate over *when* segregation began, examination of this issue necessarily opens up vital questions regarding *why* and *how* racial separation took hold as well. Most importantly, studying segregation's origins and timing underscores America's lengthy and conflicted history of racial discrimination and injustice in the land of democracy and equality. This "dilemma" remains to be resolved.

Acknowledgments

I wish to thank several people who assisted me at various stages in completing this book. David W. Blight encouraged me to undertake the project and recommended me to Bedford/St. Martin's. Edward Countryman, advisory editor for the Historians at Work series, enthusiastically supported my work, as did my editor, Chip Turner. Patricia A. Rossi and Sarah Barrash smoothed out essential details. Librarians Eric Anderson, Winston Atkins, Sebastian Hierl, Cindy Levine, Chris Meekins, Mimi Riggs, and Marihelen Stringham assisted me by procuring texts and verifying citations. So too did my graduate research assistants, Sharon Baggett, Jason Burton, Javan Frazier, and Stephen A. Ross. As usual, Jeffrey J. Crow and William C. Harris commented on my manuscript and made many helpful suggestions. W. Fitzhugh Brundage, John C. Inscoe, Marjorie Spruill Wheeler, and two anonymous readers evaluated earlier drafts. Their comments strengthened the book considerably.

JOHN DAVID SMITH

A Note for Students

Every piece of written history starts when somebody becomes curious and asks questions. The very first problem is who, or what, to study. A historian might ask an old question yet again, after deciding that existing answers are not good enough. But brand-new questions can emerge about old, familiar topics, particularly in light of new findings or directions in research, such as the rise of women's history in the late 1970s.

In one sense history is all that happened in the past. In another it is the universe of potential evidence that the past has bequeathed. But written history does not exist until a historian collects and probes that evidence *(research)*, makes sense of it *(interpretation)*, and shows to others what he or she has seen so that they can see it too *(writing)*. Good history begins with respecting people's complexity, not with any kind of preordained certainty. It might well mean using modern techniques that were unknown at the time, such as Freudian psychology or statistical assessment by computer. But good historians always approach the past on its own terms, taking careful stock of the period's cultural norms and people's assumptions or expectations, no matter how different from contemporary attitudes. Even a few decades can offer a surprisingly large gap to bridge, as each generation discovers when it evaluates the accomplishments of those who have come before.

To write history well requires three qualities. One is the courage to try to understand people whom we never can meet—unless our subject is very recent—and to explain events that no one can re-create. The second quality is the humility to realize that we can never entirely appreciate either the people or the events under study. However much evidence is compiled and however smart the questions posed, the past remains too large to contain. It will always continue to surprise.

The third quality historians need is the curiosity that turns sterile facts into clues about a world that once was just as alive, passionate, frightening, and exciting as our own, yet in different ways. Today we know how past events "turned out." But the people taking part had no such knowledge. Good history recaptures those people's fears, hopes, frustrations, failures, and achievements; it tells about people who faced the predicaments and choices that still confront us in the twenty-first century.

All the essays collected in this volume bear on a single, shared problem that the authors agree is important, however differently they may choose to respond to it. On its own, each essay reveals a fine mind coming to grips with a worthwhile question. Taken together, the essays give a sense of just how complex the human situation can be. That point—that human situations are complex—applies just as much to life today as to the lives led in the past. History has no absolute "lessons" to teach; it follows no invariable "laws." But knowing about another time might be of some help as we struggle to live within our own.

EDWARD COUNTRYMAN

Contents

Foreword   *v*
Preface   *vii*
A Note for Students   *ix*

PART ONE   **Introduction**   1

Segregation and the Age of Jim Crow   *3*
From Slavery to Segregation   3
Historians and the Origins of Racial Segregation   28

PART TWO   **Some Current Questions**   43

1. When did the South capitulate to segregation?   45

C. Vann Woodward

From *The Strange Career of Jim Crow*

"More than a decade was to pass after Redemption before the
first Jim Crow law was to appear upon the law books of a
Southern state, and more than two decades before the older
states of Virginia, North Carolina, and South Carolina were to
adopt such laws."

2. Was segregation the creation of custom or of law?   59

Joel Williamson

"*The Separation of the Races*"

"Well before the end of Reconstruction, separation had
crystallized into a comprehensive pattern which, in its essence,
remained unaltered until the middle of the twentieth century."

3. Why were the railroads the "contested terrain" of race relations in the postwar South?   85

Edward L. Ayers

From *The Promise of the New South: Life After Reconstruction*

"Most of the debates about race relations focused on the railroads of the New South."

4. What did segregation replace?   103

Howard N. Rabinowitz

"*From Exclusion to Segregation: Southern Race Relations, 1865–1890*"

"But the emphasis on the alternatives of segregation or integration has obscured the obvious 'forgotten alternative'— exclusion."

5. What role did gender play in railroad segregation?   133

Barbara Y. Welke

From "*When All the Women Were White, and All the Blacks Were Men: Gender, Class, Race, and the Road to* Plessy, *1855–1914*"

"From the first post–Civil War case, segregation by gender served as a legal analogy justifying regulations segregating passengers by race."

6. How did segregation enforce racial subordination?   153

Leon F. Litwack

From *Trouble in Mind: Black Southerners in the Age of Jim Crow*

"Although blacks had previously experienced segregation in various forms, the thoroughness of Jim Crow made it strikingly different."

Making Connections   165
Suggestions for Further Reading   167

When Did Southern Segregation Begin?

PART ONE

Introduction

Segregation and the Age of Jim Crow

Segregation and the Age of Jim Crow

From Slavery to Segregation

Writing in 1899, William Edward Burghardt Du Bois, the African American historian, sociologist, and editor, analyzed why some blacks committed crimes. One cause, Du Bois argued, was "the exaggerated and unnatural separation in the South of the best classes of whites and blacks. A drawing of the color line," he explained, "that extends to street-cars, elevators and cemeteries, which leaves no common ground of meeting, no medium of communication, no ties of sympathy between two races who live together and whose interests are at bottom one—such a discrimination is more than silly, it is dangerous."

Du Bois explained that the South's racial segregation "makes it possible for the mass of whites to misinterpret the aims and aspiration of the Negroes, to mistake self-reliance for insolence, and condemnation of lynch-law for sympathy with crime. It makes it possible for the Negroes to believe that the best people of the South hate and despise them, and express their antipathy in proscribing them, taunting them and crucifying them." The situation had only worsened two years later when Du Bois made his famous declaration that the "problem of the twentieth century is the problem of the color line." Between 1882 and 1903, when Du Bois published his manifesto *The Souls of Black Folk,* whites already had lynched at least two thousand blacks. Between 1866 and 1921, dozens of race riots also had marred the southern landscape. These included such well-known massacres as those in Memphis (1866), New Orleans (1866, 1874, 1900), Wilmington, North Carolina (1898), Atlanta (1906), and Houston (1917). Lesser-known race riots occurred in Eutaw, Alabama (1870), Laurens, South Carolina (1870), Clinton, Mississippi (1875), Danville, Virginia (1883), and Greenwood County, South Carolina (1898). Racial tension and turmoil, racial segregation and violence went hand in hand late in the century—a period that Rayford W. Logan termed the nadir of America's race relations.[1]

For black southerners living under the veil of racism at the turn of the century, it would have been a logical conclusion to believe that whites would "hate and despise" them. Although historians recognize the intense struggle of African Americans to control their own destinies, shape their own lives, form their own communities, and to resist oppression, from the moment of their emancipation in 1865, blacks fought an uphill battle against overwhelming odds. No sooner had the Civil War ended than whites moved to rivet their former slaves into new forms of labor—share wages, farm tenancy, sharecropping, the crop-lien system—that kept blacks generally landless and largely under white control. In 1865 and 1866 white southerners passed Black Codes designed to circumscribe the blacks' mobility, to restrict their economic opportunities, and to define them as a subordinate racial class.

To be sure, the Thirteenth, Fourteenth, and Fifteenth Amendments, and the Congressional Reconstruction Acts of 1867, promised freedom, citizenship, and suffrage, and African Americans scored many triumphs during and after Reconstruction. They created strong and resilient families, sent their children to school, formed their own churches, voted and organized politically, and labored mightily in hopes of owning family farms. Despite many accomplishments and moments of genuine biracial cooperation, from 1865 onward black southerners consistently encountered hostility from whites who sought to block their rise from slavery. Through manipulative paternalism, political chicanery, economic exploitation, physical intimidation and, when necessary to retain racial control, torture and mob murder, whites worked to keep black advancement in check. Over the course of the postwar decades, white southerners, committed to and obsessed with maintaining their supremacy, used every means at their disposal first to define a special, unequal sphere for African Americans and then to keep blacks in their place.

The intersection of "race," "place," and "space" is the subject of this book. It delves into specific disagreements and debates among historians about when, why, and how segregation in the American South began and their broader meaning. Our central concern will be what David Delaney has termed the "origins, emergence, change, and discontinuity in inherited geographies of race and racism." Inclusion, exclusion, space, distance, boundaries, margins, and lines of demarcation—whether created by custom or law—were essential components of what Delaney calls "the evolving spatiality of southern race relations." How whites and blacks negotiated space—in both public and private places—following emancipation is essential to our understanding of when and why segregation began and the emergence of the Jim Crow South.[2]

A larger issue is the meaning of the South's biracial system itself. Jim Crow laws defined what it meant to be "white" and "Negro" across class lines in the South. The color of his or her skin rendered the poorest, most ignorant "poor" white superior to the most accomplished person of color. The nation's overall commitment to white supremacy, its dismissive treatment of people of color and immigrants, coincided with America's burgeoning urbanization and industrialization and with its imperialistic forays into the Pacific and the Caribbean during the Spanish-American War and its treatment of "subject" peoples in the war's aftermath. It is significant to note that African Americans were not the only minority to be segregated in late-nineteenth-century America. Native Americans, Asian Americans, and Mexican Americans were all marginalized and segregated by the white majority. The spatial ordering of peoples was invasive, extensive, and national in scope during the age of Jim Crow.[3]

Indeed, turn-of-the-century America was a period when whites in both the North and South largely defined culture and society in racial terms, relegating people of color to the bottom of the socioeconomic ladder. Whites considered blacks subordinates and pariahs. African Americans were caught in a double bind. White southerners believed that slavery had been blacks' "natural" condition and that emancipation was a backward step in the race's development. White northerners blamed slavery for what they considered the freedpeople's degradation and, aside from their labor, considered blacks a social menace. Turn-of-the-century America was a time when whites were obsessed with "the Negro question," defining African Americans less as people and more as a "problem." The vast majority of whites viewed black assertiveness—boycotts, strikes, protests, political fusion with white farmers and laborers—as a threat. As James R. Grossman explains, whites believed that "black labor needed to be coerced to be reliable" and that "black people were dangerous, not quite as civilized as white people, and certainly not as orderly." By the 1890s whites were determined to keep blacks in their place, both literally and figuratively, as a permanently separate and dependent underclass.[4]

According to John W. Cell, "the most satisfactory explanation" for the start of segregation "is that the American nation, including the South, was undergoing rapid and massive change. Segregation was a means of placing the race question on hold while substantial parts of the South industrialized and while the nation as a whole modernized, expanded to what it considered its natural limits, and became one of the world's great imperial powers. Not for the first time, nor for the last, black people paid a heavy price for national reconciliation and progress." As the present book suggests, legalized segregation was the result of years of experimentation by whites in searching for an effective means of racial control. Until the pitched civil rights battles of the mid–twentieth century, segregation was white southerners' solution to the "Negro problem."[5]

Though a national phenomenon, especially in urban centers, segregation was most prominent in the South, where the bulk of the country's African American population resided. Along with slavery, secession, the Confederate battle flag, and ruralism, segregation remains one of the most identifiable and powerful historical symbols of the South. It was a region, Ulrich Bonnell Phillips explained in 1928, whose "white folk" held "a common resolve indomitably maintained—that it shall be and remain a white man's country." Having grown to manhood in Georgia in the 1890s, Phillips understood that white supremacy, "whether expressed with the frenzy of a demagogue or maintained with a patrician's quietude, is the cardinal test of a Southerner and the central theme of Southern history."[6]

As students will discover in the six readings that follow, historians rarely have discussed segregation apart from the various discriminations that African Americans experienced in the second half of the nineteenth century. William Cohen argues that segregation and racial proscriptions were in fact inseparable. During the period from slavery to segregation, "the drive to white domination in the South occurred on many fronts simultaneously and . . . disfranchisement, lynching, segregation, and the opposition to miscegenation were linked to one another in the white determination to put blacks back 'in their place.' The laws and practices that southerners accepted in order to achieve that end bespeak a society in which the ideology of white supremacy reigned almost unchallenged. The world without slavery was also to be a world where white hegemony was complete." Spatial segregation based on alleged racial distinctions thus was just one mode of racial control developed by whites after the Civil War. For almost a century segregation hovered over the American South like a miasma, debilitating all it touched, choking everyone, black and white. The cloud of segregation polluted the South until the civil rights movement of the 1960s swept into the region like a gust of fresh air.[7]

Segregation in the American South, commonly referred to as Jim Crow, was the elaborate process constructed by whites of physically separating the races based on social custom or legal distinction. The term *Jim Crow* derived from nineteenth-century minstrelsy. Thomas Dartmouth "Daddy" Rice, a white entertainer, performed in blackface a song-and-dance routine, "Jump Jim Crow," that portrayed the Negro as a comical, shuffling character. Rice based his caricature on a performance that he had seen in Louisville in 1828 by an elderly slave owned by a Mr. Crow. Historians have used the terms *segregation* and *Jim Crow* both specifically and loosely to describe the process of setting the races apart, often confusing or conflating customary or informal segregation with statutory or formal segregation. As a result, they have disagreed as to when, why, and how segregation originated. Many of their differences of opinion thus have stemmed from historians' failure to specify to which form of racial separation they have referred.[8]

Roger A. Fischer was right in 1969 when he argued that historians should adopt "an evolutionary concept of segregation in the South." Though its modern form unfolded late—in the 1890s South—the history of segregation actually ranges over the entire course and geography of American history. The key element in sorting out segregation's history is differentiating between segregation by custom, habit, or practice (de facto segregation) and segregation by specific law (de jure segregation). Historians have frequently erred by focusing too narrowly—on de jure segregation only—thereby missing long-standing patterns of informal racial separation that have stained the fabric of interracial contact throughout American history.[9]

Despite their disagreements, historians generally concur that Jim Crow became formalized in the 1890s, when one southern state after another passed a patchwork of interrelated laws codifying blacks' customary second-class legal and social status. Following a pattern that emerged in the 1870s and 1880s when the federal courts failed to enforce the Reconstruction amendments, in 1896 the U.S. Supreme Court added its imprimatur to Jim Crow in the flawed *Plessy v. Ferguson* case, upholding "separate-but-equal" facilities on public conveyances. This was applied to other public facilities, including schools. The segregation system, an American apartheid, thus was in place in the South before World War I and divided much of the region into separate and unequal black and white worlds.

Segregation enveloped every element of southern culture. According to Cell, it "covered all areas of life, love, work, leisure, and even death." Though racially defined separation shaped white as well as black lives, its power and pervasiveness proved most burdensome and oppressive to African Americans. Cell explains:

> When they rode public transportation, they sat in the black section in the rear. If they wanted to drink, eat, or go to the toilet, they might be lucky enough to find facilities reserved for them; otherwise they had to do without. Parks, beaches, golf courses, tennis courts, and swimming pools excluded them; again comparatively rarely they might find separate but undoubtedly inferior facilities. If they ran afoul of the law, they were sworn on separate-but-equal Bibles and, if convicted by usually all-white juries, were sentenced by white judges to segregated jails. When they died, they were embalmed in black funeral parlors . . . and buried in black cemeteries.[10]

Du Bois, whose career spanned this period, recalled the many indignities of life under segregation. Jim Crow waiting rooms, he complained, generally had "no heat in winter and no air in summer; undisturbed loafers and white train hands and broken disreputable settees; to buy a ticket is torture: you stand and stand and wait and wait until every white person at the 'Other Window' is waited on. Then . . . [the white ticket agent] browbeats and contradicts you, hurries and confuses the ignorant; gives many the wrong change . . . and sends all out on the platform burning with indignation and hatred." Blacks then boarded a Jim Crow car positioned behind the engine and full of soot, sparks, and dirt. While traveling, Du Bois complained, "It is difficult to get lunch or drinking water. Lunch rooms either 'don't serve niggers' or serve them at some dirty and ill-attended hole in the wall. Toilet rooms are often filthy. If you have to change cars be wary of junctions which are usually without accommodation and filled with quarrelsome whites who hate a 'darky dressed up.' "[11]

As an institutionalized legal system of racial and social control, segregation emerged first in Mississippi (1890) and then in South Carolina (1895) when those states "reformed" their state constitutions. Their sister southern states quickly followed, imposing new legal codes that placed rigid regulations on African Americans and redefined social relations between the races. Proscribing blacks, white southerners argued, was a Progressive "reform" for several reasons.

Disfranchising African Americans would cleanse the political system by eliminating them as a source of corruption among Democrats, Republicans, and Populists who, during the tumultuous 1890s, had vied for their votes. Minimizing racial contact, whites explained, would maintain law, order, and stability, thereby allowing the two races to develop and establish their own identities at their own pace. Regulating the conditions of black life would curb what whites considered a dangerous assertiveness on the part of African Americans, especially the generations born since emancipation, who were considered too "uppity" and unwilling to accept their proper "place" in southern society. Isolating blacks spatially, whether on streetcars, railroad cars, schools, churches, or neighborhoods, would protect whites from "contamination" from African American disease and degeneracy. For these reasons and more, late-nineteenth-century white southerners implemented segregation in every corner of southern life. In doing so they codified what they had done informally since emancipation.

In terms of day-to-day practice, "Jim Crow" referred to a broad range of racially differentiated state laws and statutes and municipal ordinances that outlined appropriate formal spatial relations between the races, often restricting contact between them, and also establishing codes of racial etiquette governing informal contact as well. Specifically, segregation laws earmarked separate residential, educational, recreational, and social services for African Americans. They applied to transportation, lodging, dining facilities, prisons, hospitals, asylums, mental institutions, orphanages, old-age homes, funeral homes, and cemeteries. Perhaps the most bizarre example of segregation statutes were the Florida and North Carolina laws that mandated separate storage facilities for textbooks used by white and black students. Encouraged by the prevailing legal system, individuals and businesses constructed their own segregationist practices that became institutionalized over time and were as powerful as legal precedents. These included separate drinking fountains, toilets, and ticket windows; bleachers at sporting events; seats in theaters; and special entrances and dining areas in restaurants that served "colored" guests. So thoroughly did the South become segregated that brothels, telephone booths, even courtroom Bibles became differentiated by color. After World War I, segregation evolved along with changing technology. Segregated bus depots, taxis, ambulances, blood supplies, air terminals, swimming pools, and soda fountains dotted the South's urban landscape. Until well into the 1960s, facilities for African Americans were both separate and decidedly unequal as well.

For more than a century white southerners defended segregationist law and practice as the natural result of racial animosities and differences, arguing that segregation provided the best means to avoid racial friction and the tensions that had been contained before 1865 by the bonds of slavery. Segregation structured formal and informal racial contact between whites and blacks in virtually every avenue of southern life. As this introduction suggests, the history of segregation is complex, often contradictory, and its meaning and implications remain ambiguous. To a certain degree nuances of circumstance, class, and temperament among African Americans themselves helped determine Jim Crow's meaning and influence.

For example, blacks consistently protested segregation and challenged it in the courts. In launching the Niagara Movement (the forerunner of the National Association for the Advancement of Colored People) in 1905, Du Bois blasted the assignment of African Americans to "the 'Jim Crow' car, since its effect is and must be to make us pay first-class fare for third-class accommodations, render us open to insults and discomfort and to crucify wantonly our manhood, womanhood and self-respect." But blacks also realized that racial separation provided what Grace Elizabeth Hale terms "relatively autonomous black spaces, even autonomous black bodies." Segregation "created spaces for black doctors, black colleges, and increasingly black business districts—from Auburn Avenue in Atlanta to Beale Street in Memphis—as southern African Americans moved into growing southern cities. The creation of a separate white southern world, a culture of segregation, implied that somewhere there existed a separate black one. As whites strove to create an all-encompassing system of segregation . . . they also risked aiding African Americans in the very struggle for more autonomy that white supremacy sought to deny."[12]

Howard N. Rabinowitz, Herman Belz, and Michael Naragon have written convincingly that although blacks resisted the inequality bred by segregation, many accepted it as an improvement over the exclusion from hospitals, theaters, and social services they experienced as slaves and free blacks before the war. Belz notes that "blacks accepted segregation because it was better than exclusion and because it appealed to their sense of separate identity." "Savvy and shrewd," Naragon writes, "African Americans used local courts to press not for integrated accommodations but for funding and resources equal to that provided white institutions."[13]

Even the exact meaning of the physical separation of the races itself remains murky. Did segregation allow for interracial interaction? If so, in what ways? Neil R. McMillen explains that in Mississippi, which issued the first Black Code in 1865 and the first rigid segregation statutes twenty-five years later, " 'place,' as whites defined it, was always more behavioral than spatial in nature. The dominant race understood that it was often neither possible nor desirable to separate physically two people living and working together in close proximity. Valuing hierarchy more than they feared propinquity, whites casually rubbed elbows with blacks in contexts that sometimes startled northerners. Yet the requirements of caste, most particularly of social distance, were zealously enforced." The contours and nuances of segregation obviously differed from time to time and from place to place, depending heavily on basic idiosyncratic and subtle human relationships.[14]

Viewed broadly, segregation began much earlier than the 1890s. It existed informally throughout much of the country's antebellum history, in towns, cities, and along the expanding frontier—wherever blacks and whites lived in close proximity and competed for jobs and living space. Before the Civil War, whites routinely segregated blacks in private and public places—in housing, neighborhoods, streetcars, railroad cars, theaters, lecture halls, schools, and churches—on both sides of the Mason-Dixon line. To complicate segregation's periodization, local municipalities, north and south, before and after the Civil War and before the 1890s, also passed segregation laws. Depending on time and place, these laws were strictly enforced, enforced haphazardly, rescinded, ignored, or applied selectively based on numerous local factors. The key point is that long before the 1890s, whites employed both de facto *and* de jure segregation to regulate slaves, free blacks, and postwar freedmen and women. The two modes of controlling race and place frequently existed simultaneously. And without a doubt, the post–Civil War South was characterized by evolving patterns of racial exclusion and segregation concerning transportation, housing, and social services that were inseparable from other issues such as disfranchisement and outlawing miscegenation. "What is primarily involved here," Otto H. Olsen explains, "is the role of race distinction and division as an instrument in the maintenance of white supremacy, and what has changed with time has been the precise manner and intensity with which such separation has been maintained."[15]

Fischer has explained that though racial segregation had been part of the national experience before the Civil War, "only in the South did it develop into a virtually total system of racial control for such a prolonged period of time." Slavery on the South's isolated farms and plantations was a multifaceted system of labor, social, and racial control that was regulated by federal law, state slave codes, local ordinances, and close supervision by whites. Segregation thus was unnecessary, if not unworkable, there. Conditions differed, however, in the Old South's towns and cities, where African American laborers enjoyed degrees of anonymity, freedom from strict surveillance, and independence unknown to plantation slaves. Dispersed clusters of free blacks and slaves, many of whom hired themselves out (or, in the case of slaves, were hired out by their masters), resided in Charleston, Mobile, New Orleans, Savannah, Richmond, and other cities where, according to Richard C. Wade, "public etiquette was needed to govern the relations of races when the blacks were beyond the supervision of their owners."[16]

In many antebellum southern urban centers, local custom dictated where blacks could live and work as well as where and how they could congregate. Most urban slaves lived in close proximity to their masters—in a stable, a kitchen, an adjoining outbuilding, a barracks, or a shack in a back alley behind their master's home. When local mores failed to regulate urban blacks sufficiently, cities passed ordinances that either excluded blacks without providing them alternative facilities or segregated them from contact with whites. As the Civil War approached, public spaces such as restaurants, bars, hotels, and walking grounds were uniformly off-limits to free blacks and slaves. Most cities, however, provided African Americans segregated sections of jails, hospitals, cemeteries, theatres, churches, and public conveyances. Free blacks in some locales attended segregated classrooms, while slaves were denied access to schools altogether.

Free blacks in the antebellum North experienced similar conditions. According to Leon F. Litwack, "while statutes and customs circumscribed the Negro's political and judicial rights, extralegal codes . . . relegated him to a position of social inferiority. . . . In virtually every phase of existence, Negroes found themselves systematically separated from whites." On railroads and streetcars, stagecoaches and steamboats, blacks either were excluded totally or segregated in Jim Crow cars or seats. The term *Jim Crow* became, as Joel Williamson explains, "a label for one stereotype of the American Negro," and the term was first used to designate segregated railroad facilities in Massachusetts in 1841 and later in the North, not in the

South. If they gained admittance to theaters and lecture halls, blacks were required to sit in out-of-the-way sections. Custom barred most northern blacks from entering hotels, inns, restaurants, and resorts, and forced them to worship in special Negro pews in white churches. An observer remarked that in the antebellum North, racial discrimination "haunts its victim wherever he goes,—in the hospitals where humanity suffers,—in the churches where he kneels to God,—in the prisons where he expiates its offences,—in the graveyards where it sleeps the last sleep." Not surprisingly, during the Civil War the Union Army's 179,000 U.S. Colored Troops served in segregated regiments officered by whites.[17]

The war ultimately emancipated the South's four million slaves and had dramatic effects on race relations in the region. Both Presidential Reconstruction (1865–1867) and Congressional Reconstruction (1867–1877) were periods of tense experimentation for southerners of both races. As Reconstruction unfolded, both sides jockeyed for position, and there was little common ground to ease racial friction. Access to public and private spaces, mostly in the South's cities and towns (which experienced dramatic increases in black population), became contested terrain on which whites and blacks fought many of the battles of Reconstruction. Whites, frightened by the specter of emancipated slaves in their midst and determined to maintain white supremacy, sought to retain as many of slavery's controlling features as possible. White southerners feared "Africanization" of the South and denounced as "uppity" African Americans who refused to behave as inferiors. They also feared radical whites who, they believed, would use blacks for political purposes. Most white southerners longed for the racial etiquette of slavery and demanded social distance from their former bondsmen.

Blacks, in contrast, were equally determined to shed the symbols and badges of slavery—to be freed men and women in word as well as deed. They were eager to enjoy the hard-won fruits of freedom, including land ownership, economic and residential mobility, education for their children, and social services. Excluded or segregated as slaves from many public places or conveyances, newly emancipated black southerners sought equality with whites and openly challenged the racial hegemony of their former masters. Black access to public spaces conveyed an equality unacceptable to most white southerners. As Litwack explains, "When . . . [blacks] chose to test their freedom by entering public places from which they had previously been barred or by sitting indiscriminately in public conveyances where their presence had previously been restricted, the worst fears of the white South were realized and the utmost vigilance demanded."[18]

In late 1865 and in 1866, white southerners quickly made their intentions known by passing a series of blatantly discriminatory Black Codes—

state labor and police regulations that circumscribed many of the freed-people's freedoms. In these laws whites outlined the ex-slaves' new rights and responsibilities and, sensitive to the number of blacks "on the move after emancipation," detailed apprenticeship, convict, enticement, and vagrancy laws that would keep them immobile, dependent, and nearby to labor. Some of these Black Codes drew a color line in public places. Florida, Mississippi, and Texas passed special Jim Crow laws excluding blacks from first-class railroad cars. Mississippi's 1865 code, for example, declared it "unlawful for . . . any freedman, negro, or mulatto, to ride in any first class passenger cars, set apart, or used by, and for white persons" except "in the case of negroes or mulattoes, travelling with their mistress, in the capacity of maids."[19]

The Black Codes were soon struck down by Freedmen's Bureau officials and Congress in the Reconstruction Acts of 1867. With blacks voting and Republicans in control of the southern states, no corpus of state laws replaced the Black Codes. Not until later in the century did states and municipalities pass detailed segregationist statutes, although such actions were unnecessary because, as Litwack explains, during Reconstruction "racial distinctions . . . were almost always understood rather than stated." "In most instances," he adds, "the 'color line' simply perpetuated distinctions that had been made during slavery." Though rarely codified, "the practices and customs governing racial contact in public places and accommodations acquired the force of statutes, backed as they were by a nearly unanimous white public opinion and local police power." Responding to the prospect of integrated schools, a white Georgian remarked: "Sir, we accept the death of slavery but, sir, surely there are some things that are not tolerable. Our people have not been brought up to associate with negroes. They don't think it decent; and the negroes will be none the better for being thrust into the places of white men's sons."[20]

Drawing heavily on northern and southern antebellum social practice, the freedpeople during Reconstruction commonly found themselves relegated to separate and inferior facilities apart from whites. For example, blacks almost always attended separate schools from whites. During Reconstruction, the southern states enacted many school segregation statutes. Tennessee, Arkansas, and Texas led the way in 1866; in the period from 1868 through 1888, the former Confederate states, despite black voters and Republicans in control, passed eighteen such laws, with thirteen more added between 1889 and 1915. As Cohen explains, "The later laws were often redundant assertions of the mood of the white South rather than remedies against specific vestiges of equality."[21]

Whites also left little doubt about their feelings toward riding next to blacks in public conveyances or sitting next to them in public places.

During Reconstruction freedpeople rode in specially marked horse-drawn streetcars, traveled in second-class railroad compartments or freight cars, and slept on the open decks of steamboats. If they gained admittance to theaters and churches, blacks either took seats behind whites or sat in separate galleries. Hospitals, asylums, and social services throughout the South often differentiated service by color. Some southern cities specified discrete walkways and promenades for whites and blacks. African Americans patronized black-owned hotels and restaurants because white establishments almost never welcomed them. Blacks even served in separate militia companies.[22]

During Reconstruction the southern states also passed numerous anti-miscegenation statutes that were clearly designed to place legal obstacles in the way of the most intimate contact between blacks and whites. By 1867 five states—Alabama, Georgia, Mississippi, South Carolina, and Arkansas—banned racial intermarriage or established penalties for those who engaged in interracial sexual relations. Later, between 1870 and 1884, nine states either initiated new legislative action or passed additional statutes banning intermarriage. "At bottom," Cohen insists, "the miscegenation acts were the ultimate segregation laws. They embodied the very essence of the beliefs southern whites held about race: that whites were racially superior to blacks and that any mixing of the two groups was bound to sully the whites."[23]

Incensed by second-class treatment, blacks by 1867 forcefully challenged streetcar segregation in New Orleans, Richmond, Charleston, Louisville, Mobile, Savannah, Nashville, and Baltimore, though, as Rabinowitz remarked, "the extent of integration within the cars, however, remains a subject of controversy." Between 1868 and 1873, Radical governments in Mississippi, South Carolina, Louisiana, and Florida forbade segregated public accommodations; South Carolina and Louisiana also prohibited segregated public schools. Seven southern states passed civil rights laws in one form or another during Congressional Reconstruction that applied to public carriers and public accommodations. This policy was codified on the federal level by the Civil Rights Act of 1875. Republican senator Charles Sumner's dogged efforts led to the passage of this bill, guaranteeing all persons, regardless of color or condition, full and equal access to "inns, public conveyances on land or water, theaters, and other places of public amusement." In its original form, the Civil Rights Act of 1875 would have outlawed segregation in public schools and cemeteries, provisions that were excluded in the final bill. Though the act promised federal enforcement, Eric Foner maintains that, on balance, the "law was more a broad assertion of principle than a blueprint for further coercive action by the federal government. It left the initiative for enforcement primarily with black litigants suing for their rights in the already overburdened federal courts. Only a handful of blacks came forward to challenge acts of discrimination by hotels, theaters, and railroads."[24]

Overall, during Reconstruction there were few documented successes in breaking the color line. Between 1870 and 1877 some New Orleans public schools were integrated, as was the University of South Carolina in the years 1873 to 1877. But most southern schools remained segregated. Some integration came to pass in public conveyances on the Atlantic seaboard. Blacks who tested the Civil Rights Act in Louisiana and North Carolina garnered limited success at integrating theaters, restaurants, and inns. "On the whole, however," Fischer insists, during Congressional Reconstruction "segregation survived relatively unscathed. Few Negroes asserted their legal rights, and most Radical governments tolerated or even encouraged *de facto* segregation in institutions under their control." This pattern generally continued as Reconstruction officially ground to a halt in 1877. During the 1870s, as Republican-controlled governments collapsed in one southern state after another and Republican politicians in Washington turned their backs on the interests of the freedpeople, African Americans had every reason to fear for the future. As long as they retained the right to vote, however, blacks hoped to forestall yet more attempts by whites to segregate them into separate spaces and inferior lives.[25]

Despite common misconceptions, in the post-Reconstruction years black southerners continued to live in a world that was not yet rigidly segregated. African American life in the first New South was far less monolithic than many historians have assumed. As David Levering Lewis notes, "Formal disfranchisement, in naked violation of the Fifteenth Amendment, had not yet come about; nor had institutionalized 'Jim Crow'— banning black people from commercial establishments and public places and herding them into the last seats and rickety add-ons in trains and streetcars. This would begin in earnest a decade later." Many blacks indeed voted and were politically active, and a surprisingly large number held public office well into the 1890s. During the years 1877 through 1901 eleven African Americans were elected to the U.S. Congress. In Mississippi, blacks continued to sit in the state legislature throughout the 1880s; six served in 1890, and one remained in 1899. "Dozens of Southern cities," Herbert Aptheker reports, "had Negroes appointed and elected officers on all levels of administrative responsibility . . . in the 1880's and 1890's." North Carolina's George H. White served two terms in the U.S. Congress (1897–1901) and was the last African American to sit in Congress until 1929.[26]

Black assertiveness and resiliency, however, convinced whites that African Americans needed to be put in their place, which was to be as close to their former slave status as possible. In order to control them, Democrats in the 1870s launched a campaign to disfranchise freedpeople, a movement that picked up momentum in the 1880s and ultimately triumphed in the 1890s and early 1900s. As Foner explains, "Long before their outright disenfranchisement around the turn of the century, blacks saw their political rights progressively eroded." White conservatives realized that before they could systematically segregate blacks, they first had to remove them from the political process. They did so, Cohen says, "with deliberate speed."[27]

Mindful of the Fifteenth Amendment's protection of voting rights, southern legislators carefully crafted legislation designed to reduce, impede, restrict, or deny suffrage to blacks. In 1871 Georgia passed the first poll tax (which discriminated against the poor of both races), followed by Texas (1874), Virginia (1876), and Florida (1889). In order to vote, African Americans sometimes also had to pay property taxes. In 1874 Texas became the first state to require special voter registration procedures that discriminated against blacks, a practice followed by Alabama (1875), Mississippi and Texas (1876), North Carolina (1877), South Carolina (1882), Virginia (1884), Florida (1887), and Tennessee (1889). When these devices proved insufficient to curb black voting, the states devised new ones, including multiple ballot boxes, secret ballots, and the apportionment of voting districts.[28]

In 1890 Mississippi enacted an "understanding clause" to test a potential voter's comprehension of the state constitution. This examination allowed for the enfranchisement of selected individuals based presumably on their knowledge of the constitution. In reality, the examiner framed the questions and evaluated the answers based on the race or class of the examinee. Similar tests were adopted by South Carolina (1895), Louisiana (1898), and other states. In some states black voters also had to pass literacy tests. To provide a way for poor whites to circumvent these disfranchisement measures, in 1898 Louisiana (followed by North Carolina and Oklahoma) established "grandfather clauses." Men, presumably whites, who either had voted prior to January 1, 1867 (when blacks first were allowed to vote in the South), or who had descended from such voters were enfranchised; men who did not qualify under the "grandfather clause," presumably blacks, could not. Alabama and Georgia even had "fighting grandfather clauses" that exempted veterans, including former Confederate soldiers, from other voting requirements. Cohen argues that these early disfranchisement measures worked. Between 1880 and 1888, the number of black voters in Georgia and South Carolina dropped by 50 percent and 63 percent, respectively. By 1910 provisions were on the books in North Carolina, Alabama, Virginia, Georgia, and Oklahoma that largely disfranchised blacks in those states. When legal barriers designed to disfranchise blacks failed, whites resorted to extralegal means—force, fraud, and intimidation—to keep blacks away from the polls. "By 1880," Cohen writes, "only 34 percent of Mississippi's eligible black voters were going to the polls."[29]

During these years, a period that white conservative southerners referred to as Redemption, lawmakers moved slowly but steadily first to negate the few desegregation measures passed during Reconstruction, and then to add new segregation statutes to their laws. For example, the races were separated once again in New Orleans public schools, and black students were removed from the University of South Carolina in Columbia to "a special college set up for them by the State at Orangeburg." In May 1877, South Carolina's *Edgefield Advertiser* gloated that at long last "our beloved and honored University is freed forever from the Radical and the negro!" In 1883 white southerners received an impetus to draw the color line even more boldly when, in the *Civil Rights Cases*, the U.S. Supreme Court declared the Civil Rights Act of 1875 unconstitutional. Writing for the majority, Justice Joseph Bradley argued that the Fourteenth Amendment had no jurisdiction in private, as opposed to state, cases of discrimination. Bradley also argued that at some point the Negro had to assume "the rank of a mere citizen" and cease being "the special favorite of the laws." In his dissent, Justice John Marshall Harlan, ironically a member of a former slaveholding Kentucky family, maintained that the Court's decision was "too narrow and artificial": inns, amusements, and conveyances, according to Harlan, did not qualify as "private persons," but rather operated by state authority and thus were subject to federal civil rights action.[30]

Even before the Supreme Court struck down the Civil Rights Act, Tennessee in 1881 moved to segregate its public conveyances, adding another statute a year later that required passengers paying for first-class tickets to ride in first-class cars. The legislature in Nashville took special pains to ensure that railroads, hotels, restaurants, and other businesses would be protected from civil rights suits. The 1882 law and another passed in 1884 specified that the facilities should be "separate but equal," which, as Cohen notes, "simply meant that blacks paying the first-class fare were entitled to their own segregated section." In 1885, Atlanta's New South spokesman Henry W. Grady remarked, "On the railroads, as elsewhere, the solution of the race problem is, equal advantages for the same money,—equal in comfort, safety, and exclusiveness,—but separate."[31]

Other states soon followed Tennessee's lead. Between 1887 and 1894, one state after another (Florida, Mississippi, Texas, Louisiana, Alabama, Arkansas, Georgia) passed railroad segregation laws or strengthened earlier laws, with most incorporating the "separate but equal" principle. In

1898 South Carolina segregated its railroads, followed a year later by North Carolina and Virginia. Meanwhile nine of the states passed laws requiring the segregation of streetcars as well. By the turn of the century, then, each of the former Confederate states had legally separated blacks and whites in public transportation.[32]

It is essential to remember, however, that the implementation of statutory segregation was not inevitable, but rather hinged on disfranchisement—the exclusion of African American males from the political process. Before disfranchisement, interracial and "independent" political coalitions of farmers and laborers, mechanics and miners, Republicans and Democrats, Greenbackers and later Populists, existed in the South. "Between 1865 and the turn of the twentieth century," Jane Dailey explains, "every state south of the Mason-Dixon line experimented with political alliances that spanned the color line. . . . To scratch the surface of the 'solid South' in the late nineteenth century was to discover multiple competing interest groups divided by region, race, ideology, and class." Independent coalition parties like Virginia's Readjusters in the 1880s and North Carolina's Fusionists in the 1890s achieved significant, though short-term, success in postponing the ultimate triumph of legalized Jim Crow in their respective states. In fact, Lawanda Cox has argued, black politicians who allied with whites in these years "were sufficiently effective to have helped trigger their own undoing," ushering in "the white racist reaction that led to the displacement of partial by total disfranchisement and the hardening of *de facto* into legal segregation." Black politicians' success forced conservative Democrats to take the interracial political coalitions seriously—dead seriously.[33]

North Carolina's pitched political battles in the 1890s provide an excellent case study of efforts to promote political cooperation across the color line. In Tar Heel elections in 1894, reform-minded white Populists joined with both black and white Republicans to gain control of the state from Democrats by a 116 to 54 majority in the General Assembly in 1895, electing Republican Daniel L. Russell governor a year later. Eleven black legislators were elected to the General Assembly in 1897, and hundreds of blacks held county-level political appointments. Determined to remove the Fusionists from power, and disparaging "Negro rule," Democrats in 1898 launched a violent white supremacy campaign. According to party chairman Furnifold M. Simmons, the Democrats would "re-establish in North Carolina the supremacy of the white race." To accomplish this, paramilitary mounted riflemen ("Red Shirts" and "Rough Riders") harassed, intimidated, and attacked Fusionist voters, especially blacks, to keep them away from the polls. In late 1898, eastern North Carolina was on the verge of race war.[34]

Democratic spokesmen also fanned the fires of distrust between the races by publicizing and taking out of context what they considered to be an inflammatory editorial by Alex Manly, editor of Wilmington's *Record,* North Carolina's only African American daily newspaper. Responding to justifications by whites for the lynching of black men because they allegedly were prone to rape white women, Manly wrote, "our experience among poor white people in the country teaches us that women of that race are not more particular in the matter of clandestine meetings with colored men, than are the white men with colored women." The editor went on to malign whites as "a lot of harping hypocrites . . . you cry aloud the virtue of your women while you seek to destroy the morality of ours. Don't think ever that your women will remain pure while you are debauching ours. You sow the seed—the harvest will come in due time." Not surprisingly, such language inflamed white supremacists. The state, especially the Republican-controlled port city of Wilmington, which had a black majority, was a tinder box ready to spark.[35]

Amid all manner of violence, including threats of political assassinations, and voter fraud, the Democrats won the highly charged election of November 8, 1898, regaining control of the General Assembly 134 to 36. To punctuate their control, two days after the election Democrats fomented a coup d'état in Wilmington designed specifically to oust the city's Republican municipal government and to destroy Manly's newspaper. White mobs invaded African American neighborhoods, burning homes and businesses and forcing black residents either to flee to surrounding swamps or to leave the state. According to one informant, "a lot of them was running from the white men and they ran to the river and they couldn't swim and a lot of them drowned." An eyewitness remembered that "Wagon loads of Negro bodies were hauled through the streets." Though newspaper reports were inconclusive as to the number of fatalities, as many as thirty blacks may have died in the Wilmington massacre. Whites sustained only a handful of injuries.[36]

Having silenced the Populist-Republican reform alliance, North Carolina's Democrats next took steps to ensure that working-class whites and blacks would remain powerless. Revising the state's electoral system in ways that kept many local offices appointive, not elective, the General Assembly also proposed a suffrage amendment designed essentially to disfranchise blacks and poor whites. A poll tax, literacy test, and grandfather clause virtually guaranteed that few African Americans would vote. Resolute in its determination to control blacks, the legislature in 1899 also passed legislation that segregated blacks on steamboats and railroads. In the election of 1900 (another contest in which Democrats used threats of violence, including murder, to discourage Populist and Republican voters) the suffrage amendment passed by more than 50,000 votes. Just as racial violence snuffed out the Populist-Republican alliance, disfranchisement smothered the political hopes of North Carolina's blacks and symbolized the victory of the state's white supremacists. Denied access to the polls, blacks were powerless to challenge the segregation laws that enshrouded the South by the turn of the century. "Once enacted," Idus A. Newby has written, "they constituted a code of racial conduct that was just as extensive as and probably more rigidly enforced than the slave codes of the antebellum era."[37]

This new wave of de jure segregation posed an especially irritating problem for middle-class blacks as early as the mid-1880s, when whites openly barred blacks from "white" hotels, restaurants, barber and beauty shops, and theaters. Because of the expansion of railroad travel in the South by the mid-1880s, trains became the most contested public space of all, especially when African Americans insisted on their right to equal access to first-class railroad cars. In 1883, for example, J. A. Scott, a black lawyer, complained about what he described as the "universal discrimination" in Alabama, "and indeed, all over the South, in the treatment of the colored people as to [railroad] cars they are permitted to ride in." Blacks sought entry to first-class coaches not because they wanted social equality, he explained, but rather because "there are better accommodations there." Scott noted that "in the cars allotted to the colored people a white man comes in and smokes cigars, and chews tobacco, and curses and swears, and all that kind of thing, and the conductors on the various roads don't exercise their powers for the protection of the colored passengers." "Our people do not care whether they are put in the front of the train or in the middle or at the tail end, so long as they have proper accommodation and proper protection."[38]

Scott's words were largely disingenuous because blacks did indeed care where they were put. But his remarks raise interesting questions about the dynamics of segregation in public places and in neighborhoods in the New South's cities. As Thomas W. Hanchett explains, during the post-emancipation decades the two races routinely shared urban space — train stations, parks, streetcars — in southern cities. Nonetheless, a pattern of separate black and white neighborhoods emerged slowly in southern cities in the 1890s. After 1900, self-contained black neighborhoods sprouted up throughout the South. They commonly included a black main street that was distinct from the white business district. To what extent did blacks accept segregation if it guaranteed "proper accommodation and proper protection"?[39]

Rabinowitz maintains that late in the century most southern urban blacks lived in small segregated scattered clusters, not ghettos, and that a significant degree of the segregation was "voluntary as blacks sought out their 'own kind.' " They were attracted by African American cultural institutions, including churches, schools, theaters, fraternal organizations, restaurants, and places of entertainment, as well as by jobs, black-owned businesses, and offices of black professional men. As Rabinowitz explains, "for most southern urban blacks residential segregation clearly meant more than simply the absence of white neighbors—it was the foundation of the region's biracial society." Whites, however, interpreted it differently. After 1900, fears of blacks moving into traditionally white neighborhoods spirited cities to pass racial zoning laws.[40]

Baltimore began this trend in 1910 when it required segregated neighborhoods; other southern cities, including Richmond and Atlanta, followed soon after. By 1916 Louisville, New Orleans, Oklahoma City, and St. Louis had passed residential segregation statutes. Though the U.S. Supreme Court declared such laws unconstitutional in *Buchanan v. Warley* (1917), similar laws continued to appear on the books, and restrictive covenants and other arrangements designed to keep neighborhoods white continued for many decades.[41]

The evolution of segregation in Charlotte, North Carolina, provides an interesting case history. The races generally coexisted harmoniously in the city's train stations until 1893 when, in response to a minor disturbance by blacks, whites demanded separate waiting rooms. Hanchett identifies a direct relationship between the 1890s political alliance of Populists and black Republicans on the one hand, and the rise of segregated facilities in Charlotte on the other. The first "For White People" and "For Colored People" signs appeared at the city's Seaboard Air Line train station in 1895. A year later, in *Plessy v. Ferguson,* the U.S. Supreme Court sanctioned "separate but equal" facilities for blacks, and this doctrine was soon applied to every avenue of their lives. Responding to the racially coded signs at its train station, the editor of Charlotte's black religious newspaper, *The Star of Zion,* complained: "They ought to be disregarded by all decent people." Soon Charlotte's whites took further steps to create more spatial distance between themselves and blacks. In 1899 municipal regulations required segregation in Charlotte's public buildings and parks.[42]

Though for years whites and blacks in Charlotte had shared public parks for games, meetings, picnics, and religious revivals, in 1903 whites moved to ban blacks from recreation grounds. As Edward Dilworth Latta, a white industrialist and philanthropist, observed, "the negroes have absolutely no place for recreation or to hold meetings of any kind. The white people have the county court house, Academy of Music, the fair grounds and other places, but the colored race is debarred from these places." By 1905 park segregation was on the books in Charlotte. In late 1906 white Charlotteans, fearful of race riots like one that had erupted in Atlanta in September of that year, pushed to segregate the city's street-cars. "The feeling between whites and blacks is undoubtedly growing more acute," one citizen remarked, "and it behooves us to use every reasonable precaution to prevent such trouble such as they are having in Atlanta." As a solution, he added, "one thing which might be done here to very greatly lessen the danger of trouble would be to have separate compartments for the races in the street cars. I am a constant patron of the street cars and I have observed lately that the negroes are making themselves more and more objectionable to the white passengers by their insolent behavior."[43]

In 1906 the Southern Railway Company built a four-foot-high iron fence to separate the white and colored sections of its new station on West Trade Street in Charlotte. When whites complained that this fence was an insufficient barrier between them and blacks, the company replaced the fence with a floor-to-ceiling wall. A year later North Carolina passed a statute requiring segregated seating on all trolleys and streetcars in the state. "Henceforth," Hanchett notes, "on mass transit (including buses, when introduced), black Charlotteans would sit in the back and whites would sit in the front."[44]

In addition to the spatial distance that literally separated the races in neighborhoods and public places, whites kept blacks figuratively in their place, in informal and seemingly casual settings, through a complex web of racial etiquette. This racial etiquette was as much rooted in segregation as the "Whites Only" and "Colored Only" signs separating the races in public space. The racially defined code of behavior, according to Grossman, was a protocol "by which blacks were first taught and then reminded that they lacked civic dignity, that they were something less than second-class citizens." Du Bois initially encountered this in the 1880s when he went south for the first time to attend Fisk University in Nashville—a time, Du Bois recalled, when "the full force of legal caste in the South had not yet fallen on Negroes. Streetcars were not yet separate and there was still some Negro voting." Yet he sensed a strange social distance between the races. "No one but a Negro going into the South without previous experience of color caste can have any conception of its barbarism," Du Bois remembered many years later. "It is not a matter of law or ordinance; it is a question of instinctive feeling; of inherited and inborn knowledge."[45]

Blacks of all ages were expected to exhibit deference in all contacts with whites—even poor whites, whom they mocked privately as "peckerwoods." Blacks were to address whites as "Mr." or "Mrs." or "captain" or some other title of respect. On the other hand, whites were to call blacks by their first names, much as adults talk to children. Black men were expected to look down when they spoke to whites, especially white women. Blacks were to wait patiently in any line until all whites had been served. They were to enter a white home only by the back door. And they were to step from the sidewalk into the street to allow whites to pass when walking and were to yield the right of way to whites when driving.[46]

Du Bois remembered vividly his first brush with southern racial etiquette in Nashville.

> I quite accidentally jostled a white woman as I passed. She was not hurt in the slightest, nor even particularly inconvenienced. Immediately in accord with my New England training, I raised my hat and begged her pardon. I acted quite instinctively and with genuine regret for a little mistake. The woman was furious; why I never knew; somehow I cannot say how, I had transgressed the interracial mores of the South. Was it because I showed no submissiveness? Did I fail to debase myself utterly and eat spiritual dirt? Did I act as equal among equals? I do not know. I only sensed scorn and hate; the kind of despising which a dog might incur.

This confrontation so angered Du Bois that "for at least half a century I avoided the necessity of showing them [white southerners] courtesy of any sort."[47]

Du Bois's unintentional jostling of a white woman underscores the central role of gender in late-nineteenth-century white supremacist thought in general, and in the rise of racial segregation in particular. As early as 1855, the former slave and black abolitionist Frederick Douglass remarked that "women—white women, I mean—are idols at the south . . . and if these *idols* but nod, or lift a finger, woe to the poor victim: kicks, cuffs and stripes are sure to follow." Almost nine decades later, in *The Mind of the South* (1941), Wilbur J. Cash explained that post–Civil War white southerners constructed the "cult of Southern Womanhood," idealizing and transforming the southern lady into the region's "standard for its rallying, the mystic symbol of its nationality in the face of the foe." After the war white southerners wrote continually, longingly, and nostalgically about how in the Old South and during the war itself masters trusted their male slaves to protect their women. Circumstances changed dramatically, however, following Appomattox, whites explained. Denied slavery's discipline, and encouraged by northern and southern Republicans to seek social and political equality with whites, blacks allegedly regressed toward savagery. In the post-emancipation southern white mind, the once loyal black male slaves had become "black savage rapists."[48]

From Reconstruction to Redemption, and from the Progressive Era and beyond, white southerners anguished over black male contact—sexual and otherwise—with white women. Fearful of their females' safety at the hands of black men, whites structured their laws and social etiquette around maintaining what they deemed "racial purity." Throughout these decades white southerners were obsessed with protecting their women from allegedly savage and wanton blacks who reportedly craved them and who were determined to rape them. As late as 1937, John Dollard observed "that rape is the most intensely hostile act a Negro can perform within the purview of southern regional culture. . . . Rape and the wish to commit it seem to be constantly posited by the white caste as features of the Negro psychology." Cash dubbed this psychosis among whites "the Southern rape complex." Driven to protect the sexual purity of "Southern womanhood" and to maintain racial control, whites subjected black men to extralegal violence—burnings and lynchings. In the postwar South, according to Forrest G. Wood, "virtually every racist action could be justified . . . on the grounds that it perpetuated, exalted, and, indeed, sanctified the myth of white womanhood."[49]

Descriptions of alleged black male bestiality and justifications for the brutal murder of alleged black rapists run like a leitmotif through late-nineteenth-century southern literature and commentary. In 1889, for example, Virginian Philip Alexander Bruce interpreted the raping of white women by black men as symptomatic of the general retrogression and assertiveness of black males since emancipation. "There is something strangely alluring and seductive to them in the appearance of a white woman; they are aroused and stimulated by its foreignness to their experience of sexual pleasures, and it moves them to gratify their lust at any cost," he wrote. Plantation novelist Thomas Nelson Page blamed the "ravishing and murdering" of white women by blacks on Reconstruction-era "talk of social equality" and the absence of discipline among blacks following slavery's demise. "The intelligent Negro," Page explained, "may understand what social equality truly means, but to the ignorant and brutal young Negro, it signifies but one thing: the opportunity to enjoy, equally with white men, the privilege of cohabiting with white women." Northerners, Virginian Myrta Lockett Avary complained in 1909, failed to grasp the constant threat of sexual assault that white southern women endured. "Only people on the spot," she wrote, "writhing under the agony of provocation, comprehended the fury of response to the crime of crimes."[50]

Unquestionably, fear of "the crime of crimes" spurred white southerners to regulate contact between black men and white women and served as a major justification for segregation. In fact, the earliest form of segregation in public transit, dating back to Presidential Reconstruction, began when southern railway companies tried to exclude blacks from first-class accommodations (in what was commonly referred to as the "ladies' car") and relegate African Americans to crowded, filthy, and often unsafe smoking cars or freight boxcars. Railway companies, sensitive to local social cus-

toms, sought to eliminate the possibility of racial contact and thus established a dual-class structure of travel. "Few whites," Litwack explains,
"needed to be reminded of what was ultimately at stake. Behind every discussion and skirmish involving racial separation lurked the specter of
unrestrained black lust and sexuality, with that most feared of consequences—racial amalgamation. . . . Much of the furor over racial separation in public vehicles grew out of fears that white women and black men
might otherwise find themselves seated next to each other."[51]

Having triumphed over slavery and gained citizenship, blacks not surprisingly refused to accept their exclusion from accommodations available
to whites without a fight. During the post-emancipation decades African
Americans brought numerous civil lawsuits against carriers challenging
racial segregation. The most famous case occurred in 1892, when Homer
Adolph Plessy, a thirty-four-year-old, light-skinned Louisiana mulatto, purchased a first-class ticket on an East Louisiana Railroad train from New
Orleans to Covington, Louisiana, and took a seat in the first-class coach, a
car reserved for whites. Determined to provoke a case that would test the
constitutionality of segregation, Plessy openly violated Louisiana's 1890 law
requiring "equal but separate accommodations for the white and colored
races" on passenger trains. Applauding that railroad car bill, the New
Orleans *Daily Times-Democrat* remarked that while white southerners held
"no spirit of hostility to the negroes," they nevertheless had concluded
"that the two races shall live separate and distinct from each other in all
things, with separate schools, separate hotels and separate cars."[52]

As prearranged by his lawyers and the railroad company (the carrier
cooperated because it considered segregated cars expensive and feared
boycotts by blacks), Plessy refused the conductor's request to leave the
"white" compartment and sit in the car designated for blacks. He was sum-
marily removed from the train, arrested and charged with violating the
state statute, and bound over to criminal court. After hearing Plessy's plea
that the Louisiana law violated the Thirteenth and Fourteenth Amendments, Judge John H. Ferguson upheld the state statute. So too did
Louisiana's Supreme Court. Charging that Louisiana's separate car law was
an act of enforced discrimination, one that catered to white supremacy
and degraded blacks, Plessy's attorneys took his case to the U.S. Supreme
Court. On May 19, 1896, the Court handed down its decision in *Plessy v.
Ferguson*.[53]

By a seven-to-one vote, the Court upheld Louisiana's separate car law.
Speaking for the majority, Justice Henry Billings Brown argued that Louisiana's statute did not violate the Thirteenth or Fourteenth Amendments by
abridging the privileges or immunities of U.S. citizens or depriving persons
of liberty or property without due process of law. Ignoring the distinction

between private and state action that had been at issue in the 1883 *Civil Rights Cases,* the Court rejected Plessy's plea on three main grounds.

First, Justice Brown explained, "We consider the underlying fallacy of the plaintiff's argument to consist in the assumption that the enforced separation of the two races stamps the colored race with a badge of inferiority. If this be so, it is not by reason of anything found in the act, but solely because the colored race chooses to put that construction on it." Second, he wrote that the Fourteenth Amendment "could not have been intended to abolish distinctions based upon color, or to enforce social, as distinguished from political equality, or a commingling of the two races upon terms unsatisfactory to either. Laws permitting, and even requiring, their separation in places where they are liable to be brought into contact do not necessarily imply the inferiority of either race to the other, and have been generally, if not universally, recognized as within the competency of the state legislatures in the exercise of their police power." Finally, the majority of the Court argued that social prejudice could not be overturned by statutes, and disagreed with the principle "that equal rights cannot be secured to the negro except by an enforced commingling of the two races. . . . If the two races are to meet upon terms of social equality, it must be the result of natural affinities, a mutual appreciation of each other's merits and a voluntary consent of individuals." With this decision the Supreme Court affirmed the "separate but equal" doctrine.[54]

Justice Harlan, who had dissented in 1883 in the *Civil Rights Cases,* cast the lone negative vote in *Plessy.* In his opinion, Louisiana's law violated the spirit of the Thirteenth and Fourteenth Amendments. Harlan believed that "the arbitrary separation of citizens, on the basis of race, while they are on a public highway, is a badge of servitude wholly inconsistent with the civil freedom and the equality before the law established by the Constitution. It cannot be justified on legal grounds." He feared that legalized segregation on trains would spread to segregation in other areas of American life as well. Though whites had proclaimed themselves "the dominant race," Harlan reminded the Court that "in the eye of the law, there is in this country no superior, dominant ruling class of citizens. There is no caste here. Our Constitution is color-blind, and neither knows nor tolerates classes among citizens." Fearful of its implications for race relations, Harlan described the *Plessy* decision as a dangerous step backward toward slavery. He predicted that it "will, in time, prove to be quite as pernicious as the decision made by this tribunal in the *Dred Scott case.*"[55]

Justice Harlan proved most prescient. The *Plessy* case opened the flood gates for the rising tide of Jim Crow—a half century of across-the-board legalized segregation of black southerners. While *Plessy* confirmed the right of the states to legislate equal but separate accommodations for blacks, it never addressed the issue of guaranteeing true equality for people of color. Once freed from constitutional restraint, municipalities and states throughout the South passed racially coded criminal and segregation statutes that defined special space for blacks and kept them in their place.

"In every significant, openly visible aspect of his life," explains Louis H. Pollak, the black man "was segregated by the law from—which is to say, ostracized by—his white fellow citizens." Blacks either were excluded from public or quasi-public facilities or provided separate but never equal accommodations. Well into the 1950s and even the 1960s, African Americans lived in racially segregated neighborhoods, attended segregated schools, traveled in segregated buses and trains, and had access to generally inferior libraries, museums, hospitals, churches, theaters, stadiums, restaurants, hotels, parks, and beaches. African Americans remained disfranchised and, accordingly, were underrepresented in government and unprotected in the courts. As Fischer has explained, the entire notion of separate but equal was a charade. As the plaintiffs in the landmark *Brown v. Board of Education* (1954) argued, the mere act of legally separating the races was inherently unequal. Until the "Second Reconstruction" of the 1960s, then, "Negroes rode in the rear of buses, drank from rusted spigots a few inches away from spotless ones for whites, and buried their dead in weedy, overgrown plots usually separated from neatly trimmed white ones by only a hedge or picket fence. Often Negroes were denied even separate facilities, especially in business establishments, where black restrooms, fitting rooms, and lunch counter sections were uncommon."[56]

The history of race relations from slavery to segregation underscores the persistent determination of whites, as Ulrich Bonnell Phillips understood, to subordinate and degrade blacks. Though the essays that follow disagree on when, why, where, and how segregation developed, their authors concur that white racism lay at its core. They also agree that Jim Crow, whether by custom or code, in the Old South or the New, exposed the nation's hypocrisy—its shallow commitment to racial equality, fairness, and justice for African Americans. Overt racial discrimination in various forms continued to haunt Americans until the 1960s, when the civil rights revolution, through the courts and legislation, restored to blacks constitutional rights that had been denied as Reconstruction unraveled. Just as Jim Crow had a "strange" and circuitous "career," so too did true freedom for African Americans.

Summarizing in 1915 why he opposed segregation, Booker T. Washington said that he found it unfair, unjust, unnecessary, inconsistent, and harmful to race relations. A decade earlier a black editor put it even more succinctly when he asked: "Who can be satisfied to be humiliated?"[57]

Historians and the Origins of Racial Segregation

During much of the last century historians interpreted race relations in the age of Jim Crow in a familiar pattern, characterized by George Brown Tindall as "somewhat flat and static." According to William Cohen, "Their view was of a near-monolithic white South rising up in the 1870s to overthrow corruption and northern oppression and to establish white supremacy. More by implication than by direct statement," Cohen adds, "the works left the impression that, Reconstruction aside, segregation and disfranchisement were part of the natural order of things." Following World War II, however, revisionist scholars began to question the traditional interpretation of the rise of Jim Crow, deemphasizing its linear qualities and underscoring its ambiguities, complexities, and inconsistencies. As Tindall explained, southern race relations following Reconstruction "had undergone a lengthy period of flux."[58]

Vernon Lane Wharton led the way in 1947. His *The Negro in Mississippi, 1865–1890* outlined the Janus-faced qualities of race relations in that state. "By 1890 almost all white men in Mississippi agreed that the Negro was in his place," he wrote, "and that, at all costs, he should be kept there. That place, like the place of the slave, was carefully defined, and, theoretically unalterable." But Wharton added that despite the draconian racial repression black Mississippians experienced at the turn of the century, they also had "gained limited rights of movement, self-expression, and self-determination."[59]

In 1950 Herbert Aptheker, the much maligned and often ignored Marxist scholar, presented the most revisionist interpretation of Jim Crow's origins up to that date. Segregation, Aptheker argued, was neither "natural" nor "inevitable" but was "man-made; ruling class–made, to be exact." It was of recent vintage, he insisted, "from the late 1880's to the early 1900's," and resulted from the determination of white elites to "smash the rising unity of Negro and white" laborers "and to re-subject the Negro people to special oppression. . . ." Two years later, in *South Carolina Negroes, 1877–1900,* Tindall identified a pattern following Reconstruction of "race relations in a fluid and uncertain condition," yet one that gradually solidified, "by statute, by custom, by direction of the dominant whites, and by the institutional segregation of schools, churches, and private organizations."[60]

In a series of lectures he delivered at the University of Virginia in 1955, a year after the *Brown v. Board of Education* case declared "separate-but-equal" school facilities unconstitutional, C. Vann Woodward revolutionized the interpretation of race relations between the end of Reconstruction in 1877 and the 1890s. As Rabinowitz later explained, Woodward was "largely responsible" for identifying "segregation, disfranchisement, and mob violence against blacks under the rubric of Jim Crow due to their overlap in terms of timing and causation." Joel Williamson describes Woodward as "the first to grasp firmly the idea that the story of race relations in the South and in America had been diverse and evolutionary, and that it had not frozen with the end of either slavery or Reconstruction into an absolutely monolithic, rigid, and lasting pattern. He opened a new field of study on American history." Drawing upon the earlier work of Wharton and Tindall, but ignoring Aptheker's 1950 contribution, Woodward soon sparked "an ongoing debate over the origins of segregation after the Civil War."[61]

In *The Strange Career of Jim Crow* (1955), excerpts of which appear in this volume, Woodward overturned the longstanding myth that late-nineteenth-century segregation was a throwback to race relations under slavery. The history of race relations in the South, he insisted, changed over time, and degrees of experimentation, tolerance, and variety characterized southern race relations between the end of the Civil War and the 1890s. Rigid, formal, pervasive racial segregation was a child of the New South, Woodward said, not of the Old South.

Under slavery, he explained, masters and slaves lived unsegregated lives, in various types of close but unequal relationships. During Reconstruction, once federal officials overthrew the Black Codes and imposed military rule, the freedpeople engaged fully in the South's economic, social, and political life. While racial friction certainly was evident, southern black life nonetheless was relatively "open," uncircumscribed by racially defined laws. Even, in the late 1870s and 1880s, after the Democrats "redeemed" the region, Woodward said, African Americans continued to vote, hold office, and have equal access to public conveyances. There were "forgotten alternatives" then, Woodward suggested, between the relative calm of race relations following Reconstruction and the explosion of virulent racism (with its accompanying race baiting, lynchings, disfranchisement, and spatial segregation) that enveloped the South as the century closed.

Woodward interpreted the rise of formal segregation as an abrupt aberration. The jarring change in race relations, he explained, occurred during the tumultuous 1890s, an era when white conservative elites, responding to a political coalition of white and black Populists, revived and manipulated latent racial and class antagonisms and moved to destroy the insurgents. Woodward termed this the South's "capitulation to racism." Constructing an image of barbaric blacks as a threat to southern civilization, especially to white womanhood, white Democrats solidified their own power, denied blacks political and social power by disfranchising them, and then instituted rigid Jim Crow legislation that systematically segregated the races in the last years of the century. Woodward described the Jim Crow laws of the

1890s as "the public symbols and constant reminders" of black inferiority. Whites constructed a closed society based upon a strict "segregation code." "That code lent the sanction of law to a racial ostracism that extended to churches and schools, to housing and jobs, to eating and drinking. Whether by law or custom, that ostracism eventually extended to virtually all forms of public transportation, to sports and recreation, to hospitals, orphanages, prisons, asylums, and ultimately to funeral homes, morgues, and cemeteries."[62]

Published at a pivotal time in history—what historians term the start of the "Second Reconstruction"—*The Strange Career of Jim Crow* stressed that segregation was not spawned by slavery, that race relations in the South had not always been strained or fixed, and that laws, not folkways or mores, constructed the edifice of Jim Crow. Woodward's book reminded readers during the racially tense 1950s that because segregationist laws had been passed for political and social ends, they could just as easily be banned by legislation. So influential was Woodward's thesis that the Reverend Martin Luther King Jr. referred to *The Strange Career of Jim Crow* as "the Bible of the civil rights movement."[63] State studies by Charles E. Wynes (Virginia); Frenise A. Logan (North Carolina); Henry C. Dethloff and Robert P. Jones, John W. Blassingame, and Dale A. Somers (Louisiana); Margaret Law Callcott (Maryland); Eric Anderson (North Carolina); and John William Graves (Arkansas) have largely supported what historians continue to refer to as the "Woodward thesis."[64] These historians, according to Joseph H. Cartwright, generally "depicted the era between reconstruction and the turn of the century as one delicately poised between a reactionary white supremacist ethic and a trend toward biracial political activity and flexibility in interracial contacts." As late as 1985 Edward L. Ayers remarked that "Woodward's thesis is still the standard by which all others are measured. . . ."[65]

Other historians, however, disagreed sharply with Woodward and "certain dogmatic Woodwardian disciples" who, according to Roger A. Fischer, tended to accept *Strange Career* "as holy writ." Woodward's critics identified continuity, not discontinuity, in race relations between the Old South and the New South, and argued that Woodward undervalued early broad patterns of racial segregation in the antebellum North, the Old South, during Reconstruction, and beyond. In his influential *Slavery in the Cities: The South, 1820–1860* (1964), Richard C. Wade maintained that "even before slavery had been abolished, a system of segregation had grown up in the cities. Indeed," he continued, "the whites thought some such arrangement was necessary if they were to sustain their traditional supremacy over the Negroes."[66]

The continuity thesis is most clearly identified with Joel Williamson's pathbreaking scholarship. While agreeing with Woodward that formalized, legal (de jure) segregation first appeared in the last decade of the century, in *After Slavery: The Negro in South Carolina During Reconstruction, 1861–1877* (1965) Williamson nonetheless faulted him for overvaluing the importance of legal discrimination, for paying short shrift to the extensive pattern of informal or customary (de facto) segregation that Williamson had uncovered in Reconstruction-era South Carolina, and for providing too rosy a portrait of race relations following Appomattox. "Well before the end of Reconstruction," Williamson explained, "separation had crystallized into a comprehensive pattern which, in its essence, remained unaltered until the middle of the twentieth century." Williamson's research led him to conclude that "the pattern of separation was fixed in the minds of the whites almost simultaneously with the emancipation of the Negro." As Rabinowitz observed, once Williamson challenged Woodward, "historians jumped in on both sides of the debate." A chapter from Williamson's book appears in this work.[67]

If Williamson was Woodward's most thoughtful critic, David Hackett Fischer was perhaps Woodward's sharpest and most unfair critic. In *Historians' Fallacies: Toward a Logic of Historical Thought* (1970) Fischer proclaimed that the works of Wade, Williamson, Litwack, V. Jacque Voegeli, Winthrop D. Jordan, and others had proven "Woodward's argument . . . wrong in all its major parts—wrong because he made a long story short." Fischer insisted that there was "abundant evidence of a 'capitulation to racism' by Americans, both above and below the Mason-Dixon line, long before 1890." In Fischer's estimate, Woodward "telescoped" the history of racial segregation "into the narrow span of his own special period, and thereby falsified it." He went so far as to charge that "the thesis of the *Strange Career of Jim Crow* truncates one of the enduring themes of American history." Fischer, whose attack was based on his reading of secondary sources, used Woodward's book as an example of a flawed historical method, a reliance on what he termed the "telescopic" and the "overwhelming exception" fallacies.[68]

These criticisms led Woodward to defend and refine his thesis repeatedly over the course of many years. In a 1970 interview, for example, he explained that "formal, legalized, universal segregation was not an immediate consequence of Reconstruction, but an evolution over a period of years. . . . What I meant by segregation was physical separation—physical distance, not social distance, which has always been great." Responding to Wade and Williamson, Woodward said that both scholars missed the significance of racial integration that existed concomitantly with racial segregation. "Reconstruction brought the races into physical contact in many ways in which they had never been before."[69]

A year later, Woodward charged that some of his critics, including "partisans in a raging debate over public policy," had misread, distorted, and misused his *Strange Career*. Clarifying his original arguments, Woodward explained: "No, he had not said that segregation was superficially rooted or easily eradicated; it was rooted in prejudices older than slavery and might be as difficult to uproot. No, he had never suggested that the period after Reconstruction was a golden age of race relations. Yes, he was quite aware that *de facto* segregation normally antedated *de jure* segregation and that it was widely practiced in several areas before the 1890's." Woodward continued to refine his argument in three revised editions (1957, 1966, and 1974), and *Strange Career* remains among the most heavily analyzed, most significant texts in American historiography, one that has defined the field and shaped the contours of the scholarship on the origins of segregation for almost a half century.[70]

So influential was *Strange Career* that most scholars who studied the origins of segregation felt compelled to respond to Woodward and his critics. In 1971, for example, August Meier and Elliott Rudwick identified patterns in the history of racial segregation in Savannah, Georgia, that generally reconciled Woodward's and Williamson's theses. Meier and Rudwick's research suggested that although whites introduced streetcar segregation in Savannah in the early 1870s, black protests and boycotts forced streetcar integration until the turn of the century.[71]

In *The Segregation Struggle in Louisiana, 1862–1877* (1974), Roger A. Fischer identified a long-standing pattern of racial segregation in antebellum New Orleans and documented the vigorous campaigns African Americans waged during Reconstruction to remove segregation in the state's schools, streetcars, theaters, and taverns. Ira Berlin's research on free blacks in the Old South echoed Fischer's findings. As the Civil War approached, "segregation had extended to almost every corner of Southern life," he wrote, and following the war "the informal pattern of separation, well entrenched long before Emancipation, persisted." In *The Shaping of Southern Politics: Suffrage Restriction and the Establishment of the One-Party South, 1880–1910* (1974), J. Morgan Kousser questioned Woodward's analysis of disfranchisement, specifically, just who were the disfranchisers. In his heavily quantified study Kousser concluded that "Woodward exaggerated the support which the Redeemers or 'paternalists' gave to black suffrage."[72]

In several influential essays (one of which is reproduced here) and in his *Race Relations in the Urban South, 1865–1890* (1978), Rabinowitz sided with Williamson in recognizing that both de jure and de facto segregation appeared during Reconstruction. But, moving beyond the old debate,

Rabinowitz concluded that "segregation . . . ironically often signified an improvement" for blacks because "what it replaced was not integration but exclusion." As freedpeople, blacks for the first time accessed public and private accommodations, schools, social welfare, and public services denied them as slaves. In the South's cities they served in separate black militia companies and were admitted to segregated almshouses, hospitals, insane asylums, and institutions for the deaf, dumb, and blind. "Rather than the flexible system of race relations portrayed by Woodward," Rabinowitz explained, "by 1873 the urban landscape for blacks was dominated by segregated galleries in the theaters; exclusion from leading hotels, restaurants, and bars and segregated access in others; segregated or no waiting rooms in railroad stations; and second-class or smoking cars on the railroads." The combination of white racism and voluntary black self-segregation resulted in separate churches, clubs, and neighborhoods.[73]

In his comparative *The Highest Stage of White Supremacy: The Origins of Segregation in South Africa and the American South* (1982), John W. Cell agreed with Rabinowitz. Cell argued that southern cities led the way, long before the 1890s, in inventing and testing "the various devices—including separate housing and social services, poll taxes, educational qualifications for the ballot, white party primaries—that were to be fused into the legal system of segregation across the South."[74]

In *Dark Journey: Black Mississippians in the Age of Jim Crow* (1989), Neil R. McMillen described the veil that Jim Crow cast over Mississippi from the perspective of black Mississippians. Though the state had led the way in passing segregation laws during Reconstruction, McMillen insists that much of the racial control was informal, not legal, and that exclusion played as much of a role in regulating blacks as segregation. As McMillen explained, segregation resulted

> in part of the frustrations of agricultural depression in the eighties and nineties and the fear that Populism threatened both white cohesion and a renewed black political influence . . . [and] was sustained by a cluster of related national currents ranging from the vogue of Social Darwinian "survival of the fittest" and Anglo-Saxon scientific racism to the immigration restriction movement and the American assumption of the "white man's burden" in Hawaii and the Philippines. Not least of all, the excesses of the period were encouraged by a growing Yankee readiness to accept a "southern solution" to the race problem.

Not until segregation came under fire in the 1950s did municipalities enforce the color line in such service establishments as barber shops and beauty parlors, and in such public accommodations as hotels, restaurants, theaters, and billiard halls. Such discrimination empowered blacks to develop strategies of survival and resistance and hammer out a group identity of their own.[75]

In *At Freedom's Edge: Black Mobility and the Southern White Quest for Racial Control, 1861–1915* (1991) Cohen challenged Woodward by interpreting the process of legalized segregation of the 1890s "to a large extent" as an "intensification of processes that had been at work at least since the end of Reconstruction." During Redemption, Cohen documents, one former Confederate state after another restricted suffrage, determined to exclude blacks from state governments.[76]

Edward L. Ayers's *The Promise of the New South: Life After Reconstruction* (1992), an excerpt from which is reprinted in this book, builds and expands upon Woodward's pioneering work. Ayers interprets the decision to segregate blacks legally as a complex process, a result of "the growing ambition, attainments, and assertiveness of blacks, by the striking expansion and importance of the railroad system in the 1880s, by a widespread distrust and dislike for the railroad corporations, by the course of legal cases at the state and circuit level, and by the example each state set for others." He attributes the Jim Crow laws to the impersonal forces of capitalism and modernism that cloaked the New South. Segregation "was the product of no particular class, of no wave of hysteria or displaced frustration, no rising tide of abstract racism, no new ideas about race." It "grew out of concrete situations, out of technological, demographic, economic, and political changes. . . ." Ayers explains Jim Crow not as an aging symbol of antebellum slavery, but rather as a new and powerful force, one as revolutionary and progressive in its transforming powers as the railroads that crisscrossed the region. Jim Crow was "a badge of sophisticated, modern, managed race relations."[77]

Grace Elizabeth Hale also frames segregation within the myriad institutional adjustments that spirited and created order in the increasingly impersonal social relations of the New South. In *Making Whiteness: The Culture of Segregation in the South, 1890–1940* (1998), she interprets segregation as one of the "spatial mediations of modernity"—the unending process of "separating peoples as a way of making and fixing absolute racial difference. . . ." Hale maintains that "African Americans were clearly inferior in the South because they occupied inferior spaces like Jim Crow cars, often literally marked as colored. . . ." "Systemized spatial relations replaced the need to know others personally in order to categorize them," she argues. Racial violence, including "spectacle lynchings," also "were about making racial difference in the new South, about ensuring the separation of all southern life into whiteness and blackness. . . ."[78]

The relationship between racial violence and racial privilege lies at the heart of Leon F. Litwack's *Trouble in Mind: Black Southerners in the Age of Jim*

Crow (1998), an excerpt from which is presented in this book. As several of Woodward's detractors noted, Litwack's *North of Slavery: The Negro in the Free States, 1790–1860* (1961) exposed numerous forms of segregation and racial discrimination in the antebellum North that prefigured the South's Jim Crow system. Similarly, Litwack's *Been in the Storm So Long: The Aftermath of Slavery* (1979) underscored how quickly white southerners moved during Reconstruction to establish or to reestablish segregation in public places and conveyances. In *Trouble in Mind,* a work that focuses on white barbarity and repression, Litwack reiterates his previous argument that "racial segregation was hardly a new phenomenon" at the end of Reconstruction. He argues that segregation, a legal and social system predicated on racial fear and hate, reached its zenith from the late 1870s until the 1920s. "To maintain and underscore its absolute supremacy, the white South systematically disfranchised black men, imposed rigid patterns of racial segregation, manipulated the judicial system, and sustained extraordinary levels of violence and brutality." This combination of legal and extralegal control mechanisms, Litwack concludes, formed the New South's solidifying and driving force, its "racial creed," as the twentieth century dawned.[79]

By viewing this violent, racialized society through the lens of gender, recent scholars have contributed among the most original and insightful studies on the segregation era. Examining, for example, the role of sexuality in nineteenth-century southern culture and society, Peter W. Bardaglio concluded that "it embodied the relations of race, class, and gender, and was itself one of the motors that drove the unequal distribution of power in this society." During Reconstruction, Martha Hodes has argued, "expressions of white anxiety about sex between black men and white women reached an unprecedented intensity." As citizens and no longer slaves, blacks threatened the foundation of southern white society. "The idea of manhood," Hodes adds, "which had long implied the right and responsibilities of citizenship in American political thought, now assumed connotations in white minds of black men engaging in sex with white women." The mere charge of "Negro domination," Jacqueline Dowd Hall writes, inclined white men to make white women the focal point of violent disfranchisement battles. "Manufacturing rape scares, they whipped up support by charging that black men's access to politics, however limited, had aroused their desire for that other prerequisite of white manhood: access to white women."[80]

Gender, definitions of manhood and womanhood, the fear of black men as rapists, and the assertiveness of black women colors much of the latest scholarship on race relations in the age of Jim Crow. When, by the late 1880s and early 1890s, as Barbara Y. Welke explains in the excerpt that appears in this book, custom and common law proved inadequate to exclude blacks from first-class cars on southern railroads, southern state legislatures intervened to pass Jim Crow statutes. "For southern whites," Welke notes, "women of color riding as the equals of white women in ladies' accommodations was a direct threat to the status of white womanhood, and hence to white superiority generally. . . . The specter of black men riding in ladies' accommodations raised the worst fears of Southern whites." Because they led the way in challenging segregation in the courts, Welke considers "women of color . . . the foot soldiers in the battle against inequality and segregation."[81]

Laura F. Edwards and Glenda Elizabeth Gilmore also place gender at the center of the evolution of race relations in the post-emancipation South. In *Gendered Strife and Confusion: The Political Culture of Reconstruction* (1997), Edwards maintains that African American women led the fight in forcing whites to recognize the integrity of their households. In her opinion, "freedpeople's struggles for fair wages, reasonable terms of employment, education, civil rights, and political power depended on their ability to establish and maintain their own households." Edwards positions marriages, especially those of the freedpeople, at the heart of postwar social relations. While the former slaves understood the legalization of their marriages as the institutional recognition of family life and the basis for claiming civil and political rights, white elites interpreted them as a means of consolidating state power over them.[82]

Gilmore's *Gender and Jim Crow: Women and the Politics of White Supremacy in North Carolina, 1896–1920* (1996) spotlights the gendered underpinnings of North Carolina's white supremacy campaigns of 1898 and 1900 and how black females vigorously assumed various "political" roles during the Progressive era. "After black men's banishment from politics," she explains, "North Carolina's black women added a network of women's groups that crossed denominational—and later party—lines and took a multi-issue approach to civic action. In a nonpolitical guise, black women became the black community's diplomats to the white community." Like white Progressives, black women organized mothers' clubs, sponsored community cleanup days, built playgrounds, and promoted public health and temperance. "To achieve these goals," Gilmore writes, "southern black women entered political space, appearing before local officials and interacting with white bureaucrats." By 1920, she concludes, black women, though committed to overturning Jim Crow, had reconciled themselves to refining it—to make segregation better for their people. Focused and determined, "they set their shoulders, fixed their facial expressions, watched their language, and undertook interracial work without illusion because they knew that racial progress depended upon it."[83]

While Welke, Edwards, Gilmore, and other historians have raised the consciousness of students to the role of African American women in combating racial injustice, their work unfortunately tends to fall short of examining segregation's timing. An extended study of the role of gender on Jim Crow's initial emergence and sustenance—and how it relates to the continuity or discontinuity theses—remains to be made. Such an investigation will fill an important gap in this ongoing and lively debate.

Notes

1. W. E. B. Du Bois, "The Negro and Crime," *Independent,* 51 (May 18, 1899): 1355–57, and "The Freedmen's Bureau," *Atlantic Monthly,* 87 (March 1901): 365; Robert L. Zangrando, *The NAACP Crusade Against Lynching, 1909–1950* (Philadelphia: Temple University Press, 1980), [6] (Table 2); H. Leon Prather, "Race Riots," in Charles Reagan Wilson and William Ferris, eds., *Encyclopedia of Southern Culture* (Chapel Hill: University of North Carolina Press, 1989), 1496–97; Rayford W. Logan, *The Negro in American Life and Thought: The Nadir, 1877–1901* (New York: Dial Press, 1954).

2. David Delaney, *Race, Place, & the Law, 1836–1948* (Austin: University of Texas Press, 1998), 99.

3. See Roger Daniels, *Not Like Us: Immigrants and Minorities in America, 1890–1924* (Chicago: Ivan R. Dee, 1997).

4. James R. Grossman, "A Certain Kind of Soul," in James Oliver Horton and Lois E. Horton, eds., *A History of the African American People* (New York: Smithmark Publishers, 1995), 100.

5. John W. Cell, "Race Relations," in Wilson and Ferris, eds., *Encyclopedia of Southern Culture,* 188.

6. Ulrich Bonnell Phillips, "The Central Theme of Southern History," *American Historical Review,* 34 (October 1928): 31.

7. William Cohen, *At Freedom's Edge: Black Mobility and the Southern White Quest for Racial Control, 1861–1915* (Baton Rouge: Louisiana State University Press, 1991), 220–21.

8. Charles Reagan Wilson, "Jim Crow," in Wilson and Ferris, eds., *Encyclopedia of Southern Culture,* 213–14.

9. Roger A. Fischer, "Communications," *American Historical Review,* 75 (October 1969): 327.

10. Cell, "Race Relations," in Wilson and Ferris, eds., *Encyclopedia of Southern Culture,* 189.

11. *The Autobiography of W. E. B. Du Bois: A Soliloquy of Viewing My Life from the Last Decade of Its First Century* (New York: International Publishers, 1968), 234–35.

12. W. E. B. Du Bois, "Niagara's Declaration of Principles, 1905," in Herbert Aptheker, ed., *A Documentary History of the Negro People in the United States,* 7 vols. (New York: Citadel Press, 1951–1994), 2:903; Grace Elizabeth Hale, *Making Whiteness: The Culture of Segregation in the South, 1890–1940* (New York: Pantheon Books, 1998), 199–200.

13. Howard N. Rabinowitz, *Race Relations in the Urban South, 1865–1890* (New York: Oxford University Press, 1978); Herman Belz, *Emancipation and Equal Rights: Politics and Constitutionalism in the Civil War Era* (New York: W. W. Norton, 1978),

147; Michael Naragon, "Segregation," in Seymour Drescher and Stanley L. Enger-man, eds., *A Historical Guide to World Slavery* (New York: Oxford University Press, 1998), 352.

14. Neil R. McMillen, *Dark Journey: Black Mississippians in the Age of Jim Crow* (Urbana: University of Illinois Press, 1989), 23.

15. Otto H. Olsen, ed., *The Thin Disguise: Turning Point in Negro History. Plessy v. Ferguson: A Documentary Presentation (1864–1896)* (New York: Humanities Press, 1967), 4.

16. Roger A. Fischer, "Segregation," in David C. Roller and Robert W. Twyman, eds., *The Encyclopedia of Southern History* (Baton Rouge: Louisiana State University Press, 1979), 1088; Richard C. Wade, *Slavery in the Cities: The South, 1820–1860* (New York: Oxford University Press, 1964), 266.

17. Leon F. Litwack, *North of Slavery: The Negro in the Free States, 1790–1860* (Chicago: University of Chicago Press, 1961), 97; Joel Williamson, ed., *The Origins of Segregation* (Boston: D. C. Heath and Company, 1968), v.

18. Leon F. Litwack, *Been in the Storm So Long: The Aftermath of Slavery* (New York: Alfred A. Knopf, 1979), 261.

19. Theodore B. Wilson, *The Black Codes of the South* (University: University of Alabama Press, 1965); Fischer, "Segregation," 1088; Walter Lynwood Fleming, ed., *Documentary History of Reconstruction,* 2 vols. (1906–1907; reprint, New York: McGraw-Hill, 1966), 1:281–82.

20. Litwack, *Been in the Storm So Long,* 262, 489.

21. Cohen, *At Freedom's Edge,* 214–17.

22. Litwack, *Been in the Storm So Long,* 262–63; Otis A. Singletary, *Negro Militia and Reconstruction* (Austin: University of Texas Press, 1957).

23. Cohen, *At Freedom's Edge,* 213–16.

24. Fischer, "Segregation," 1088; Litwack, *Been in the Storm So Long,* 263; Howard N. Rabinowitz, "Continuity and Change: Southern Urban Development, 1860–1900," in Blaine A. Brownell and David R. Goldfield, eds., *The City in Southern History: The Growth of Urban Civilization in the South* (Port Washington, N.Y.: Kennikat Press, 1977), 100; Loren Schweninger, "Civil Rights Act of 1875," in Charles D. Lowery and John F. Marszalek, eds., *Encyclopedia of African-American Civil Rights: From Emancipation to the Present* (Westport, Conn.: Greenwood Press, 1992), 105; Eric Foner, *Reconstruction: America's Unfinished Revolution, 1863–1877* (New York: Harper & Row, 1988), 556.

25. Fischer, "Segregation," 1088.

26. David Levering Lewis, *W. E. B. Du Bois: Biography of a Race, 1868–1919* (New York: Henry Holt and Company, 1993), 35; J. Morgan Kousser, "Disfranchisement," in Roller and Twyman, eds., *The Encyclopedia of Southern History,* 362; Herbert Aptheker, "American Imperialism and White Chauvinism," *Jewish Life,* 4 (July 1950): 23; Benjamin R. Justesen, *George Henry White: An Even Chance in the Race of Life* (Baton Rouge: Louisiana State University Press, 2001).

27. Foner, *Reconstruction,* 590; Cohen, *At Freedom's Edge,* 202–3.

28. Cohen, *At Freedom's Edge,* 202–5.

29. Richard H. Collin, "Understanding Clause," in Roller and Twyman, eds., *The Encyclopedia of Southern History,* 1260; Kousser, "Grandfather Clause," in ibid., 552; Cohen, *At Freedom's Edge,* 205, 207; John Hope Franklin and Alfred A. Moss, Jr., *From Slavery to Freedom: A History of African Americans,* 7th ed. (New York: McGraw-Hill, 1994), 261.

30. Fischer, "Segregation," 1088; Daniel Walker Hollis, *University of South Carolina: College to University,* 2 vols. (Columbia: University of South Carolina Press, 1956), 2:80, 83; James E. Sefton, *"Civil Rights Cases,"* in Lowery and Marszalek, eds., *Encyclopedia of African-American Civil Rights,* 110–11; Alan Westin, "John Marshall Harlan and the Constitutional Rights of Negroes: The Transformation of a Southerner," *Yale Law Journal,* 66 (April 1957): 674–85.

31. Cohen, *At Freedom's Edge,* 217–20; Henry W. Grady, "In Plain Black and White: A Reply to Mr. Cable," *Century Magazine,* 29 (April 1885): 915.

32. Cohen, *At Freedom's Edge,* 217–20.

33. Jane Dailey, *Before Jim Crow: The Politics of Race in Postemancipation Virginia* (Chapel Hill: University of North Carolina Press, 2000), 2, 4; Lawanda Cox, "From Emancipation to Segregation: National Policy and Southern Blacks," in John B. Boles and Evelyn Thomas Nolen, eds., *Interpreting Southern History: Historiographical Essays in Honor of Sanford W. Higginbotham* (Baton Rouge: Louisiana State University Press, 1987), 248.

34. Jeffrey J. Crow and Robert F. Durden, *Maverick Republican in the Old North State: A Political Biography of Daniel L. Russell* (Baton Rouge: Louisiana State University Press, 1977), 125, 126–28; Paul D. Escott, *Many Excellent People: Power and Privilege in North Carolina, 1850–1900* (Chapel Hill: University of North Carolina Press, 1985), 247–54; Richard L. Watson, Jr., "Furnifold M. Simmons and the Politics of White Supremacy," in Jeffrey J. Crow, Paul D. Escott, and Charles L. Flynn, Jr., eds., *Race, Class, and Politics in Southern History: Essays in Honor of Robert F. Durden* (Baton Rouge: Louisiana State University Press, 1989), 131–33.

35. Wilmington *Record,* August 18, 1898, in Jeffery J. Crow, "Cracking the Solid South: Populism and the Fusionist Interlude," in Lindley S. Butler and Alan D. Watson, eds., *The North Carolina Experience* (Chapel Hill: University of North Carolina Press, 1984), 348–49.

36. Ray Gavins, "Recasting the Black Freedom Struggle in Wilmington, 1898–1930," *Carolina Comments,* 48 (November 2000): 143.

37. Watson, "Furnifold M. Simmons and the Politics of White Supremacy," 133–40; Idus A. Newby, *The South: A History* (New York: Holt, Rinehart and Winston, 1978), 351.

38. J. A. Scott quoted in Fleming, ed., *Documentary History of Reconstruction,* 2:446–47.

39. Thomas W. Hanchett, *Sorting Out the New South City: Race, Class, and Urban Development in Charlotte, 1875–1975* (Chapel Hill: University of North Carolina Press, 1998), 116.

40. Howard N. Rabinowitz, "Segregation, Residential," in Wilson and Ferris, eds., *Encyclopedia of Southern Culture,* 1442.

41. Ibid.

42. Hanchett, *Sorting Out the New South City,* 118–19.

43. Ibid., 119–20.

44. Ibid., 120.

45. Grossman, "A Certain Kind of Soul," 102; *The Autobiography of W. E. B. Du Bois,* 122, 121.

46. McMillen, *Dark Journey,* 24.

47. *Autobiography of W. E. B. Du Bois,* 121.

48. Frederick Douglass, *My Bondage and My Freedom* (1855; reprint, New York: Dover Publications, 1969), 59; Wilbur J. Cash, *The Mind of the South* (New York:

Alfred A. Knopf, 1941), 86; Lawrence J. Friedman, "Rape Complex, Southern," in Roller and Twyman, eds., *The Encyclopedia of Southern History,* 1029.

49. John Dollard, *Caste and Class in a Southern Town* (1937; Garden City, N.Y.: Doubleday Anchor Books, 1957), 296, 297; Cash, *The Mind of the South,* 115; Forrest G. Wood, *Black Scare: The Racist Response to Emancipation and Reconstruction* (Berkeley: University of California Press, 1970), 143.

50. Philip Alexander Bruce, *The Plantation Negro as a Freeman: Observations on His Character, Condition, and Prospects in Virginia* (New York: G. P. Putnam's Sons, 1889), 83; Thomas Nelson Page, *The Negro: The Southerner's Problem* (New York: Charles Scribner's Sons, 1904), 111–13; Myrta Lockett Avary, *Dixie After the War: An Exposition of Social Conditions Existing in the South, During the Twelve Years Succeeding the Fall of Richmond* (1906; reprint, New York: Negro Universities Press, 1969), 381.

51. Claude H. Nolen, *The Negro's Image in the South* (Lexington: University of Kentucky Press, 1967), 36; Litwack, *Been in the Storm So Long,* 262, 265.

52. Olsen, ed., *The Thin Disguise,* 54, 53.

53. Brook Thomas, ed., *Plessy v. Ferguson: A Brief History with Documents* (Boston: Bedford Books, 1997), 5; Charles A. Lofgren, *The Plessy Case: A Legal-Historical Interpretation* (New York: Oxford University Press, 1987), 41; Olsen, ed., *The Thin Disguise,* 14–16.

54. Olsen, ed., *The Thin Disguise,* 111–12, 109, 112.

55. Ibid., 119, 117.

56. Louis H. Pollak, "Emancipation and Law: A Century of Process," in Robert A. Goldwin, ed., *100 Years of Emancipation* (Chicago: Rand McNally, 1963), 170; Fischer, "Segregation," 1089.

57. Booker T. Washington, "My View of Segregation Laws," *New Republic,* 5 (December 5, 1915): 113–14, reprinted in Louis R. Harlan, ed., *The Booker T. Washington Papers,* 14 vols. (Urbana: University of Illinois Press, 1972–1989), 13:357–60; Hanchett, *Sorting Out the New South City,* 120.

58. George Brown Tindall, "Southern Negroes Since Reconstruction: Dissolving the Static Image," in Arthur S. Link and Rembert W. Patrick, eds., *Writing Southern History: Essays in Historiography in Honor of Fletcher M. Green* (Baton Rouge: Louisiana State University Press, 1965), 339, 355; Cohen, *At Freedom's Edge,* 201.

59. Vernon Lane Wharton, *The Negro in Mississippi, 1865–1890* (Chapel Hill: University of North Carolina Press, 1947), 274–75.

60. Aptheker, "American Imperialism and White Chauvinism," 21, 23; George Brown Tindall, *South Carolina Negroes, 1877–1900* (Columbia: University of South Carolina Press, 1952), 303, 302.

61. Howard N. Rabinowitz, "Jim Crow: Segregation and Disfranchisement in the South, 1870s–1917," in Peter J. Parish, ed., *Reader's Guide to American History* (London: Fitzroy Dearborn Publishers, 1997), 365; Joel Williamson, *The Crucible of Race: Black-White Relations in the American South Since Emancipation* (New York: Oxford University Press, 1984), 492–93.

62. C. Vann Woodward, *The Strange Career of Jim Crow: A Brief Account of Segregation* (New York: Oxford University Press, 1955), 7, 8.

63. John Herbert Roper, *C. Vann Woodward, Southerner* (Athens: University of Georgia Press, 1987), 198.

64. Charles E. Wynes, *Race Relations in Virginia, 1870–1902* (Charlottesville: University Press of Virginia, 1961); Frenise A. Logan, *The Negro in North Carolina, 1786–1894* (Chapel Hill: University of North Carolina Press, 1964); Henry C.

Dethloff and Robert P. Jones, "Race Relations in Louisiana, 1877–98," *Louisiana History*, 9 (Fall 1968): 301–23; John W. Blassingame, *Black New Orleans, 1860–1880* (Chicago: University of Chicago Press, 1973); Dale A. Somers, "Black and White in New Orleans: A Study in Urban Race Relations, 1865–1900," *Journal of Southern History*, 40 (February 1974): 19–42; Margaret Law Callcott, *The Negro in Maryland Politics, 1870–1912* (Baltimore: The Johns Hopkins University Press, 1969); Eric Anderson, *Race and Politics in North Carolina, 1872–1901* (Baton Rouge: Louisiana State University Press, 1981); John William Graves, *Town and Country: Race Relations in an Urban-Rural Context, Arkansas, 1865–1905* (Fayetteville: University of Arkansas Press, 1990).

65. John H. Cartwright, *The Triumph of Jim Crow: Tennessee Race Relations in the 1880s* (Knoxville: University of Tennessee Press, 1976), vii; Edward L. Ayers, "The Birth of Jim Crow," *Virginia Quarterly Review*, 61 (Spring 1985): 338.

66. Fischer, "Communications," 327; "A Pioneer Protest: The New Orleans Street-Car Controversy of 1867," *Journal of Negro History*, 53 (July 1968): 219–33; "Racial Segregation in Ante Bellum New Orleans," *American Historical Review*, 64 (February 1969): 926–37; *The Segregation Struggle in Louisiana, 1862–77* (Urbana: University of Illinois Press, 1974), 159; Wade, *Slavery in the Cities*, 277.

67. Joel Williamson, *After Slavery: The Negro in South Carolina During Reconstruction, 1861–1877* (Chapel Hill: University of North Carolina Press, 1965), 274, 275, 298; Rabinowitz, "Jim Crow: Segregation and Disfranchisement in the South, 1870s–1917," 366.

68. David Hackett Fischer, *Historians' Fallacies: Toward a Logic of Historical Thought* (New York: Harper & Row, 1970), 148–49. Fischer refers to V. Jacque Voegeli's *Free But Not Equal: The Midwest and the Negro During the Civil War* (Chicago: University of Chicago Press, 1967) and Winthrop D. Jordan's *White Over Black: American Attitudes Toward the Negro, 1550–1812* (Chapel Hill: University of North Carolina Press, 1968).

69. John A. Garraty, "C. Vann Woodward: The Negro in American Life: 1865–1918," *Interpreting American History: Conversations with Historians*, 2 vols. (London: Macmillan Company, 1970), 2:51–52.

70. C. Vann Woodward, *American Counterpoint: Slavery and Racism in the North/South Dialogue* (1971; New York: Oxford University Press, 1983), 237–38. For later responses to his critics, see Woodward's *Thinking Back: The Perils of Writing History* (Baton Rouge: Louisiana State University Press, 1986), 81–99, and "*Strange Career* Critics: Long May They Persevere," *Journal of American History*, 75 (December 1988): 857–68.

71. August Meier and Elliott Rudwick, "A Strange Chapter in the Career of 'Jim Crow,'" in Meier and Rudwick, eds., *The Making of Black America: Essays in Negro Life & History*, 2 vols. (New York: Atheneum, 1971), 2:14–19.

72. Ira Berlin, *Slaves without Masters: The Free Negro in the Antebellum South* (New York: Pantheon, 1974), 326, 383; J. Morgan Kousser, *The Shaping of Southern Politics: Suffrage Restriction and the Establishment of the One-Party South, 1880–1910* (New Haven: Yale University Press, 1974), 275.

73. Rabinowitz, *Race Relations in the Urban South*, 127, 182, 331–32; and "Continuity and Change: Southern Urban Development, 1860–1900," in Brownell and Goldfield, eds., *The City in Southern History*, 100. Also see Rabinowitz's "From Exclusion to Segregation: Health and Welfare Service for Southern Blacks, 1865–1890," *Social Service Review*, 48 (September 1974): 327–54; "From Exclusion to Segregation:

Southern Race Relations, 1865–1890," *Journal of American History*, 63 (September 1976): 325–50; "The Conflict between Blacks and the Police in the Urban South, 1865–1900," *The Historian*, 39 (November 1976): 62–76; "The Not-So-Strange Career of Jim Crow," *Reviews in American History*, 12 (March 1984): 58–64; "A Comparative Perspective on Race Relations in Southern and Northern Cities, 1860–1900, with Special Emphasis on Raleigh," in Jeffery J. Crow and Flora J. Hatley, eds., *Black Americans in North Carolina and the South* (Chapel Hill: University of North Carolina Press, 1984), 137–59; "More than the Woodward Thesis: Assessing *The Strange Career of Jim Crow*," *Journal of American History*, 75 (December 1988): 842–56; and "Segregation and Reconstruction," in Eric Anderson and Alfred Moss, Jr., eds., *The Facts of Reconstruction: Essays in Honor of John Hope Franklin* (Baton Rouge: Louisiana State University Press, 1991), 79–98.

74. John W. Cell, *The Highest Stage of White Supremacy: The Origins of Segregation in South Africa and the American South* (Cambridge, Eng.: Cambridge University Press, 1982), 133.

75. McMillen, *Dark Journey*, 7.

76. Cohen, *At Freedom's Edge*, 202, 203–10.

77. Edward L. Ayers, *The Promise of the New South: Life After Reconstruction* (New York: Oxford University Press, 1992), 145.

78. Hale, *Making Whiteness*, 6, 7, 8, 130, 203.

79. Leon F. Litwack, *Trouble in Mind: Black Southerners in the Age of Jim Crow* (New York: Alfred A. Knopf, 1998), 229, 218–19.

80. Peter W. Bardaglio, *Reconstructing the Household: Families, Sex, and the Law in the Nineteenth-Century South* (Chapel Hill: University of North Carolina Press, 1995), 39; Martha Hodes, *White Women, Black Men: Illicit Sex in the Nineteenth-Century South* (New Haven: Yale University Press, 1997), 147; Jacqueline Dowd Hall, " 'You Must Remember This': Autobiography as Social Critique," in Nancy Bercaw, ed., *Gender and the Southern Body Politic* (Jackson: University Press of Mississippi, 2000), 8.

81. Barbara Y. Welke, "When All the Women Were White, and All the Blacks Were Men: Gender, Class, Race, and the Road to *Plessy*, 1855–1914," *Law and History Review*, 13 (Fall 1995): 282, 278n.

82. Laura F. Edwards, *Gendered Strife and Confusion: The Political Culture of Reconstruction* (Urbana: University of Illinois Press, 1997), 46.

83. Glenda Elizabeth Gilmore, *Gender and Jim Crow: Women and the Politics of White Supremacy in North Carolina, 1896–1920* (Chapel Hill: University of North Carolina Press, 1996), 148, 151, 178.

PART TWO

Some Current Questions

The selections that follow deal with some of the issues about the origins of Southern segregation that now interest historians. Other questions and other selections could have been chosen, but these show the current state of the conversation. Each selection is preceded by a headnote that introduces both its specific subject and its author. After the headnote come Questions for a Closer Reading. The headnote and the questions offer signposts that will allow you to understand more readily what the author is saying. The selections include the original notes that provide suggestions for further exploration. If an issue that the author raises intrigues you, use the notes to follow it up. At the end of all the selections are more questions, under the heading Making Connections. Turn to these after you have read the selections, and use them to bring the whole discussion together. In order to answer them, you may find that you need to reread the texts. Most historical texts require more than one reading for careful analysis and reflection.

C. Vann Woodward

From *The Strange Career
of Jim Crow*

C. Vann Woodward (1908–1999), Sterling Professor of History Emeritus at Yale University, ranked as one of the most influential historians of the United States in the twentieth century. According to Drew Gilpin Faust, among Woodward's foremost achievements was "the central place he established for Southern history in our understanding of the nation's identity and moral character." Woodward's *Tom Watson, Agrarian Rebel* (1938) exhibited his skills at political biography. His *Origins of the New South* (1951) showed his abilities at synthesis and reinterpretation, while *The Burden of Southern History* (1960) underscored Woodward's mastery of graceful prose, careful generalization, and subtle irony. His *Mary Chesnut's Civil War* (1981) marked Woodward as an accomplished historical sleuth and editor, earning him the Pulitzer Prize. But it was *The Strange Career of Jim Crow* (1955), Woodward's most popular book, that raised fundamental questions about when, why, and how segregation enveloped race relations in the American South. Writing during the first wave of the civil rights revolution, Woodward spoke directly to the post–*Brown v. Board of Education* generation. He argued that segregation was not the "natural" relationship between whites and blacks and that it occurred much later than previous scholars had assumed. If, as Woodward maintained, laws gave birth to Jim Crow in the late nineteenth century, then laws could just as readily bury it in the mid–twentieth century. Woodward considered segregation, like the rest of southern history, both "burden and opportunity." The excerpt that follows comes from the first edition of Woodward's influential work.[1]

Questions for a Closer Reading

1. How did slavery make the segregation of the races difficult in the Old South?

2. By defining segregation as solely the product of Jim Crow laws, did Woodward overlook other forms of racial proscription?

3. How did differences within the South lead to the start of segregation?

4. What forces led white southerners to adopt the "extreme racism" that led to passage of the Jim Crow laws? When, in Woodward's estimate, did this occur?

5. Did de facto segregation continue after the start of de jure segregation?

6. What "forgotten alternatives" in race relations, according to Woodward, were available to white southerners following Reconstruction?

Note

1. Michael O'Brien, "Making the South New: Sympathy and Scholarship in C. Vann Woodward," London *Times Literary Supplement,* April 14, 2000, 18; Drew Gilpin Faust, "C. Vann Woodward: Helping to Make History," *Chronicle of Higher Education,* January 14, 2000, B7; Gaines M. Foster, "Woodward and Southern Identity," *The Southern Review,* 21 (April 1985): 358.

The Strange Career of Jim Crow

Forgotten Alternatives

In the first place it is necessary to clear away some prevailing misconceptions about this latest of lost causes. One of them grows out of a tendency to identify and confuse it with an earlier lost cause. The assumption is often made that Reconstruction constituted an interruption of normal relations between the races in the South. Once the carpetbaggers were overthrown and "Home Rule" was established, the founding fathers of the New South, after conceding that slavery was finished and the Negro was now a freedman and more vaguely a citizen, are presumed to have restored to normality the disturbed relations between whites and blacks. To conceive of the new order of race relations as a restoration, however, is to forget the nature of relations between races under the old regime. For one thing segregation would have been impractical under slavery, and for another the circumstances that later gave rise to the segregation code did not exist so long as the Negro was enslaved. "Before and directly after the war," writes W. E. B. Du Bois, "when all the best of the Negroes were domestic servants in the best of the white families, there were bonds of intimacy, affection, and sometimes blood relationship, between the races. They lived in the same home, shared in the family life, often attended the same church, and talked and conversed with each other." These conditions could certainly not be said to have been "restored" by segregation.

A second misconception is more common and is shared by a number of historians. While recognizing that the new order was new and not the restoration of an old system, they sometimes make the assumption that it followed automatically upon the overthrow of Reconstruction as an immediate consequence of Redemption. Those who cherish the new order of segregation, Jim Crowism, and disfranchisement, therefore, often attribute it to the Redeemers, the founding fathers of the New South. Their defense

C. Vann Woodward, from *The Strange Career of Jim Crow* (New York: Oxford University Press, 1955), 13–26, 51–56, 81–87.

of the system clothes it with the moral prestige they attribute to Redemption, and their indignation against any attack upon it is fired by the zeal of the historic struggle for home rule and the emotional heritage of the Civil War period. Their identification of the two causes is understandable but unjustified, and it lingers to complicate and confuse adjustment to the New Reconstruction.

As a matter of fact, some important aspects of segregation were achieved and sanctioned by the First Reconstruction. One of these was segregation of the great Protestant churches, a process accomplished by the voluntary withdrawal of the Negroes and their establishment of independent organizations of their own. Whatever the intentions of the framers of the Fourteenth Amendment were regarding segregation in the public schools—a controversy that even the Supreme Court in its historic decision of 17 May 1954 declined to settle—the fact is that segregation became the almost universal practice in the public schools of the South during Reconstruction, with or without explicit sanction of the radicals. In a third important field, the military services, segregation was strengthened by the Civil War and left unaltered during Reconstruction. As for equality in social gatherings of a private nature, there is little evidence that even the high Negro officials of Reconstruction governments in the South were extended that recognition—even by the white radicals.

After Redemption was achieved the new governments of the Southern states retained such segregation practices as had been established during or before Reconstruction, but showed little immediate disposition to expand the code into new fields. Much less was there evidence of a movement to make segregation universal, such as it was to become in the twentieth century. More than a decade was to pass after Redemption before the first Jim Crow law was to appear upon the law books of a Southern state, and more than two decades before the older states of Virginia, North Carolina, and South Carolina were to adopt such laws.

Suspicions of the South's intentions toward the freedmen after the withdrawal of federal troops were naturally rife in the North. In 1878 Colonel Thomas Wentworth Higginson went south to investigate for himself. The report of his findings, published in the *Atlantic Monthly*, is of particular interest in view of the Colonel's background. One of the most militant abolitionists, Higginson had been one of the "Secret Six" who conspired with John Brown before the Harpers Ferry raid, and during the war he had organized and led a combat regiment of Negro troops. In Virginia, South Carolina, and Florida, the states he visited in 1878, he found "a condition of outward peace" and wondered immediately if there did not lurk beneath it "some covert plan for crushing or reenslaving the colored race." If so, he decided, it would "show itself in some personal ill usage of the blacks, in the withdrawal of privileges, in legislation endangering their rights." But, he reported, "I can assert that, carrying with me the eyes of a tolerably suspicious abolitionist, I saw none of these indications." He had expected to be affronted by contemptuous or abusive treatment of Negroes. "During this trip," however, he wrote, "I had absolutely no occasion for any such attitude." Nor was this due to "any cringing demeanor on the part of the blacks, for they show much more manhood than they once did." He compared the tolerance and acceptance of the Negro in the South on trains and street cars, at the polls, in the courts and legislatures, in the police force and militia, with attitudes in his native New England and decided that the South came off rather better in the comparison. "How can we ask more of the States formerly in rebellion," he demanded, "than that they should be abreast of New England in granting rights and privileges to the colored race? Yet this is now the case in the three states I name; or at least if they fall behind in some points, they lead at some points." Six years later, in a review of the situation in the South, Higginson found no reason to change his estimate of 1878.

The year 1879 provides testimony to the point from a foreign observer. Sir George Campbell, a member of Parliament, traveled over a large part of the South, with race relations as the focus of his interest. He was impressed with the freedom of association between whites and blacks, with the frequency and intimacy of personal contact, and with the extent of Negro participation in political affairs. He commented with particular surprise on the equality with which Negroes shared public facilities. He remarked that "the humblest black rides with the proudest white on terms of perfect equality, and without the smallest symptom of malice or dislike on either side. I was, I confess, surprised to see how completely this is the case; even an English Radical is a little taken aback at first."

In the first year of Redemption a writer who signed himself "A South Carolinian" in the *Atlantic Monthly* corroborated the observations of the Englishman regarding the Negro's equality of treatment on common carriers, trains, and street cars. "The negroes are freely admitted to the theatre in Columbia and to other exhibitions, lectures, etc.," though the whites avoided sitting with them "if the hall be not crowded," he added. "In Columbia they are also served at the bars, soda water fountains, and ice-cream saloons, but not generally elsewhere."

Twenty years later, in 1897, a Charleston editor referring to a proposed Jim Crow law for trains wrote: "We care nothing whatever about Northern or outside opinion in this matter. It is a question for our own decision according to our own ideas of what is right and expedient. And our opinion is that we have no more need for a Jim Crow system this year than we had last year, and a great deal less than we had twenty and thirty years ago." In his view such a law was "unnecessary and uncalled for," and furthermore it would be "a needless affront to our respectable and well behaved colored people."

Southern white testimony on the subject has naturally been discounted as propaganda. If only by way of contrast with later views, however, the following editorial from the Richmond *Dispatch,* 13 October 1886, is worth quoting: "Our State Constitution requires all State officers in their oath of office to declare that they 'recognize and accept the civil and political equality of all men.' We repeat that nobody here objects to sitting in political conventions with negroes. Nobody here objects to serving on juries with negroes. No lawyer objects to practicing law in court where negro lawyers practice. . . . Colored men are allowed to introduce bills into the Virginia Legislature; and in both branches of this body negroes are allowed to sit, as they have a right to sit." George Washington Cable, the aggressive agitator for the rights of Negroes, protested strongly against discrimination elsewhere, but is authority for the statement made in 1885, that "In Virginia they may ride exactly as white people do and in the same cars."

More pertinent and persuasive is the testimony of the Negro himself. In April 1885, T. McCants Stewart set forth from Boston to visit his native state of South Carolina after an absence of ten years. A Negro newspaperman, corresponding editor of the New York *Freeman,* Stewart was conscious of his role as a spokesman and radical champion of his race. "On leaving Washington, D.C.," he reported to his paper, "I put a chip on my shoulder, and inwardly dared any man to knock it off." He found a seat in a car which became so crowded that several white passengers had to sit on their baggage. "I fairly foamed at the mouth," he wrote, "imagining that the conductor would order me into a seat occupied by a colored lady so as to make room for a white passenger." Nothing of the sort happened, however, nor was there any unpleasantness when Stewart complained of a request from a white Virginian that he shift his baggage so that the white man could sit beside him. At a stop twenty-one miles below Petersburg he entered a station dining room, "bold as a lion," he wrote, took a seat at a table with white people, and was courteously served. "The whites at the table appeared not to note my presence," he reported. "Thus far I had found travelling more pleasant . . . than in some parts of New England." Aboard a steamboat in North Carolina he complained of a colored waiter who seated him at a separate table, though in the same dining room with whites. At Wilmington, however, he suffered from no discrimination in dining arrangements. His treatment in Virginia and North Carolina, he declared, "contrasted strongly with much that I have experienced in dining rooms in the North." Another contrast that impressed him was the ease and frequency with which white people entered into conversation with him for no other purpose than to pass the time of day. "I think the whites of the South," he observed, "are really less afraid to [have] contact with colored people than the whites of the North."

Stewart continued his journey southward rejoicing that "Along the Atlantic seaboard from Canada to the Gulf of Mexico — through Delaware, Maryland, Virginia, the Carolinas, Georgia and into Florida, all the old slave States with enormous Negro populations . . . a first-class ticket is good in a first-class coach; and Mr. [Henry W.] Grady would be compelled to ride with a Negro, or, walk." From Columbia, South Carolina, he wrote: "I feel about as safe here as in Providence, R.I. I can ride in first-class cars on the railroads and in the streets. I can go into saloons and get refreshments even as in New York. I can stop in and drink a glass of soda and be more politely waited upon than in some parts of New England." He also found that "Negroes dine with whites in a railroad saloon" in his native state. He watched a Negro policeman arrest a white man "under circumstances requiring coolness, prompt decision, and courage"; and in Charleston he witnessed the review of hundreds of Negro troops. "Indeed," wrote Stewart, "the Palmetto State leads the South in some things. May she go on advancing in liberal practices and prospering throughout her borders, and may she be like leaven to the South; like a star unto 'The Land of Flowers,' leading our blessed section on and on into the way of liberty, justice, equality, truth, and righteousness."

One significant aspect of Stewart's newspaper reports should be noted. They were written a month after the inauguration of Grover Cleveland and the return of the Democrats to power for the first time in twenty-four years. His paper had opposed Cleveland, and propaganda had been spread among Negro voters that the return of the Democrats would mean the end of freedmen's rights, if not their liberty. Stewart failed to find what he was looking for, and after a few weeks cut his communications short with the comment that he could find "nothing spicy or exciting to write." "For the life of [me]," he confessed, "I can't 'raise a row' in these letters. Things seem (remember I write seem) to move along as smoothly as in New York or Boston. . . . If you should ask me, 'watchman, tell us of the night'. . . I would say, 'The morning light is breaking.'"

So far nearly all the evidence presented has come from the older states of the eastern seaboard. In writing of slavery under the old regime it is common for historians to draw distinctions between the treatment of slaves in the upper and older South and their lot in the lower South and the newer states. In the former their condition is generally said to have been better than it was in the latter. It is worth remarking an analogous distinction in the treatment of the race in the era of segregation. It is clear at least that the newer states were inclined to resort to Jim Crow laws earlier than the older commonwealths of the seaboard, and there is evidence that segregation and discrimination became generally practiced before they became law. Even so, there are a number of indications that segregation and ostracism were not nearly so harsh and rigid in the early years as they became later.

In his study of conditions in Mississippi, Vernon Wharton reveals that for some years "most of the saloons served whites and Negroes at the same bar. Many of the restaurants, using separate tables, served both races in the same room. . . . On May 21, 1879, the Negroes of Jackson, after a parade of their fire company, gave a picnic in Hamilton Park. On the night of May 29, 'the ladies of the [white] Episcopal Church' used Hamilton Park for a *fete*. After their picnic the Negroes went to Angelo's Hall for a dance. This same hall was used for white dances and parties, and was frequently the gathering place of Democratic conventions. . . . Throughout the state common cemeteries, usually in separate portions, held the graves of both whites and Negroes." Wharton points out, however, that as early as 1890 segregation had closed in and the Negroes were by that date excluded from saloons, restaurants, parks, public halls, and white cemeteries.

At the International Exposition in New Orleans in 1885 Charles Dudley Warner watched with some astonishment as "white and colored people mingled freely, talking and looking at what was of common interest. . . . On 'Louisiana Day' in the Exposition the colored citizens," he reported, "took their full share of the parade and the honors. Their societies marched with the others, and the races mingled in the grounds in unconscious equality of privileges." While he was in the city he also saw "a colored clergyman in his surplice seated in the chancel of the most important white Episcopal church in New Orleans, assisting the service."

A frequent topic of comment by Northern visitors during the period was the intimacy of contact between the races in the South, an intimacy sometimes admitted to be distasteful to the visitor. Standard topics were the sight of white babies suckled at black breasts, white and colored children playing together, the casual proximity of white and Negro homes in the cities, the camaraderie of maidservant and mistress, employer and employee, customer and clerk, and the usual stories of cohabitation of white men and Negro women. The same sights and stories had once been favorite topics of comment for the carpetbaggers and before them of the abolitionists, both of whom also expressed puzzlement and sometimes revulsion. What the Northern traveler of the 'eighties sometimes took for signs of a new era of race relations was really a heritage of slavery times, or, more elementally, the result of two peoples having lived together intimately for a long time and learned to like and trust each other—whatever their formal relations were, whether those of master and slave, exploiter and exploited, or superior and inferior.

It would certainly be preposterous to leave the impression that any evidence I have submitted indicates a golden age of race relations in the period between Redemption and segregation. On the contrary, the evidence of race conflict and violence, brutality and exploitation in this very period is overwhelming. It was, after all, in the 'eighties and early 'nineties that lynching attained the most staggering proportions ever reached in the history of that crime. Moreover, the fanatical advocates of racism, whose doctrines of total segregation, disfranchisement, and ostracism eventually triumphed over all opposition and became universal practice in the South, were already at work and already beginning to establish dominance over some phases of Southern life. Before their triumph was complete, however, there transpired a period of history whose significance has been hitherto neglected. Exploitation there was in that period, as in other periods and in other regions, but it did not follow then that the exploited had to be ostracized. Subordination there was also, unmistakable subordination; but it was not yet an accepted corollary that the subordinates had to be totally segregated and needlessly humiliated by a thousand daily reminders of their subordination. Conflict there was, too, violent conflict in which the advantage lay with the strong and the dominant, as always; but conflict of some kind was unavoidable short of forceful separation of the races. . . .

The South's adoption of extreme racism was due not so much to a conversion as it was to a relaxation of the opposition. All the elements of fear, jealousy, proscription, hatred, and fanaticism had long been present, as they are present in various degrees of intensity in any society. What enabled them to rise to dominance was not so much cleverness or ingenuity as it was a general weakening and discrediting of the numerous forces that had hitherto kept them in check. The restraining forces included not only Northern liberal opinion in the press, the courts, and the government, but also internal checks imposed by the prestige and influence of the Southern conservatives, as well as by the idealism and zeal of the Southern radicals. What happened toward the end of the century was an almost simultaneous—and sometimes not unrelated—decline in the effectiveness of restraint that had been exercised by all three forces: Northern liberalism, Southern conservatism, and Southern radicalism.

The acquiescence of Northern liberalism in the Compromise of 1877 defined the beginning, but not the ultimate extent, of the liberal retreat on the race issue. The Compromise merely left the freedman to the custody of the conservative Redeemers upon their pledge that they would protect him in his constitutional rights. But as these pledges were forgotten or violated and the South veered toward proscription and extremism, Northern opinion shifted to the right, keeping pace with the South, conceding point after point, so that at no time were the sections very far apart on race policy. The failure of the liberals to resist this trend was due in part to political factors. Since reactionary politicians and their cause were identified with the bloody-shirt issue and the demagogic exploitation of sectional animosities, the liberals naturally felt themselves strongly drawn toward the cause of sectional reconciliation. And since the Negro was the symbol of sectional strife, the liberals joined in deprecating further agitation of his cause and in defending the Southern view of race in its less extreme forms. It was quite common in the 'eighties and 'nineties to find in the *Nation, Harper's Weekly,* the *North American Review,* or the *Atlantic Monthly* Northern liberals and former abolitionists mouthing the shibboleths of white supremacy regarding the Negro's innate inferiority, shiftlessness, and hopeless unfitness for full participation in the white man's civilization. Such expressions doubtless did much to add to the reconciliation of North and South, but they did so at the expense of the Negro. Just as the Negro gained his emancipation and new rights through a falling out between white men, he now stood to lose his rights through the reconciliation of white men.

The cumulative weakening of resistance to racism was expressed also in a succession of decisions by the United States Supreme Court between 1873 and 1898 that require no review here. In the *Slaughter House Cases* of 1873 and in *United States v. Reese* and *United States v. Cruikshank* in 1876, the court drastically curtailed the privileges and immunities recognized as being under federal protection. It continued the trend in its decision on the *Civil Rights Cases* of 1883 by virtually nullifying the restrictive parts of the Civil Rights Act. By a species of what Justice Harlan in his dissent described as "subtle and ingenious verbal criticism," the court held that the Fourteenth Amendment gave Congress power to restrain states but not individuals from acts of racial discrimination and segregation. The court, like the liberals, was engaged in a bit of reconciliation—reconciliation between federal and state jurisdiction, as well as between North and South, reconciliation also achieved at the Negro's expense. Having ruled in a previous case (*Hall v. de Cuir,* 1877) that a state could not *prohibit* segregation on a common carrier, the Court in 1890 (*Louisville, New Orleans, and Texas Railroad v. Mississippi*) ruled that a state could constitutionally *require* segregation on carriers. In *Plessy v. Ferguson,* decided in 1896, the Court subscribed to the doctrine that "legislation is powerless to eradicate racial instincts" and laid down the "separate but equal" rule for the justification of segregation. Two years later, in 1898, in *Williams v. Mississippi* the Court completed the opening of the legal road to proscription, segregation, and disfranchisement by approving the Mississippi plan for depriving Negroes of the franchise.

Then, in that same year, 1898, the United States plunged into imperialistic adventures under the leadership of the Republican party. These adventures in the Pacific and the Caribbean suddenly brought under the jurisdiction of the United States some eight million people of the colored races, "a varied assortment of inferior races," as the *Nation* described them, "which, of course, could not be allowed to vote." As America shouldered the White Man's Burden she took up at the same time many Southern attitudes on the subject of race. "If the stronger and cleverer race," said the editor of the *Atlantic Monthly*, "is free to impose its will upon 'new-caught, sullen peoples' on the other side of the globe, why not in South Carolina and Mississippi?" The doctrines of Anglo-Saxon superiority by which Professor John W. Burgess of Columbia University, Captain Alfred T. Mahan of the United States Navy, and Senator Albert Beveridge of Indiana justified and rationalized American imperialism in the Philippines, Hawaii, and Cuba differed in no essentials from the race theories by which Senator Benjamin R. Tillman of South Carolina and Senator James K. Vardaman of Mississippi justified white supremacy in the South. The Boston Evening *Transcript* of 14 January 1899, admitted that Southern race policy was "now the policy of the Administration of the very party which carried the country into and through a civil war to free the slave." And *The New York Times* of 10 May 1900 reported editorially that "Northern men . . . no longer denounce the suppression of the Negro vote [in the South] as it used to be denounced in the reconstruction days. The necessity of it under the supreme law of self-preservation is candidly recognized."

In the South leaders of the white-supremacy movement thoroughly grasped and expounded the implication of the new imperialism for their domestic policies. "No Republican leader," declared Senator Tillman, "not even Governor Roosevelt, will now dare to wave the bloody shirt and preach a crusade against the South's treatment of the negro. The North has a bloody shirt of its own. Many thousands of them have been made into shrouds for murdered Filipinos, done to death because they were fighting for liberty." And the junior Senator from South Carolina, John J. McLaurin, thanked Senator George F. Hoar of Massachusetts "for his complete announcement of the divine right of the Caucasian to govern the inferior races," a position which "most amply vindicated the South." Hilary A. Herbert, an advocate of complete disfranchisement of the Negro in Alabama rejoiced in May 1900 that "we have now the sympathy of thoughtful men in the North to an extent that never before existed."

At the dawn of the new century the wave of Southern racism came in as a swell upon a mounting tide of national sentiment and was very much a part of that sentiment. Had the tide been running the other way, the

Southern wave would have broken feebly instead of becoming a wave of the future. . . .

Within this context of growing pessimism, mounting tension, and unleashed phobias the structure of segregation and discrimination was extended by the adoption of a great number of the Jim Crow type of laws. Up to 1900 the only law of this type adopted by the majority of Southern states was that applying to passengers aboard trains. And South Carolina did not adopt that until 1898, North Carolina in 1899, and Virginia, the last, in 1900. Only three states had required or authorized the Jim Crow waiting room in railway stations before 1899, but in the next decade nearly all of the other Southern states fell in line. The adoption of laws applying to new subjects tended to take place in waves of popularity. Street cars had been common in Southern cities since the 'eighties, but only Georgia had a segregation law applying to them before the end of the century. Then in quick succession North Carolina and Virginia adopted such a law in 1901, Louisiana in 1902, Arkansas, South Carolina, and Tennessee in 1903, Mississippi and Maryland in 1904, Florida in 1905, and Oklahoma in 1907. These laws referred to separation within cars, but a Montgomery city ordinance of 1906 was the first to require a completely separate Jim Crow street car. During these years the older seaboard states of the South also extended the segregation laws to steamboats.

The mushroom growth of discriminatory and segregation laws during the first two decades of this [twentieth] century piled up a huge bulk of legislation. Much of the code was contributed by city ordinances or by local regulations and rules enforced without the formality of laws. Only a sampling is possible here. For up and down the avenues and byways of Southern life appeared with increasing profusion the little signs: "Whites Only" or "Colored." Sometimes the law prescribed their dimensions in inches, and in one case the kind and color of paint. Many appeared without requirement by law—over entrances and exits, at theaters and boarding houses, toilets and water fountains, waiting rooms and ticket windows.

A large body of law grew up concerned with the segregation of employees and their working conditions. The South Carolina code of 1915, with subsequent elaborations, prohibited textile factories from permitting laborers of different races from working together in the same room, or using the same entrances, pay windows, exits, doorways, stairways, "or windows [*sic*]" at the same time, or the same "lavatories, toilets, drinking water buckets, pails, cups, dippers or glasses" at any time. Exceptions were made of firemen, floor scrubbers, and repair men, who were permitted association with the white proletarian elite on an emergency basis. In most instances segregation in employment was established without the aid of statute. And in many crafts and trades the written or unwritten policies of Jim Crow unionism made segregation superfluous by excluding Negroes from employment.

State institutions for the care of the dependent or incapacitated were naturally the subject of more legislation than private institutions of the same sort, but ordinarily the latter followed pretty closely the segregation practices of the public institutions. The fact that only Mississippi and South Carolina specifically provided for general segregation in hospitals does not indicate that non-segregation was the rule in the hospitals of other states. The two states named also required Negro nurses for Negro patients, and Alabama prohibited white female nurses from attending Negro male patients. Thirteen Southern and border states required the separation of patients by races in mental hospitals, and ten states specified segregation of inmates in penal institutions. Some of the latter went into detail regarding the chaining, transportation, feeding, and working of the prisoners on a segregated basis. Segregation of the races in homes for the aged, the indigent, the orphans, the blind, the deaf, and the dumb is the subject of numerous state laws.

Much ingenuity and effort went into the separation of the races in their amusements, diversions, recreations, and sports. The Separate Park Law of Georgia, adopted in 1905, appears to have been the first venture of a state legislature into this field, though city ordinances and local custom were quite active in pushing the Negro out of the public parks. Circuses and tent shows, including side shows, fell under a law adopted by Louisiana in 1914, which required separate entrances, exits, ticket windows, and ticket sellers that would be kept at least twenty-five feet apart. The city of Birmingham applied the principle to "any room, hall, theatre, picture house, auditorium, yard, court, ball park, or other indoor or outdoor place" and specified that the races be "distinctly separated . . . by well defined physical barriers." North Carolina and Virginia interdicted all fraternal orders or societies that permitted members of both races to address each other as brother.

Residential segregation in cities developed along five different patterns in the second decade of the century. The type originating in Baltimore in 1910 designated all-white and all-Negro blocks in areas occupied by both races. This experiment was imitated in Atlanta and Greenville. Virginia sought to legalize segregation by a state law that authorized city councils to divide territories into segregated districts and to prohibit either race from living in the other's district, a method adopted by Roanoke and Portsmouth, Virginia. The third method, invented by Richmond, designated blocks throughout the city black or white according to the majority of the residents and forbade any person to live in any block "where the majority of residents on such streets are occupied by those with whom said person is forbidden to intermarry." This one was later copied by Ashland, Virginia, and Winston-Salem, North Carolina. A still more complicated law origi- nated in Norfolk, which applied to both mixed and unmixed blocks and fixed the color status by ownership as well as occupancy. And finally New Orleans developed a law requiring a person of either race to secure con- sent of the majority of persons living in an area before establishing a resi- dence therein. After these devices were frustrated by a Supreme Court decision in 1917, attempts continued to be made to circumvent the deci- sion. Probably the most effective of these was the restrictive covenant, a private contract limiting the sale of property in an area to purchasers of the favored race.

The most prevalent and widespread segregation of living areas was accomplished without need for legal sanction. The black ghettos of the "Darktown" slums in every Southern city were the consequence mainly of the Negro's economic status, his relegation to the lowest rung of the lad- der. Smaller towns sometimes excluded Negro residents completely simply by letting it be known in forceful ways that their presence would not be tol- erated. In 1914 there were six such towns in Texas, five in Oklahoma, and two in Alabama. On the other hand there were by that time some thirty towns in the South, besides a number of unincorporated settlements, inhabited exclusively by Negroes. In August 1913, Clarence Poe, editor of the *Progressive Farmer,* secured the unanimous endorsement of a conven- tion of the North Carolina Farmer's Union for a movement to segregate the races in rural districts.

The extremes to which caste penalties and separation were carried in parts of the South could hardly find a counterpart short of the latitudes of India and South Africa. In 1909 Mobile passed a curfew law applying exclusively to Negroes and requiring them to be off the streets by 10 P.M. The Oklahoma legislature in 1915 authorized its Corporation Commission to require telephone companies "to maintain separate booths for white and colored patrons." North Carolina and Florida required that textbooks used by the public-school children of one race be kept separate from those used by the other, and the Florida law specified separation even while the books were in storage. South Carolina for a time segregated a third caste by establishing separate schools for mulatto as well as for white and Negro children. A New Orleans ordinance segregated white and Negro prosti- tutes in separate districts. Ray Stannard Baker found Jim Crow Bibles for Negro witnesses in Atlanta courts and Jim Crow elevators for Negro pas- sengers in Atlanta buildings.

2. Was segregation the creation of custom or of law?

Joel Williamson

"The Separation of the Races"

Since 1960, Joel Williamson (b. 1929) has taught southern history at the University of North Carolina at Chapel Hill, where he is Lineberger Professor in the Humanities. The complex intersection of race and southern identity is the focus of his books, including *New People: Miscegenation and Mulattoes in the United States* (1980), *The Crucible of Race: Black-White Relations in the American South Since Emancipation* (1984), and *William Faulkner and Southern History* (1993). In *The Crucible of Race,* which won the Francis Parkman Prize, Williamson argued that emancipation ended the "peculiar integration" of slavery and ushered in "a great increase in the separation of the races," oftentimes the result of black separatism. Williamson first made this point in his landmark *After Slavery: The Negro in South Carolina During Reconstruction, 1861–1877* (1965), described by a contemporary as "a revolutionary reinterpretation" that challenged Woodward's "popular view . . . that segregation was a late nineteenth-century phenomenon. . . ." Though mindful of significant economic and political change in Reconstruction-era South Carolina, Williamson nevertheless insisted that both races remained enslaved by the "mental separation" of the past.[1]

Questions for a Closer Reading

1. Were the plantations and cities of the Old South segregated? Why or why not?

2. What forces, according to Williamson, swayed white South Carolinians to distance themselves from blacks during Reconstruction?

3. What forces, according to Williamson, swayed black South Carolinians to distance themselves from whites during Reconstruction?

4. What was the impact of South Carolina's 1868 antidiscrimination statute on segregation in public conveyances and accommodations?

5. Would it be accurate to term the pattern of white "withdrawal" that Williamson describes as "self-segregation"?

6. Was the segregation Williamson analyzes de facto or de jure?

7. In terms of their evidence and argument, which historian is more persuasive, Woodward or Williamson?

Note

1. Joel Williamson, *The Crucible of Race: Black-White Relations in the American South Since Emancipation* (New York: Oxford University Press, 1984), 249, 250; Walter L. Brown, review of *After Slavery: The Negro in South Carolina During Reconstruction, 1861–1877,* by Joel Williamson, *American Historical Review,* 71 (April 1966): 1079.

"The Separation of the Races"

The physical separation of the races was the most revolutionary change in relations between whites and Negroes in South Carolina during Reconstruction.

Separation had, of course, marked the Negro in slavery; yet the very nature of slavery necessitated a constant, physical intimacy between the races. In the peculiar institution, the white man had constantly and closely to oversee the labor of the Negro, preserve order in domestic arrangements within the slave quarters, and minister to the physical, medical, and moral needs of his laborers. In brief, slavery enforced its own special brand of interracial associations; in a sense, it married the interests of white to black at birth and the union followed both to the grave. Slavery watched the great mass of Negroes in South Carolina, but those Negroes who lived outside of the slave system were not exempt from the scrutiny of the whites. Even in Charleston, the free Negro community was never large enough to establish its economic and racial independence. In the mid-nineteenth century, as the bonds of slavery tightened, the whites were forced to bring free Negroes under ever more stringent controls and to subject their lives to the closest surveillance.

During the spring and summer of 1865, as the centripetal force of slavery melted rapidly away, each race clearly tended to disassociate itself from the other. The trend was evident in every phase of human endeavor: agriculture, business, occupations, schools and churches, in every aspect of social intercourse and politics. As early as July of 1865, a Bostonian in Charleston reported that "the worst sign here . . . is the growth of a bitter and hostile spirit between blacks and whites—a gap opening between the races which, it would seem may at some time result seriously."[1] Well before the end of Reconstruction, separation had crystallized into a comprehensive pattern which, in its essence, remained unaltered until the middle of the twentieth century.

Joel Williamson, "The Separation of the Races," from *After Slavery: The Negro in South Carolina During Reconstruction, 1861–1877* (Chapel Hill: University of North Carolina Press, 1965), 274–99.

There is no clear, concise answer to the question of why separation occurred. Certainly, it was not simply a response of Negroes to the prejudiced fiat of dominant whites; nor was it a totally rationalized reaction on the part of either race. Actually, articulate whites and Negroes seldom attempted to explain their behavior. Yet, the philosophies and attitudes each race adopted toward the other lend a certain rationality to separation, and, if we are always mindful that this analysis presumes a unity which they never expressed, can be applied to promote an understanding of the phenomenon.

For the native white community, separation was a means of avoiding or minimizing problems which, they felt, would inevitably arise from the inherent inferiority of the Negro, problems which the North, in eradicating slavery and disallowing the Black Code, would not allow them to control by overt political means. In this limited sense, segregation was a substitute for slavery.

Thus, first, total separation was essential to racial purity, and racial purity was necessary to the preservation of a superior civilization which the whites had labored so arduously to construct, and suffered a long and bloody war to defend. After the war, that civilization was embattled, but not necessarily lost. Unguarded association with an inferior caste would obviously endanger white culture. In this view, children were peculiarly susceptible to damage. "Don't imagine that I allow my children to be with negroes out of my presence," wrote the mistress of a lowcountry plantation in 1868, "on one occasion only have they been so with my knowledge."[2] Even the Negro wet nurse, that quintessence of maternalism upon which the slave period paternalist so often turned his case, emerged as the incubus of Southern infancy. "We gave our infants to the black wenches to suckle," lamented an elderly white, "and thus poisoned the blood of our children, and made them *cowards* . . . the Character of the people of the state was ruined by slavery and it will take 500 years, if not longer, by the infusion of new blood to eradicate the hereditary vices imbibed with the blood (milk is blood) of black wet nurses."[3] Adults, of course, were not immune to racial contamination. Casual associations across the color line might lead to serious ones and to the total pollution of the superior race. Particularly might this be so of the poor, the ignorant, and the feeble-minded, but even the aristocracy had to be watched. Shortly after Redemption, an anonymous Carolinian was incensed at a rumor that Wade Hampton had dined at a table with Negroes in the home of the president of Claflin, the leading Negro university in the state. "Who shall say where it will stop?" he warned. "Will not dining lead to dancing, to social equality, to miscegenation, to mexicanization and to general damnation."[4]

Separation also facilitated the subordination of the inferior race by constantly reminding the Negro that he lived in a world in which the white man was dominant, and in which the non-white was steadfastly denied access to the higher caste. Further, the impression of Negro inferiority would be constantly re-enforced by relegating the baser element, whenever possible, to the use of inferior facilities. The sheer totality of the display alone might well serve to convince members of the lower caste that such, indeed, was in the natural order of things.

Many whites had envisioned the early elimination of the freedman from the Southern scene, and many had eagerly anticipated this event. In time, however, it became evident to all that the Negro would be neither dissolved nor transported to Africa. In a sense, separation was a means of securing the quasi elimination of Negroes at home. It was, perhaps, a more satisfactory solution than their demise or emigration, since it might produce many of the benefits of their disappearance without losing an advantageous, indeed, a necessary supply of labor.

Finally, separation was a logical solution to the problem posed by the widespread conviction that the races were inherently incompatible outside of the master-slave relationship. If the white man could not exist in contentment in the proximity of Negroes, then partial satisfaction might be achieved by withdrawal from associations with members of the inferior caste. This spirit was evident among some of the wealthier whites who voluntarily dispensed entirely with the services of Negro domestics. Elderly William Heyward, in 1868 still second to none in the ranks of the rice aristocracy, stopped taking his meals at the Charleston Hotel because, as he said, he found "the negro waiters so defiant and so familiar in their attentions." "A part of the satisfaction is," he explained to a friend, "that I am perfectly independent of having negroes about me; if I cannot have them as they used to be, I have no desire to see them except in the field."[5] Planters were often manifesting precisely the same sentiment when they deserted their land and turned to grain culture, or to the use of immigrant labor. Separation was also a way of avoiding interracial violence. B. O. Duncan and James L. Orr, both native white Republicans, argued against mixing in the public schools because they were convinced that minor irritations between children would generate major altercations between parents of different races. Conceived as a means of avoiding violence, separation, ironically, was subsequently enforced by the use of violence.

The Southern white did not always have a clear reason why racial "mixing" (as they called it) in a given situation was wrong, why the color bar should be leveled in one place and not in another. Nevertheless, he had no difficulty in recognizing a breach of the proprieties when he saw it. A young Carolinian visiting New York in the summer of 1867 was outraged by the degree of mixing he observed there: "I can now say that I have seen the city of cities, and after I have seen it it is nothing but vanity and vexation of spirit. Here you can see the negro all on equal footing with white man. White man walking the street with negroe wenches. White man and negroe riding to gether. White man and negroes sit in the same seat in church or in a word the negro enjoys the same privileges as the white man. They address each other as Mr and Miss but notwithstanding all this we (the southern boys) say what we please and when we please. . . ."[6]

Contrary to common belief, the separation of the races was not entirely the work of the whites. Suspicious, resentful, and sometimes hateful toward the whites, chafed by white attitudes of superiority, and irritated by individual contacts with supercilious whites, Negroes, too, sought relief in withdrawal from association with the other race. In many instances, the disassociation was complete — that is, many Negroes left the state. During the war, Corporal Simon Crum of the First South Carolina declared his intention of leaving South Carolina after the capitulation because, as he phrased it, "dese yer Secesh will neber be cibilized in my time."[7] For those who could not or would not leave, alternative forms of withdrawal were possible. A major facet in the new pattern of agriculture was the removal of Negro labor from the immediate supervision of white men. As the Negro agriculturalist moved his labor away from the eye of the white man, so also did he move his family and his home. Plantation villages became increasingly rare as Negro landowners and renters either built new houses on their plots or, in a rather graphic symbolic display, laboriously dragged their cabins away from the "Negro street." Negroes in the trades and in domestic service followed similar trends. Furthermore, Negroes chose to withdraw from white-dominated churches, though they were often urged to stay, and they attended racially separated schools in spite of the legal fact that all schools were open to all races. Negroes also tended to withdraw from political association with members of the white community.

Finally, on those few occasions when Negroes entered into polite social situations with whites, Northern as well as Southern, they were often ill at ease. For instance, while driving along a road near Columbia, a planter and his wife met William, "a fine looking light mulatto" who had been their stableboy as a slave. William was driving a buggy and seated beside him was a young white woman, elegantly attired. The woman was a "Yankee school marm," probably one of the new teachers in Columbia's Negro school. As he passed his late master and mistress, the Negro averted his gaze and did not speak. The following day, he approached the planter and apologized for having been escort to a "white woman." He had met the teacher at a celebration, he explained, and she had insisted on his taking her to see the countryside.[8]

During Reconstruction, the Negro's withdrawal was never a categorical rejection of the white man and his society. In the early days of freedom, it was primarily a reaction against slavery, an attempt to escape the unpleasant associations of his previous condition and the derogatory implications of human bondage. However, as the memory of slavery faded, a more persistent reason for withdrawal emerged. Essentially, it was the Negro's answer to discrimination. Almost invariably, attempts by individual Negroes to establish satisfactory relations across the race line were unsuccessful, and, all too often, the pain of the experience was greater than the reward for having stood for principle. During Reconstruction and afterward, only a few were willing to undergo such pain without the certainty of success. It was much easier, after all, simply to withdraw.

Withdrawal as a solution to the race problem was by no means satisfactory to the Negro leadership. Implicit in the behavior of Negro leaders during Reconstruction was a yearning for complete and unreserved acceptance for members of their race by the white community. However, overtly, and rather politically, they carefully distinguished between "social equality" and what might be appropriately termed "public equality." For themselves, they claimed only the latter. "Our race do not demand social equality," declared W. J. Whipper, a member from Beaufort, on the floor of the house of representatives in Columbia. "No law can compel me to put myself on an equality with some white men I know," he continued, and, turning cynically on a native white Republican who had vigorously defended separation, concluded, "but talk about equality and the member imagines he must take you into his arms as he probably would your sister, if she was good looking."[9] Two years later, Martin Delany, a man who expressed pride in his blackness, said much the same thing to a large Charleston audience. "I don't believe in social equality; there is no such thing," he shouted. "If we want to associate with a man, we'll do it, and without laws."[10]

What the Negro leadership did insist upon was public equality, that is, absolute civil and political parity with whites and full and free access to most public facilities. These latter included restaurants, bars, saloons, railway and street cars, shipboard accommodations, the theater, and other such places of public amusement. Once they gained political power, Negro leaders hastened to embody this attitude in legislation. Within a week after the first sitting of the Constitutional Convention of 1868, a Negro delegate introduced a resolution which was eventually included in the state's bill of rights: "Distinction on account of race or color, in any case whatever, shall be prohibited, and all classes of citizens shall enjoy equally all common, public, legal and political privileges."[11] Similarly, one of the first bills passed by the Republican legislature prohibited licensed businesses from discriminating "between persons, on account of race, color, or previous condition, who shall make lawful application for the benefit of such business, calling or pursuit." Convicted violators were liable to a fine of not less than $1,000 or imprisonment for not less than a year.[12] During the debate on the measure in the house, not a single Negro member spoke against the bill, and only five of the twenty-four votes registered against it were cast by Negroes, while fifty-three of the sixty-one votes which secured its passage were those of Negro legislators.[13]

Negro Congressmen were no less ardent in championing the same cause in Washington, particularly in 1874, when a federal civil rights bill was up for consideration. ". . . is it pretended anywhere," asked Congressman R. B. Elliott, who had only recently been denied service in the restaurant of a railway station in North Carolina on his journey to the capital, "that the evils of which we complain, our exclusion from the public inn, from the saloon and table of the steamboat, from the sleeping-coach on the railway, from the right of sepulture in the public burial-ground, are an exercise of the police power of the State? . . . Are the colored people to be assimilated to an unwholesome trade or to combustible materials, to be interdicted, to be shut up within prescribed limits?" Several days later, in the same place, Congressman R. H. Cain declared, "We do not want any discrimination to be made. I do not ask any legislation for the colored people of this country that is not applied to the white people of this country. All that we seek is equal laws, equal legislation, and equal rights throughout the length and breadth of this land."[14]

It was upon this emotional, uneven ground that an essentially new color line was drawn. It was established in a kind of racial warfare, of assaults and withdrawals, of attacks and counterattacks. Nevertheless, well before the end of Reconstruction, both forces had been fully engaged and the line was unmistakably formed.

Even before the Radicals came into power in South Carolina in 1868, native whites had already defined a color line in government-supported institutions, on common carriers, in places of public accommodation and amusement, and, of course, in private social organizations. The degree of separation in each of these areas varied. In many instances, obviously, some compromise between expense and the desire for complete separation had to be made. Usually, the compromise involved the division of available facilities in some manner. If this was thought to be inconvenient, Negroes were totally excluded.

Typical was the treatment of Negro and white prisoners in the state penitentiary under the James L. Orr regime. Criminals of both races were confined in the same institution but were quartered in separate cells. Ironically, the racial concepts of white prison officials sometimes redounded to the benefit of Negro inmates. Minor violations of prison rules were punished every Sunday by the offenders being tied closely together, blindfolded, and forced to work their way over a series of obstacles in the prison yard. The chief guard explained that the white offenders were placed in the most difficult middle positions of the "blind gang" because "they have more intelligence than the colored ones and are better able to understand the rules of the institution."[15]

It is paradoxical that the Negro leadership, once in office, pressed vigorously for an end to separation in privately owned facilities open to the public but they allowed a very distinct separation to prevail in every major governmental facility. The most obvious instance was the schools, but the distinction also stretched into the furthermost reaches of gubernatorial activity. For example, a visitor to the state insane asylum in Columbia in 1874 found that "The Negro female inmates occupy a separate part of the same building" in which the white women were housed.[16]

On the other side, within a month after they had gained the vote, Negroes in South Carolina opened a frontal attack against racial discrimination on common carriers. Typical was their assault on the Charleston Street Car Company. At the time of its inauguration, the facilities of the company consisted of double tracks running the length of the peninsula with a spur branching off near the mid-point. Horsedrawn cars, each manned by a driver and a conductor, ran along the tracks at regular intervals. The cars contained seats in a compartment, and front and rear platforms. Before the cars began to run in December, 1866, the question of the accommodation of Negro passengers was thoroughly canvassed. "Proper arrangements will in due time be made to allow persons of color to avail themselves of the benefits of the railway," the management assured the Negro community, but it had not then decided between providing "special cars" for the Negroes as was done in New Orleans, or "assigning to them a portion of the ordinary cars as is more usual in other cities."[17] Negro leaders rejected both alternatives. As a Northerner wrote from Charleston in January, 1867, "Every scheme that could be devised that did not contemplate the promiscuous use of the cars by whites and negroes alike, was scouted by the Negro paper here; and the result is that negroes are now debarred the use of the cars altogether, unless they choose to ride upon the platform."[18]

But here the matter did not rest, as the following press account from the *New York Times* will show:

On Tuesday afternoon, March 27, after the adjournment of the Freedmen's mass meeting in Charleston, S. C., an attempt was made by some of them to test their right to ride in the street car, which is denied them by the rules of the Company. One of them entered a car, and declined to leave it when requested to do so by the conductor, who at the same time informed him of the Company's rules. The conductor, however, insisted that he should at least leave the inside of the car, and finally his friends, who found he was liable to be forcibly ejected if resistance were offered, persuaded him to yield. On its return trip the car was filled at the same place by a crowd of negroes, who rushed into it, to the great discomfort of the white passengers, and although remonstrated with and appealed to by the conductor, declined to go out. The driver then attempted, by direction of the conductor, to throw his car from the track; and failing in this, unhitched his horses and left the car. The negroes attempted to push the car forward, and threatened personal violence to the conductor, but the arrival of the police and detachments of soldiers caused the negroes to disperse. Other cars were in the meantime entered in the same way, and the negroes, finding the conductors would not permit them to ride, endeavored to interrupt the travel of the cars by placing stones on the track. . . .[19]

The military soon restored order, but the Negro community prepared to bring the case before the courts.[20] By early May, Negroes were actually riding in the cars, and, by early June, the military commander, Sickles, had issued an order prohibiting racial discrimination on railroads, horse-cars, and steamboats.[21] Sickles's successor, Canby, continued to enforce the rule.[22]

After the Negro gained political power, the battle against discrimination became more intense and assumed a wider front. The so-called antidiscrimination bill, passed in the summer of 1868, on paper was a most formidable weapon. In essence, it imposed severe penalties upon the owners of public accommodations who were convicted of discrimination. Burden of proof of innocence lay on the accused, and state solicitors (public prosecutors) who failed to prosecute suspected violators were themselves threatened with heavy punishments.

The effect of the new legislation on common carriers was immediate. A Northern teacher returning to Beaufort in the fall of 1868, after a few months' absence in the North, observed a portion of the results:

We took a small steamer from Charleston for Beaufort. Here we found a decided change since we went North. Then no colored person was allowed on the upper deck, now there were no restrictions, — there could be none, for a law had been passed in favor of the negroes. They were everywhere, choosing the best staterooms and best seats at the table. Two prominent colored members of the State Legislature were on board with their families. There were also several well-known Southerners, still uncompromising rebels. It was a curious scene and full of significance. An interesting study to watch the exultant faces of the negroes, and the scowling faces of the rebels. . . .[23]

The same legislation applied to railway facilities; and, apparently, it was applied without a great amount of dissent. Adjustment was made easier, perhaps, by the acquisition of some of the railroad companies by Radical politicians within the state, or by Northern capitalists, and by the close understanding which usually prevailed between Republican officeholders and those Conservatives who managed to retain control of their railroads. While formal discrimination was not practiced by railway operators, unofficial racial separation did occur on a large scale. On all of the major lines first- and second-class cars were available. Most Negroes apparently deliberately chose to ride in the more economical second-class accommodations, and virtually all of the whites—particularly white women—took passage on the first-class cars. The separation thus achieved was so nearly complete that the first-class car was often referred to as the "ladies' car."[24] It is highly relevant that the first Jim Crow legislation affecting railroads in South Carolina provided for the separation of the races only in the first-class cars,[25] because, of course, this was the only place on the railroads where there was any possibility of a significant degree of mixing.

During and after Reconstruction, some Negro passengers on the railroads could afford to and did share first-class accommodations with whites, but even this limited mixing was not welcomed by the mass of whites. For instance, a Northern white woman had an interesting and revealing experience while traveling from Columbia to Charleston via the South Carolina Railroad early in 1871:

> I must tell you of a scene I saw in the cars coming from Columbia. . . . After we were all seated a black man entered suitably dressed with black pants, black coat, *no* jewelry, trailing a cane. As he came on a man (white in complexion) rose up quickly and grasped the ebony hand with great impressment, and offered him the seat at his side. The colored representative, for such he was, took the seat close to the other, & they commenced a rapid conversation. My ear was arrested at once by the most painful profanity. It came from the *negro*. This [was] an exercise of his freedom, as a slave he would never have dared to utter a word of the kind.

When the Negro representative was reproved by a fellow passenger who happened to be a well known Presbyterian minister, he "took it quietly, and then went out of the car, into the one, (second class I think they called [it]) in front of us." After the minister debarked, the Negro "came back, took a seat by himself, and behaved as well as any person could."[26] A year later, a lady of the lowcountry complained of her trials on a trip by rail from Charleston to Unionville. "Grabbed snatches of sleep on the train on the way in spite of our colored neighbors," she reported to her husband."[27] Thus, until 1898, it is possible to find instances in which individual Negroes rode the rails seated in the same cars with the most aristocratic of whites; but economic and social lines re-enforced the color line, and the mixture was never generally and freely made.[28]

In the winter of 1869–1870 and through the summer which followed, a concerted attempt was made by the Negro leadership to win the full acceptance of Negroes into all places of public amusement, eating, drinking, and sleeping. Special provisions for the accommodation of Negroes at public entertainments had been made in ante-bellum times, but physical separation of the races was invariably the rule. In December, 1868, Charles Minort, a mulatto restaurateur and lesser political figure, nearly provoked a riot in a Columbia theater by presuming to seat his wife and himself in the front row, a section traditionally reserved for tardy white ladies. Presumably, he should have chosen seats among the other Negroes present who "had taken their seats, as has always been the custom, in the rear."[29] Minort yielded to the clamor of the whites in the audience, but, a year later, the Negroes of Charleston instituted judicial proceedings against the manager of the Academy of Music for refusing to mix the races in the boxes of the theater. The management barely succeeded in winning a postponement but was able to complete the season before the case came to trial.[30]

In the spring of 1870, Negro leaders in Charleston launched an attack against discrimination in restaurants, bars, and saloons. On March 25, for instance, Louis Kenake, accused of violating the antidiscrimination act, was brought before Magistrate T. J. Mackey and put on a bond of one thousand dollars while awaiting trial. Other white restaurant keepers of Charleston united to oppose and test the validity of the act, but, in the week which followed, at least six additional charges were lodged against operators of such businesses.[31] The assault was not confined to Charleston and demonstrations by Radical politicians were frequent during the campaign of 1870. In April, a Laurens woman wrote to her son in Missouri that "On Monday the yankees & some negroes went to Hayne Williams' and asked for drink, which 'Ward' refused them, that is, to drink at the gentlemans bar. They quietly marched him off to jail, & locked the doors, putting the keys in their pockets. The family are all at Spartanburg, we look for H. Williams to night, and I am afraid of a fuss, for he is a great bully."[32] In the same month, during a Radical meeting in Lancaster, a Negro was refused service in a local bar with the comment that no "nigger" could buy a drink there. Lucius Wimbush, a Negro senator, hearing of the incident, went to the bar, ordered a drink, and was refused. He immediately had the barkeeper arrested and placed under bail.[33] Strangely, not all such suits were against whites. "1st case under Civil Rights Bill today," a Greenville merchant noted in his diary in August, "negro indicts Henry Gantt [a Negro and well-known local barber] for not shaving him where he shaves white persons—What is to come from it no one knows."[34]

Negroes were also ambitious to open sleeping accommodations to their race. In the summer of 1868, as the first Negro legislators gathered in Columbia, native whites had been extremely apprehensive that they would attempt to occupy rooms in the city's hotels. Even *The Nation,* which had applauded the opening of common carriers to both races, declared that hotels were another and "delicate" matter, where separation was every-where observed.[35] The white community was vastly relieved to find that no such invasion was attempted, one upcountry newspaper having sent a spe-cial correspondent to Columbia to ascertain the fact.[36] Nevertheless, when Negro legislators debated the antidiscrimination bill early in the session, they made it very clear that hotels were included. William E. Johnson, the African Methodist Minister then representing Sumter County in the state-house, noting that the management of Nickerson's Hotel was concerned lest Negroes apply for rooms, declared that if he found private accommo-dations filled he would want to know that this resort was open to him. George Lee, a Negro member from Berkeley, observed that a group of jun-keting legislators had recently failed to find lodging in Greenville and that this law was desired to prevent that sort of occurrence. "Equal and exact justice to all," he demanded, ". . . it is what we must have."[37] Negroes were subsequently allowed to attend meetings in Columbia hotels, but it is apparent that none were ever given lodging.

Negroes also decried the fact that places of permanent rest occupied by whites, as well as those of a more temporary variety, were denied to their race. For instance, S. G. W. Dill, the native white Radical who was assassi-nated in Kershaw in the summer of 1868, and Nestor Peavy, his Negro guard who was killed in the same assault, were buried in racially separated cemeteries.[38]

Thus, from 1868 until 1889, when the antidiscrimination law was re-pealed, Negroes in South Carolina could legally use all public facilities which were open to whites. However, in actual practice, they seldom chose to do so. "The naturally docile negro makes no effort at unnecessary self-assertion," a Northern visitor in Charleston explained in 1870, "unless under the immediate instigation of some dangerous *friends* belonging to the other race, who undertake to manage his destiny."[39] This particular reporter was certainly prejudiced against the race; but four years later another Northern observer congratulated the Negroes of South Carolina on the "moderation and good sense" which they exhibited in their "intercourse with the whites." He concluded, "They seldom intrude themselves into places frequented by the whites, and considering that in South Carolina they have a voting majority of some thirty thousand and control the entire State Government, it is somewhat remarkable that they conduct themselves with so much propriety."[40] Indeed, after 1870, even the Negro leadership hardly seemed inclined to press further their political and legal advantage to end separation. Of the numerous charges lodged under the antidiscrimination law, not a single conviction was ever recorded.[41]

Even when Negroes pressed themselves in upon the prejudice of whites, the latter adjusted by total or partial withdrawal, so that a high degree of separation was always and everywhere maintained.

Some whites responded to the pressure by total withdrawal, that is, by leaving the state entirely. Of course, many of those who left South Carolina did so primarily for economic reasons, but many also departed from purely racial motives. A Winnsboro lawyer and pre-war fireeater revealed the thinking of many emigrants when he asked William Porcher Miles, in April, 1867, how he could live in a land where "Every 'mulatto' is your Equal & every 'Nigger' is your Superior." Pronouncing the Negro majority "revolting," he advised Miles to go to England. ". . . I have no doubt you could succeed & at any rate wd not have as many Negro Clients & negro witnesses to offend yr nostrils as in these USA. I can't conceive of any ones remaining here who can possibly get away—Suppose, it were certain, wh. it is not, that no U S Congress will ever pass a Law requiring that your Daughter & mine shall either marry Negroes or die unmarried. Still the Negro is already superior to them politically & to their Fathers also, & must ever be so henceforth."[42]

As the prospect of the elevation of Negroes to political power grew increasingly imminent, restlessness among white Carolinians rose. Joseph Le Conte, nationally famous scientist and a professor at the University of South Carolina, bespoke the minds of many of his colleagues in the fall of 1867. "The prostration of every interest in the Southern States first by the war, & then by the prospect of Negro supremacy, is so great that every one is at least making inquiries in anticipation of being compelled to leave for more favored regions," he wrote to a fellow academician at Yale. "If the present program is carried out it is quite certain that living in these states is simply impossible."[43] Once the Negro was in power, the flood of white emigration swelled. "Better make terms with the Wild Comanches," wrote one exiled Carolinian from the tangles of western Arkansas in 1872, "than hourds of Radicals . . ."[44]

Of course, not every white Carolinian was able to leave the state, but even among those who remained there was a strong current of sentiment for emigration. "I shd. be better satisfied to live and raise my children in a 'white man's country;' and will do so if I can," declared one Baptist clergyman on the eve of the ratification of the Constitution of 1868.[45]

For those who did remain there were lesser degrees of withdrawal. In the one area in which the Negro gained a definite ascendency, politics, a large number of whites simply refused to recognize his dominance beyond a necessary, minimal level. In 1870, and in the two state-wide elections which followed, more than ten thousand white voters actually abstained from voting because both regular and "reform" tickets recognized the political existence of the Negro. "They don't like to give up the dead issues of the past," explained a Bishopville farmer to a Virginian, "and are apprehensive that their acknowledgement of the Negroe's Civil and political equality will lead to social leveling."[46] One of those who refused to vote gave as his reason the statement that: "I wish no affiliation with niggers & a platform acknowledging the right of the negro to vote & hold office simply discourages the efforts of the Northern Democracy. The privilege may be *allowed the negro at this time to vote &c* but it is certainly not a right."[47] Many of those who voted the reform ticket did so only with grave reservations. While honoring "Hampton, Butler, Kershaw & gentlemen of that character" for their "courage and endurance" in attempting to fashion a program in 1870, a Charleston aristocrat asserted that: "Some of us have been unable to bring ourselves to admit the right to give the negro these rights of citizenship & are therefore unable to join in the canvas, but even we who are, possibly of this mistaken conscientious opinion, will vote the Reform Union (as it is called) candidates & rejoice at their success."[48] Even those who actively campaigned as Reformers, while embracing the Negro politically, kept him at arm's length socially. Attending a Reform speaking and barbecue in 1870, the Reverend Cornish noted that the participants dined at two tables, "the negroes at one & the whites at another."[49]

After Negroes were firmly entrenched in official positions in government, native whites evinced a distinct tendency to refrain from associations which recognized the authority of Negro officers over white citizens. For instance, in the heavily Negro county of Abbeville, in 1870, a distressed guardian asked one of the magistrates, who happened to be a Democrat, to dispatch a constable to return an orphan girl stolen away from his house. "When you send for Laura," he begged, "please send a white man, as she is a white girl under my charge, and I would not like to subject her to the mortification of being brought back by a colored man. Besides that I would be censured by the community as they would know nothing of the circumstances of the case."[50] Very often, avoiding communication with Negro officeholders was an easy matter for the whites. In the predominantly white counties, Conservatives were always able to retain some offices. In the counties where the Negroes were heavily in the majority, there were usually white Republicans in office through whom the local whites might and did conduct their business with the government. Contrary to tradition, when carpetbaggers and scalawags were actually in office, and there was every prospect that they would remain so throughout the foreseeable future, the white community did not think them all nearly so odious personally as subsequent reports suggested. Even in the middle counties, where the native Negro leadership predominated and scalawags did tend to be political opportunists, native whites still found means of avoiding contacts with Republican officers which, to them, would have been humiliating. A typical resort was that of the white citizens of Camden who arranged for the introduction of a bill in the legislature by a conservative representative from the white county of Lancaster because, as a Camdenite indicated, "our Representatives were coloured, and scalawags."[51]

Withdrawal was also the means by which native whites combatted attempts by Republican officials to end separation in institutions supported by the government. The withdrawal of native whites from the University and the State School for the Deaf and Blind at the prospect of Negro admissions are illustrations of white determination either to maintain separation or to dispense with the services afforded by related state institutions. If the Radicals had attempted to end separation in the common schools, it is virtually certain that the whites would have removed their children from these schools too. As one post-Redemption proponent of universal education argued, separation was essential to academic progress. Only by this means, he explained to Governor Hampton, could it be achieved "without any danger of social equality— *and this is the great bug bear.*"[52] Doubtless, it was the threat of withdrawal by the whites which dissuaded the Radical leadership from further attempts to end separation in institutions over which they had, by political means, absolute control.

Whites also refused to engage in normal civic activities in which the color line was not distinctly drawn. Thus, native whites chose not to join militia companies in which Negroes participated and were reported to be extremely apprehensive of being forced to undergo the "humiliation" of joining a mixed company.[53] Too, whites were reluctant to sit with Negroes in the jury box. An elderly Spartanburg farmer verbalized his feelings on this point in the summer of 1869: "When I go to court & see negroes on the jury & on the stand for witnesses it makes me glad that I am so near the end of my race to sit on a jury with them I dont intend to do it we have a law that exempt a man at 65 & I take the advantage of it."[54] This kind of withdrawal often reached odd extremes. In the spring of 1870, at the peak of the Negro leadership's drive for admission to privately owned public accommodations, the white Democrats of the Charleston Fire Department refused to decorate their engines and join in the annual parade because Negro fire companies were being allowed to march in the procession.[55]

This general withdrawal of whites from participation in civil affairs resulted in a tendency within the white community to govern itself outside of the official system. As Reconstruction progressed, this peculiar form of dyarchy approached its logical culmination. In its last days, the Tax Union came very close to the establishment of a separate government within the state when it considered collecting a ten-mil tax from its members and supervising its expenditure, thus depriving the incumbent Radicals of the staff of political life.[56] A year later, during the period of the dual government, a similar plan was actually implemented while the Hampton regime governed the whites and the Chamberlain government served, virtually, a Negro constituency.

Native whites also tended to withdraw from public places where the color line could not be firmly fixed and the Negro could easily assert his equality. "The whites have, to a great extent—greater than ever before—yielded the streets to the negroes," wrote a Columbian on Christmas Day, 1868.[57] Similarly, in Charleston, in the late spring of 1866, a young aristocrat noted that the battery with its music and strollers had been yielded to the ladies and gentlemen of non-noble lineage on Saturdays, and by all whites to the Negroes on Sundays. On Saturdays, he declared, "the battery is quite full of gentlemen and ladies but it is not much patronized by the elite. . . . On Sunday afternoon the ethiops spread themselves on the Battery."[58]

The same reaction was manifested by the whites wherever the Negro leadership succeeded by legal means in ending separation. For instance, when Negroes won admission to the street cars of Charleston, the whites simply withdrew. "On Sunday I counted five Cars successively near the Battery crowded [with] negroes, with but one white man, the Conductor," wrote a native white in May, 1867. "The ladies are practically excluded."[59] When the Academy of Music was threatened with a discrimination suit in 1870, the white community replied with a counter-threat to withdraw its patronage and thus close the theater.[60] Adjustment which fell short of complete separation remained unsatisfactory to whites. "Even the Theatre is an uncertain pleasure," complained a Charleston lady in 1873, "no matter how attractive the program, for you know that you may have a negro next to you."[61] Probably many of her contemporaries found the exposure too damaging and stayed home.

The social lives of native whites were, of course, absolutely closed to Negroes. Access to the homes of the whites was gained by Negroes only when they clearly acquiesced in the superior-inferior relationship dictated by the owners, and even then entrance was often denied. "I told him I would never allow negroes to go in it while I owned it," wrote a Laurentville woman, incensed that a man who had bought her former home had rented it to Negroes. In spite of the fact that some Negro domestics lived in quarters behind the houses of their employers, whites were already rejecting Negroes as neighbors. A real estate agent in Aiken in 1871 responded to this sentiment when he refused offers from Negroes for city lots at triple prices because, as he explained to the owner, "purchasers among the whites will not settle among the Negroes, and I am afraid to sell to only a few of the latter."[62] Negroes were also not permitted to join any of the numerous social organizations in which native whites participated. The Patrons of Husbandry (the Grange), waxing strong in the state in the early 1870's, was not only exclusively white in membership, but was accused of widening the racial gap by its attitudes and actions toward Negroes.[63] Of course, such separation had been practiced before, but the exclusion of the Negro in freedom from the social organizations of the whites was not so much tradition as it was deliberate decision. For instance, witness the outrage of an officer of the Donaldsville Lodge of Good Templars at a careless assertion by the Abbeville *Medium* that the Lodge had admitted Negroes to membership. "I want to inform you," he lectured the editors, "that we have no negroes in our Lodge of Good Templers as you stated in your Last paper that we had formed a Lodge of Good Templers Numbering 45 including children & negroes. we don't take negroes in our Lodge. If you Do dont send me any nother number."[64]

The average Northern white residing in South Carolina during Reconstruction was only slightly less inclined than his native white contemporary to enforce racial separation. During the war, of course, Negro troops were organized in separate regiments, bivouacked in separate camps, and, when wounded, housed in separate hospitals.[65] After the war, although still sympathetic to most of the interests of the Negro, many Northern residents continued to draw a very distinct race line. In March, 1867, presumably under the influence of a man who had commanded a Negro brigade, many of the whites on St. Helena moved to establish a separate church from which Negroes would be excluded. Further, two months later when the Negroes of the island met to form a Republican organization, most of the Northern white residents boycotted the meeting, saying they were "going to have a *white* party."[66] Apparently, at least some of this sentiment carried over into the Constitutional Convention of 1868, because, as a Northern correspondent observed, white delegates occupied the front rows while Negroes filled the seats at the rear of the hall.[67] By 1870, separation also marked the formal social life of the official community in Columbia. Governor Scott, himself, set the precedent. In January, 1869, it was noted that no Negroes attended the traditional annual ball of the governor. The omission caused a great out-cry—the loudest of which, incidentally, came from Franklin J. Moses, Jr., the native white speaker of the house who became the next governor of the state on the suffrage of a Negro electorate. Governor Scott responded to the criticism by holding open house every Thursday evening to which all comers were welcomed. It was soon observed, however, that only Negro politicians called at that time.[68]

Informally, there was considerable social intercourse between Negroes and some Northern missionaries and white Radical politicians, Southern as well as Northern in birth. For instance, as revealed through her diary, the Quaker schoolmistress Martha Schofield never thought or acted in any way discriminatory against Negroes as a race.[69] Frank Moses, politically the most successful of the scalawags, after 1868, publicly, repeatedly, and consistently supported unreserved equality for Negroes. Similarly, in Charleston, in 1870, a scandalized aristocrat declared that Mrs. Bowen, the wife of scalawag Congressman Christopher Columbus Bowen and the daughter of a unionist leader in the nullification controversy in the 1830's, "is reported to receive negro visitors. . . . thank Heaven," he added gratefully, "that Mr. Petigru cannot see her degradation. . . ."[70] Perhaps in time the quantity of interchange increased slightly. A Northern observer, visiting the state in 1874, noted that the "shoddy" Northerners living in South Carolina "hob nob" with the blacks in the bars and have them at home and that "at least two politicians of Charleston have married colored wives. . . ."[71] Taken at large, however, most white Republicans apparently accepted "public equality" for Negroes; but only a few broadened their toleration to accept Negroes into their social activities.

Separation is, of course, a relative term. It was obviously not possible for Negroes and whites to withdraw entirely from association with each other. If intimate contact led to irritation and violence, it also led to warm personal friendships—often with the superior-inferior, paternal bias, but no less real for all of that. Cordiality could and did breach the barrier of race. Yet the fact remained that it was difficult to establish a human bond across the color chasm and, once established, the tie had to be assiduously maintained against the constant erosion induced by a thousand and one external forces of social pressure.

That there was sometimes tenderness between individuals of different races is abundantly evident. On the Elmore plantation near Columbia, in the fall of 1865, the young white master was nightly importuned by the Negro children to get out his fiddle and play. Frequently he did so, the dozen or so Negro boys and girls dancing around the fire, begging for more after the fiddler had exhausted himself in a two-hour concert.[72] The concern of many late masters for their ex-slaves was matched by the interest of individual Negroes in the welfare of their recent owners. A freedman seeking relief for a white family from a Bureau officer explained his motivation: "I used to belong to one branch of that family, and so I takes an interest in 'em."[73] Occasionally, ex-slaveowners retained the friendship and assistance of their erstwhile bondsmen when all others had deserted them. Thus, in the summer of 1873, in an area of Chester county where alleged Klansmen had been active two years previously, planter Robert Hemphill noted the death of a neighbor, John McCluken. "I called one morning & found him dead & the dogs in bed with him," he reported. "Strange to say there was no white person ever called to see him. The negroes were the only persons who gave him any attention at all."[74]

Sometimes, intimacy became miscegenation. The census reports are uncertain witnesses and contemporaries are typically mute on the point; but scattered references suggest that racial interbreeding was markedly less common after emancipation than before. "Miscegenation between white men and negro women diminished under the new order of things," a Bureau officer later wrote. "Emancipation broke up the close family contact in which slavery held the two races, and, moreover young gentlemen did not want mulatto children sworn to them at a cost of three hundred dollars apiece. In short, the new relations of the two stocks tended to separation rather than to fusion."[75] A Northern traveler visiting the state in 1870 concurred: "From all I could see and learn, there are far fewer half-breed children born now than before the Rebellion. There seems, indeed, a chance that the production of original half-breeds may be almost done away with. . . ."[76]

Legal, moral, and social pressures exercised by the white community upon its members, as well as the physical separation of the races suggest that these were valid observations. The Black Code pointedly declared that "Marriage between a white person and a person of color shall be illegal and void," and when the code was revised in 1866 this portion emphatically remained in force.[77] Children born of Negro mothers and white fathers, so recently especially prized for their pecuniary value, became simply illegitimate issue and a liability to the community. In addition, the laws of bastardy came to be applied against the fathers of mulatto children. Perhaps most important was the fact that, in the minds of the native whites, children of mixed blood personified the adulteration of the superior race and embodied in living form the failure of Southern civilization. Many whites, turned to soul-searching by their defeat, fixed upon miscegenation as their great sin. "It does seem strange that so lovely a climate, and country, with a people in every way superior to the Yankees, should be overrun and destroyed by them," wrote a rice aristocrat in 1868. "But I believe that God has ordered it all, and I am firmly of opinion with Ariel that it is the judgement of the Almighty because the human and brute blood have mingled to the degree it has in the slave states. Was it not so in the French and British Islands and see what has become of them."[78]

Just as complete separation of the races was physically impossible, there was little possibility that miscegenation might entirely cease. One does not have to travel far into contemporary sources to discover instances in which white men had children by Negro women. In 1867, a lowcountry planter, accused of fathering the mulatto child of his Negro house servant, wrote plaintively to his mother: "This child was begotten during my absence in Charlotte & Charleston, from the middle of December until nearly the middle of January, & the Father of it was seen night after night in Emma's house, this I heard on my return, but as it was no concern of mine I did not give it a thought. She was *free*, the Mother of 5 Children & could have a dozen lovers if she liked. I had no control over her virtue."[79] In 1874, a planter on the Cooper River in St. John's noted the existence of circumstances on his plantation which might have led to similar results. "Found a white man staying with one of the colored people on the place," ran the laconic note in his journal. "He being engaged in rebuilding Mayrents Bridge."[80] Some of these liaisons were of prolonged duration. In 1870, Maria Middleton, a Negro woman, brought suit against a Pineville physician for failure to support her three children which he had allegedly fathered. Strangely, the defendant's lawyer did not deny the paternity, but sought dismissal on the plea that the plaintiff had no legal grounds for suit.[81]

Once in power, the Radicals hastened to repeal the prohibition against interracial marriage. Thereafter, informal arrangements were sometimes legalized. In the spring of 1869, a reporter stated that three such marriages had occurred within the state—a Massachusetts man had married a Beaufort mulatto woman, and two white women had married Negro men.[82] In 1872, the legislature explicitly recognized interracial unions by declaring that the "children of white fathers and negro mothers may inherit from the father if he did not marry another woman but continued to live with their mother."[83]

There were a surprisingly large number of cases in which white women gave birth to children by Negro fathers. During his stay in Greenville,

Bureau officer John De Forest heard of two such births and noted other instances in which white women were supported by Negro men. Such situations, he believed, were largely the result of the loss of husbands and fathers in the war and the destitution of the country generally.[84] In 1866, in neighboring Pickens District, a case came into the courts in which Sally Calhoun, "a white woman of low birth," and a Negro man were brought to trial for the murder of their child. Ironically, the Negro was freed, though obviously implicated, and the woman was convicted and imprisoned.[85] Apparently, some of these liaisons were far from casual as a Spartanburg farmer rather painfully suggested to his brother in Alabama: "My dear Brother as you have made several Enquiries of me and desiring me to answer them I will attempt and endeavor to do So to the best information that I have on the Various Subjects alluded to by you the first Interrogatory is Relative to John H. Lipscomb's daughter haveing Negro Children, I am forced to answer in the affirmative no doubt but she has had two; and no hopes of her Stopping. . . ."[86]

By the end of Reconstruction, Negroes had won the legal right to enjoy, along with whites, accommodations in all public places. In reality, however, they seldom did so. On the opposite side of the racial frontier, the pattern of separation was fixed in the minds of the whites almost simultaneously with the emancipation of the Negro. By 1868, the physical color line had, for the most part, already crystallized. During the Republican regime, it was breached only in minor ways. Once the whites regained political power, there was little need to establish legally a separation which already existed in fact. Moreover, to have done so would have been contrary to federal civil rights legislation and would have given needless offense to influential elements in the North. Finally, retention of the act had a certain propaganda value for use against liberals in the North and against Republican politicians at home. Again and again, the dead letter of the law was held up as exhibit "A" in South Carolina's case that she was being fair to the Negro in the Hampton tradition. After the federal statute was vitiated in the courts, after racial liberalism had become all but extinct in the North, and as the Negro was totally disfranchised in South Carolina, the white community was ready and able to close the few gaps which did exist in the color line, and to codify a social order which custom had already decreed.

Ultimately, the physical separation of the races is the least important portion of the story. The real separation was not that duo-chromatic order that prevailed on streetcars and trains, or in restaurants, saloons, and cemeteries. The real color line lived in the minds of individuals of each race, and it had achieved full growth even before freedom for the Negro was born. Physical separation merely symbolized and reinforced mental separation. It is true that vigorous assaults by one side or the other forced the enemy to yield his forward trenches and to alter slightly the precise line of the color front. It is also true that material changes in post-Reconstruction Southern society pushed the trenches into areas which had not existed before. This often gave the illusion of basic change, of a breakthrough by the dominate whites in the war of races, whereas, actually, it merely represented the extension of the old attitudinal conflict onto new ground, only to bring with it the stalemate that marked the struggle elsewhere. Viewed in relation to the total geography of race relations, the frontier hardly changed; and the rigidity of the physical situation, set as it was like a mosaic in black and white, itself suggested the intransigence of spirit which lay behind it. Well before the end of Reconstruction, this mental pattern was fixed; the heartland of racial exclusiveness remained inviolate; and South Carolina had become, in reality, two communities — one white and the other Negro.

Notes

1. *New York Times,* July 11, 1865, p. 4.

2. Mrs. A. J. Gonzales to her mother, May 3, 1868, Elliott–Gonzales Papers.

3. C. W. Moise to F. W. Dawson, September 15, 1885, F. W. Dawson Papers. See also: A. L. Taveau to William Aiken, April 24, 1865, A. L. Taveau Papers.

4. Anonymous MS, n.d., South Carolina Reconstruction Papers. This document was probably found among the papers of Martin Witherspoon Gary. The text indicates that it was written shortly after Redemption.

5. William Heyward to James Gregorie, June 4, 1868, Gregorie-Elliott Papers.

6. J. H. Young to J. W. White, August 5, 1867, J. W. White Papers.

7. Thomas Wentworth Higginson, *Army Life in a Black Regiment* (Boston, 1890), p. 266.

8. Sally Elmore Taylor MS Memoirs.

9. *New York Times,* August 20, 1868, p. 2.

10. *Daily Republican* (Charleston), June 24, 1870.

11. *Convention Proceedings, 1868,* pp. 72, 353–56, 789–92.

12. *Statutes at Large,* XIV, 179; see also pp. 337–38, 386–88.

13. *House Journal* (Special Session, 1868), pp. 218–23; *New York Times,* August 20, 1868, p. 2.

14. *Congressional Record,* II, Part 1, 43rd Cong., 1st Sess., 408, 566.

15. *House Journal* (Special Session, 1868), Appendix A, p. 110.

16. J. E. Bomar to his children, November 26, 1874, E. E. Bomar Papers. See also: Sally Elmore Taylor MS Memoirs.

17. *Daily Courier* (Charleston), October 15, December 17, 1866.

18. *New York Times,* January 7, 1867, p. 1.

19. Ibid., April 2, 1867, p. 1.

20. Ibid., April 20, 1867, p. 1.

21. W. E. Martin to B. F. Perry, May 7, 1867 (copy), A. L. Burt Papers.

22. *New York Times,* August 20, 1868, p. 1.

23. Elizabeth Hyde Botume, *First Days among the Contrabands* (Boston, 1893), pp. 267–69.

24. *New York Times,* October 19, 1868, p. 1; *Intelligencer* (Anderson), October 21, 1868.

25. George Brown Tindall, *South Carolina Negroes, 1877–1900* (Columbia, 1952), p. 301.

26. M. C. M. Taylor to Jeremiah Wilbur, March 13, 1871, Jeremiah Wilbur Papers.

27. Margaret Grimball to John B. Grimball, July 3, 1872, J. B. Grimball Papers.

28. Negro leaders in this period experienced more difficulty in winning admission to first-class cars in other states. For instance, in December, 1869, three Carolina Negroes sued the Richmond and Danville Railroad for ejecting them from the first class cars of that Virginia line. *Horry News* (Conway), December 24, 1869.

29. *New York Times,* December 25, 1868, p. 2.

30. Ibid., January 25, 1870, p. 2.

31. *Daily Republican* (Charleston), March 26, 28, 29; April 2, 1870.

32. Mrs. J. W. Motte to Robert Motte, April 27, 1870, Lalla Pelot Papers.

33. *Daily Republican* (Charleston), April 13, 1870.

34. William L. Mauldin MS Diary, entry for August 22, 1870.

35. *The Nation,* VII, No. 164 (August 20, 1868), 142.

36. *Intelligencer* (Anderson), August 26, 1868; *New York Times,* July 12, 1868, p. 5.

37. *New York Times,* August 20, 1868, p. 1.

38. Thomas J. Kirkland and Robert M. Kennedy, *Historic Camden,* Part Two (Columbia, 1926), p. 202.

39. N. S. Shaler, "An Ex-Southerner in South Carolina," *The Atlantic Monthly,* XXVI, No. 153 (July, 1870), 58.

40. *New York Times,* July 4, 1874, p. 5. The pattern of separation was also impervious to any effects from the Civil Rights Act of 1875.

41. Tindall, *South Carolina Negroes,* pp. 292–93, citing the Charleston *News and Courier,* November 5, 1883.

42. G. I. C. to W. P. Miles, April 13, 1867, W. P. Miles Papers.

43. Joseph Le Conte to W. D. Whitney, November 28, 1867, W. D. Whitney Papers.

44. Victor W. Johns to F. W. McMaster, January 9, 1872, F. W. McMaster Papers.

45. Basil Manly, Jr., to Charles Manly, April 15, 1868, Basil Manly, Jr., Letters and Letterbook.

46. J. M. Dennis to J. Y. Harris, May 21, 1870, J. Y. Harris Papers.

47. T. P. Bailey to R. H. McKie, May 12, 1870, R. H. McKie Papers.

48. W. G. De Saussure to W. P. Miles, September 21, 1870, W. P. Miles Papers. The writer was mistaken in including Hampton in this group.

49. J. H. Cornish MS Diary, entry for September 3, 1870.

50. E. F. Powers to R. R. Hemphill, May 21, 1870, Hemphill Papers.

51. R. A. Bonney to Dock Bonney, August 2, 1868, E. W. Bonney Papers.

52. Anonymous to Wade Hampton, November 13, 1877, Freedmen File.

53. *New York Times,* May 24, 1867, p. 2.

54. Edward Lipscomb to Smith Lipscomb, June 30, 1869, Edward Lipscomb Papers.

55. *Daily Republican* (Charleston), April 30, 1870.

56. *Intelligencer* (Anderson), December 2, 1875.

57. *New York Times,* January 2, 1869, p. 2.

58. Berkeley Grimball to Elizabeth Grimball, June 10, 1866, J. B. Grimball Papers (Duke).

59. W. E. Martin to B. F. Perry, May 7, 1867 (copy), A. L. Burt Papers.

60. *New York Times,* January 25, 1870, p. 2.

61. Eliza M. Smith to W. P. Miles, January 16, 1873, W. P. Miles Papers.

62. Mrs. Robert Pelot to her husband, March 11, 1866, Lalla Pelot Papers; F. A. Ford to James Conner, November 27, 1871, James Conner Papers.

63. William A. Law to his wife, August 29, 1874, William A. Law papers: *A History of Spartanburg County,* p. 168.

64. O. P. Gordon to R. R. Hemphill, June 21, 1874, Hemphill Papers.

65. Emma E. Holmes MS Diary, entry for April 7, 1865; Rupert S. Holland, *Letters and Diary of Laura M. Towne, 1862–1884, Written from the Sea Islands of South Carolina* (Cambridge, 1912), p. 116.

66. Holland, *Letters and Diary of Laura M. Towne,* pp. 177–78, 182.

67. *New York Times,* January 27, 1868, p. 2.

68. Ibid., February 6, 1869, p. 2; January 25, 1870, p. 2; Charleston *Daily Republican,* February 19, 1870.

69. Martha Schofield MS Diary, *passim.*

70. W. G. De Saussure to W. P. Miles, September 21, 1870, W. P. Miles Papers.

71. *New York Times,* July 9, 1874, p. 1.

72. Grace B. Elmore MS Diary, entry for October 1, 1865.

73. James H. Croushore and David M. Potter (eds.), *John William De Forest, A Union Officer in the Reconstruction* (New Haven, 1948), p. 65.

74. R. N. Hemphill to W. R. Hemphill [Summer], 1873, Hemphill Papers.

75. Croushore and Potter, *A Union Officer,* p. 132.

76. Shaler, *Atlantic Monthly,* XXVI, p. 57.

77. *Statutes at Large,* XII, 270, 366^{29}–366^{30}.

78. William Heyward to James Gregorie, January 12, 1868, Gregorie–Elliott Papers.

79. T. R. S. Elliott to his mother, October 20, 1867, T. R. S. Elliott Papers.

80. Keating S. Ball MS Plantation Journal, entry for February 5, 1874.

81. *Daily Republican* (Charleston), June 7, 1870.

82. *New York Times,* May 24, 1869, p. 2.

83. *Statutes at Large,* XIII, 62–63.

84. Croushore and Potter, *A Union Officer,* p. 138.

85. *House Journal* (Special Session, 1868), Appendix A, pp. 134–35. See also: *New York Times,* November 9, 1866, p. 1.

86. Edward Lipscomb to Smith Lipscomb, June 19, 1874, Lipscomb Family Papers.

3. Why were the railroads the "contested terrain" of race relations in the postwar South?

Edward L. Ayers

From *The Promise of the New South: Life After Reconstruction*

Born in 1953, Edward L. Ayers attended Woodward's last graduate seminar at Yale, where he learned "in his [Woodward's] person and his work the potential of Southern history." Now Hugh P. Kelly Professor of History at the University of Virginia, Ayers has authored, coauthored, or coedited several books, including *Vengeance and Justice: Crime and Punishment in the Nineteenth-Century American South* (1984); *The Edge of the South: Life in Nineteenth-Century Virginia* (1991); *All Over the Map: Rethinking American Regions* (1996); and *The Oxford Book of the American South: Testimony, Memory, and Fiction* (1997). He has also developed the *Valley of the Shadow Project* (*<http://jefferson.village.virginia.edu /vshadow2>*), a World Wide Web site devoted to two Civil War communities, for which he has won national acclaim. *The Promise of the New South: Life After Reconstruction* (1992), Ayers's most important book, emphasizes the New South's heterogeneity and complexity. The New South was a contradictory land of new technology and progress, of old hatreds and reaction. No subject was more complicated than the region's race relations, that "constituted a complex environment of symbols over which no one person had much control and through which everyone had to navigate." Segregation, Ayers insists, became entwined in the powerful historical forces of race, class, and gender that propelled it forward—most noticeably on the railroads that crisscrossed the New South.[1]

Questions for a Closer Reading

1. Does Ayers agree with Woodward on the timing of segregation?
2. How did railroads reinforce white and black social roles in the late nineteenth century?
3. What were the travel conditions like on Jim Crow cars?
4. According to Ayers, did gender figure into the decision to segregate the railroads?
5. Why were railroad companies ambivalent over separate accommodations for black and white southerners?
6. In the 1880s, what position did the appellate federal courts assume on the question of Jim Crow?
7. What explanation does Ayers offer for the passage of railroad segregation laws?

Note

1. Edward L. Ayers, *Vengeance and Justice: Crime and Punishment in the Nineteenth-Century American South* (New York: Oxford University Press, 1984), vii; and *The Promise of the New South: Life After Reconstruction* (New York: Oxford University Press, 1992), 427.

The Promise of the New South: Life After Reconstruction

In a quest to channel the relations between the races, white Southerners enacted one law after another to proscribe contact among blacks and whites. Some things about the relations between the races had been established quickly after emancipation. Schools, poor houses, orphanages, and hospitals, founded to help people who had once been slaves, were usually separated by race at their inception. Cities segregated cemeteries and parks; counties segregated court houses. Churches quickly

Edward L. Ayers, from *The Promise of the New South: Life After Reconstruction* (New York: Oxford University Press, 1992), 136–46.

broke into different congregations for blacks and whites. Hotels served one race only; blacks could see plays only from the balcony or separate seats; restaurants served one race or served them in different rooms or from separate windows. In 1885, a Memphis newspaper described how thoroughly the races were separated: "The colored people make no effort to obtrude themselves upon the whites in the public schools, their churches, their fairs, their Sunday-schools, their picnics, their social parties, hotels or banquets. They prefer their own preachers, teachers, schools, picnics, hotels and social gatherings." In the countryside as well as in town, blacks and whites associated with members of their own race except in those situations when interracial association could not be avoided: work, commerce, politics, travel.[1]

Even if the general boundaries of race relations had been drawn early on, though, many decisions had yet to be made by the 1880s. The notion of a completely circumscribed world of white and black had not yet become entrenched; the use of the word "segregation" to describe systematic racial separation did not begin until the early twentieth century. Although most whites seem to have welcomed segregation in general, others saw no need to complicate the business of everyday life with additional distinctions between the races, no need to antagonize friendly and respectable blacks, no need to spend money on separate facilities, no need to risk bringing down Northern interference. Although many blacks fought against the new laws with boycotts, lawsuits, and formal complaints, others saw no use in fighting the whites who had all the power on their side, no use in antagonizing white benefactors or white enemies, no use in going places they were not welcome. The segregation begun in the decade following the end of the Civil War did not spread inexorably and evenly across the face of the South. The 1880s saw much uncertainty and much bargaining, many forays and retreats.[2]

Most of the debates about race relations focused on the railroads of the New South. While some blacks resisted their exclusion from white-owned hotels and restaurants, they could usually find, and often preferred, accommodations in black-run businesses. Travel was a different story, for members of both races had no choice but to use the same railroads. As the number of railroads proliferated in the 1880s, as the number of stations quickly mounted, as dozens of counties got on a line for the first time, as previously isolated areas found themselves connected to towns and cities with different kinds of black people and different kinds of race relations, segregation became a matter of statewide attention. Prior to the eighties, localities could strike their own compromises in race relations, try their own experiments, tolerate their own ambiguities. Tough decisions forced themselves on the state legislatures of the South after the railroads came. The result was the first wave of segregation laws that affected virtually the entire South in anything like a uniform way, as nine Southern states enacted railroad segregation laws in the years between 1887 and 1891.[3]

By all accounts, the railroads of the 1880s were contested terrain. Trains ran cars of two classes: in the first-class car rode women and men who did not use tobacco, while in the second-class car rode men who chewed or smoked, men unaccompanied by women, and people who could not afford a first-class ticket. To travel in the second-class car was to travel with people, overwhelmingly men, who behaved very differently from those in the car ahead. The floors were thick with spit and tobacco juice, the air thick with smoke and vulgarities. The second-class car had hard seats, low ceilings, and no water; frequently, it was merely a part of the baggage car set off by a partition. The second-class car ran right behind the engine, and was often invaded by smoke and soot. The cars saw more crowding of strangers than in any other place in the New South. "The cars were jammed, all the way over here, with the dirtiest, nastiest set I ever rode with," a Louisiana man complained about a trip to Texas.[4]

A first-class, or parlor, car contained a diverse group of travelers, but their behavior tended to be more genteel than those in the smoking car. "It was the ordinary car of a Southern railroad," Ellen Glasgow wrote, with "the usual examples of Southern passengers. Across the aisle a slender mother was holding a crying baby, two small children huddling beside her." "A mulatto of the new era" sat nearby, while "further off there were several men returning from business trips, and across from them sat a pretty girl, asleep, her hand resting on a gilded cage containing a startled canary. At intervals she was aroused by the flitting figure of a small boy on the way to the cooler of iced water. From the rear of the car came the amiable drawl of the conductor as he discussed the affairs of the State with a local drummer, whose feet rested upon a square leather case." The seats were covered with soft plush fabric, the floor covered with carpet.[5]

Strangely enough, the scenes of racial contention and conflict on the trains focused on the placid first-class cars rather than on the boisterous cars ahead. Sutton Griggs, a black Virginia novelist, gave a compelling account of the random violence that hovered around blacks who rode in the parlor cars. A young black man on his way to Louisiana to become president of a small black college had traveled all the way from Richmond without incident. Absorbed in a newspaper as the car crossed the line into Louisiana, he did not notice the car gradually filling at each stop. "A white lady entered, and not at once seeing a vacant seat, paused a few seconds to look about for one. She soon espied an unoccupied seat. She proceeded to it, but her slight difficulty had been noted by the white passengers." Before the black man knew what was happening, he found himself surrounded by a group of angry whites. " 'Get out of this coach. We don't allow niggers in first-class coaches.' " The black passenger resisted moving, only to be thrown off the train altogether. "Covered from head to foot with red clay, the president-elect of Cadeville College walked down to the next station, two miles away."[6]

This sort of clash was hardly confined to fiction. Andrew Springs, a young black man on the way from North Carolina to Fisk University in Nashville in 1891, told a friend back home about his experiences. "I came very near being locked up by the police at Chattanooga. I wanted some water. I went in to the White Waiting [room] and got it as they didn't have any for Cuffy to drink. Just time I got the water here come the police just like I were killing some one and said You get out of here you black rascal put that cup down. I got a notion to knock your head off." As so often happened, the black man refused to accept such treatment without protest. "I told him I were no rascal neither were I black. I were very near as white as he was. Great Scott he started for me. . . . He didn't strike tho, but had me started to the lock up." Springs, like many blacks harassed on the railroad, used the law to stop his persecution. "I told him I had my ticket and it was the duty of the R.R. Co. to furnish water for both white [and] black." The officer let him go. The young man then took the dangerous, and atypical, step of threatening the officer: "I told him if ever I catch him in North Carolina I would fix him."[7]

Aggressive single young men were not the only ones who threatened, intentionally and unintentionally, the tenuous racial situation on the railroad. In 1889, Emanuel Love, a leader of the First African Baptist Church of Savannah, was asked by an agent of the East Tennessee, Virginia and Georgia Railroad to travel over the road to a convention in Indianapolis, assuring Love that he and his entourage could have first-class accommodations the entire day. Love assumed the delegation would have a car to themselves so they would not antagonize white first-class passengers who might be on board. As the train pulled out and the pastor walked through the car greeting the other delegates, he soon noticed that there were indeed whites in the first-class car, and they began to whisper among themselves and to the white conductor. A black railway workman warned the delegation that trouble was ahead, but there was little they could do; someone had already telegraphed news of the black effrontery to the next stop. There, at least fifty white men, carrying pistols, clubs, and pieces of iron, pushed their way into the car and assaulted the "well dressed" delegates. Some sought to defend themselves, while most fled. One who could do neither was Mrs. Janie Garnet, a graduate of Atlanta University and a school teacher, who screamed in fear. One of the white men put a cocked pistol to her breast and said "You G-d d——d heffer, if you don't hush your mouth and get out of here, I will blow your G-d d——d brains out." The delegation was treated for their broken bones and bruises and made their way, presumably in a separate car, to Indianapolis. Accounts of the violence directed at blacks often spoke of well-dressed clergymen and well-dressed women as the objects of white anger.[8]

Whites also experienced racial discomfiture that did not necessarily result in violence or even overt conflict. In 1889, a Tennessee newspaper related in a light tone a story that captured some of the risks of the "parlor car." At Nashville, "a bright, good-looking colored girl (or rather an almost white colored girl)" boarded the train. A "flashily-dressed white gentleman, usually known as the 'car masher,'" began an elaborate flirtation with the girl, whom he assumed to be white. She "very modestly" accepted his attentions, "slightly blushing probably out of compassion for the fellow's mistake, but which he evidently took as an indication of a surrender to his charms." He bought his "'lady friend' a lunch, and the two sat for half an hour enjoying their supper tete-a-tete, . . . every passenger on the train enjoying the situation. The girl was entirely innocent of any intention to entrap or deceive the fellow, but he was the victim of his own inordinate conceit and folly." He eventually found out his mistake after she had reached her destination. "He was probably the maddest man in the State when he found it all out. He was mad at the girl, mad at the passengers and doubtless wanted to kick himself all the way home." The account ended, significantly, with the information that "none enjoyed the episode more than the ladies on the train."[9]

If the situation had been reversed, if some "almost white" black man had been flirting with a white girl, deceiving her, eating with her, what then? Such a scene would have invoked the sense of pollution whites associated with blacks, no matter how clean, how well-dressed, how well-mannered they might be. As a New Orleans newspaper argued in 1890, when the state was considering the segregation of its railroad cars, "one is thrown in much closer communication in the car with one's traveling companions than in the theatre or restaurant," which were already segregated. In the railroad car, the article related in suggestive language, whites and blacks would be "crowded together, squeezed close to each other in the same seats, using the same conveniences, and to all intents and purposes in social intercourse." The lesson was clear: "A man that would be horrified at the idea of his wife or daughter seated by the side of a burly negro in the parlor of a hotel or at a restaurant cannot see her occupying a crowded seat in a car next to a negro without the same feeling of disgust." Any man "who believes that the white race should be kept pure from African taint will vote against that commingling of the races inevitable in a 'mixed car' and which must have bad results." A white woman or girl who let herself fall into easy and equal relations with a black man in such an anomalous place as the parlor car would risk her reputation.[10]

The sexual charge that might be created among strangers temporarily placed in intimate surroundings, many whites worried, could not be tolerated in a racially integrated car. In the late nineteenth century, sexual relations did not have to end in intercourse or even physical contact to be considered intimate and dangerous to a woman's reputation and self-respect. In fact, the history of segregation shows a clear connection to gender: the more closely linked to sexuality, the more likely was a place to be segregated. At one extreme was the private home, where the intimacies of the parlor, the dining table, and bedroom were never shared with blacks as equals; it was no accident that blacks were proscribed from entering a white home through its front door. Exclusive hotels, restaurants, and darkened theaters, which mimicked the quiet and privacy of the home, also saw virtually no racial mixing. Schools, where children of both genders associated in terms of intimacy and equality, saw early and consistent segregation. Places where people of only one gender associated with one another, though, tended to have relaxed racial barriers. The kitchen and nursery of a home, which "should" have been off-limits to blacks for white taboos to have remained consistent, in fact saw black women participating in the most private life of white families. Part of the lowered boundary, of course, grew out of the necessity whites perceived to use black labor, but blacks were permitted in the heart of the home because those rooms saw the interaction only of white women and black women. Male preserves, for their part, were often barely segregated at all: bars, race tracks, and boxing rings were notorious, and exciting, for the presence of blacks among whites. Some houses of prostitution profited directly from the sexual attraction black women held for some white men.[11]

The railroad would not have been such a problem, then, had blacks not been seeking first-class accommodations where women as well as men traveled, where blacks appeared not as dirty workers but as well-dressed and attractive ladies and gentlemen. When the Arkansas legislature was debating the need for a separate car in 1891, some whites argued that whites should not be forced to sit next to dirty blacks; other whites argued instead that the worst blacks were those who were educated and relatively well-to-do and who insisted on imposing themselves on the white people. A young black legislator, John Gray Lucas, a recent graduate of Boston University, confronted the white lawmakers with their inconsistency: "Is it true, as charged, that we use less of soap and God's pure water than other people. . . . Or is it the constant growth of a more refined, intelligent, and

I might say a more perfumed class, that grow more and more obnoxious as they more nearly approximate to our white friends' habits and plane of life?"[12]

With every year in the 1880s, more blacks fought their way to white standards of "respectability." Black literacy, black wealth, black businesses, black higher education, and black landowning all increased substantially. When whites discussed segregating the railroads, respectable blacks responded in fury and disbelief. "Is it not enough that the two races are hopelessly separated in nearly all the higher relations of life already?" an open letter from seven black clergymen and teachers from Orangeburg, South Carolina, asked in 1889. "Are you not content with separate places of public entertainment, separate places of public amusement, separate places of public instruction, and even separate places of public worship? Why in the name of common sense, of common humanity, of the common high-bred sensitiveness of every decent person of color, should you wish to force further unnatural separation even upon the thoroughfares of daily travel?"[13]

A Northern traveler in the South observed that "a few colored men are inclined to insist upon enjoying whatever right belongs to them under the law, because they believe that any concessions on the part of the black people, or surrender of their legal rights, would invite and produce new injuries and oppressions." Educated and assertive blacks, especially those of the younger generation, chafed at every restriction against them and looked for opportunities to exercise their legal rights to attack the very assumptions and presumptions of segregation. A black Georgia newspaper reflected this aggressive mentality: "When a conductor orders a colored passenger from the first class car it's a bluff, and if the passenger goes to the forward or smoking car, that ends it; should he refuse, it ends it also, for the trainman will reflect seriously before he lays on violent hands, for he knows that such a rash proceeding makes him amenable to the law."[14]

Mary Church, sixteen years old, boarded a train by herself only to be ushered to a Jim Crow car. She protested to the conductor that she had bought a first-class ticket. " 'This is first class enough for you,' he replied sarcastically, 'and you just stay where you are,' with a look calculated to freeze the very marrow of my bones." Having heard about "awful tragedies which had overtaken colored girls who had been obliged to travel alone on these cars at night," Church decided to get off the train. The conductor refused to let her pass, wanting to know where she was going. " 'I am getting off here,' I replied, 'to wire my father that you are forcing me to ride all night in a Jim Crow car. He will sue the railroad for compelling his daughter who has a first class ticket to ride in a second class car.' " The conductor relented.[15]

Blacks resorted to the law in increasing numbers in the 1880s, taking railroads and railroad employees to court to press for equal accommodations. Blacks actually won several of these cases, even in Southern courts. In 1885, for example, a black man named Murphy had bought a first-class ticket for a train from Georgia to Tennessee. His trip was uneventful until two white women boarded the train and their male companions told Murphy to go back to the smoking car. He refused, and the white men then threw Murphy into the other car. Murphy sued the railroad. The federal judge, a former United States senator, instructed the jury that precedent established in other, Northern, states had shown that under the common law railroads could segregate their cars by race, "so as to avoid complaint and friction." The railroads forfeited that right "when the money of the white man purchases luxurious accommodations amid elegant company, and the same amount of money purchases for the black man inferior quarters in a smoking car." The jury therefore awarded the black plaintiff damages—to be paid both by the assailants and by the railroad company whose employees "made no effort to prevent the mischief." Another decision in the same year, this one occasioned by a suit brought by a black woman who had gotten off the train rather than be shunted into the smoking car with its "swearing and smoking and whiskey drinking," also ruled in favor of the black litigant. The court judged that if the railroad provided for white ladies "a car with special privileges of seclusion and other comforts, the same must be substantially furnished for colored ladies."[16]

These 1885 rulings reflected the growing consensus of the nation's appellate and federal courts, Northern and Southern, that equal accommodations had to be provided for those who paid equal amounts for their tickets. Those rulings also stipulated that the railroads could provide separate accommodations for any groups of passengers, as long as the facilities were equal and as long as separation was consistently enforced and publicized before passengers boarded the train. The railroad's case would be strengthened if it could show that separation encouraged "peace, order, convenience, and comfort," by adjusting to dominant customs in the area through which the railroad passed. In the 1880s, black Southerners were able to use this body of law to win more equitable treatment on the railroads of the region, to force the railroads to provide them equal facilities. "There is a plain rule of justice, which ought to be recognized and enforced, viz: that every man is entitled to what he pays for," a defender of the rights of black passengers in 1890 argued. "If there be on the part of the whites an unwillingness to occupy the same cars and to sit in the same seats with the blacks, let them be separate; only let equally good cars be provided for both, if both pay for them." In 1887 and 1889, the new Interstate Commerce Commission ruled that trains crossing state lines had to "give one passenger as good accommodations as another for the same price, but they are not compelled to permit a passenger to take any car or any seat that may please his fancy." The "equality of accommodations" must be "real and not delusive." The federal government simultaneously stressed equality and sanctioned segregation, giving with one hand and taking away with the other.[17]

In the 1880s, then, blacks confronted a dangerous and uncertain situation every time they bought a first-class ticket to ride on a Southern railroad. Each road had its own customs and policy, and the events on the train might depend on the proclivity of the conductor or, worse, the mood and make-up of the white passengers who happened to be on board. Although the courts upheld the rights of several blacks who had the means to take their cases to court, there was no telling how many blacks suffered discrimination, intimidation, and violence in the meantime. Some railroads sought to avoid the problems simply by refusing to sell blacks first-class tickets; the L & N resorted to this policy until blacks threatened to boycott, then it allowed black women to travel first class, then reversed itself again two months later when whites protested. At least one railroad in Alabama, operating in the piney woods along the coast, sought to avoid the potentially costly conflicts by running its own separate and identical car for blacks as early as 1882. "The rule is made for the protection of the blacks as much as for anything else in a part of the country in which they might be subjected to drunken men's insults," a Mobile paper argued.[18]

If other railroads had followed the example of this Alabama company, rail segregation might have remained in the uncertain realm of custom and private business decisions that guided so much else in Southern race relations. Other railroads, however, especially those in parts of the South where blacks did not make up a large part of the clientele, were reluctant to go the considerable expense and trouble of running twice the number of cars. The railroads, unenthusiastic about passenger traffic in any case because, as the L and N's president put it, "You can't make a g—— d—— cent out of it," neither wanted to police Southern race relations and then be sued for it nor to run extra cars. It was clear that white Southerners could not count on the railroads to take matters in hand. Some whites came to blame the railroads for the problem, for it seemed to them that the corporations as usual were putting profits ahead of the welfare of the region.[19]

The first legislative attempt at statewide segregation, in fact, began in an unlikely setting that combined black anger and white frustration at the railroads. Republicans held half the seats in Tennessee's lower house in 1881, and four of their representatives were black men determined to overturn an 1875 state law that prevented black passengers from suing discriminatory railroads. Their straightforward attempt to repeal the law failed by the narrowest of margins, however, and a bill that would have outlawed racial discrimination by the railroads never came to a vote. Another measure raced through both houses, however, and the only votes against it came from the blacks who had worked to prohibit any kind of racial distinction. The new law dictated that "All railroad companies shall furnish separate cars, or portions of cars cut off by partition walls, which all colored passengers who pay first-class rates of fare may have the privilege to enter and occupy." The separate cars or apartments had to be kept "in good repair, with the same conveniences, and subject to the same rules governing other first-class cars for preventing smoking and obscene language." If the railroad failed to enforce the law, "the company shall pay a forfeit of $100, half to be paid to the person suing, the other half to be paid to the common school fund of the state." The next year, black legislators managed to make the punishment steeper, raising the penalty to $300. In the next two sessions of the legislature, black representatives continued to work for the outright abolition of discrimination, not the half-hearted separate-but-equal law. Although whites may have considered the law a compromise, to militant blacks it was inadequate in theory and practice, full of danger.[20]

Judged by what was to come, the language of this first separate-but-equal law stressed equality and put the burden on railroads who deprived passengers of services for which they had paid; most important, it did not actually require railroads to segregate their passengers, only to provide separate but equal accommodations that blacks had "the privilege to enter and occupy." Like the appellate decisions handed down in the nation's courts in these years, this law could have been construed as a victory of sorts for black passengers. "No white person shall be permitted to ride in a negro car or to insult or annoy any negro in such car," Florida's 1887 railroad segregation law announced.[21]

The earliest railroad segregation laws, therefore, carried an ambiguous message. They took racial division and conflict for granted but placed the blame and the burden of dispelling that conflict on the railroads. Laws demanding separate cars seemed a compromise between white sensibilities and black rights, and, to whites, the only one who seemed to lose was the railroad who had to pay the cost. Mississippi's legislature of 1888 struck the same bargain, putting its first railroad segregation law in the context of an act that created a railroad commission. The focus of the language now shifted from the rights and comforts of blacks to the powers of railroad officials to make the law operate smoothly. Texas continued the trend away from an emphasis on black rights the next year in its law, when it blandly dictated that "Railroad companies shall maintain separate coaches for the white and the colored races. They shall be equal as to comfort. They shall be designated by words or letters, showing the race for whom intended." Not only could "comfort" be open to many interpretations but the law neglected to stipulate the punishment a railroad or a conductor would suffer for failure to carry out the law.[22]

Despite the shift in emphasis, matters still remained very much in doubt in 1890, as events in Louisiana show. When the Louisiana legislature began considering a separate car law, a New Orleans newspaper felt compelled to attack the railroads who opposed the bill. "In view of the extreme liberality in which the State has treated them, there should have been at least some concessions from the powerful corporations to the people." Blacks clearly did not see a separate car as an equitable solution to the violence they suffered on the trains, and they sought to use their considerable representation in the state legislature to stop passage of the law in Louisiana. The American Citizens' Equal Rights Association of Louisiana, a black organization, sent a memorial to the legislature protesting the law, a memorial that also bore the signatures of the state's eighteen black legislators. Working with white delegates friendly to the railroads, the black lawmakers were able to defeat the bill in the senate. As soon as their votes were no longer needed to override a veto on an unrelated bill, however, the black legislators found themselves betrayed: white delegates joined together to write a separate-car law after all.[23]

Two blacks in New Orleans, furious at the turn of events, decided to make a test case of the Louisiana law. They sought the help of a white Northern lawyer long dedicated to black rights, Albion Tourgée, who responded enthusiastically. "Submission to such outrages," he wrote, tends "only to their multiplication and exaggeration. It is by constant resistance to oppression that the race must ultimately win equality of right." Accordingly, they enlisted a man named Homer Adolph Plessy, seven-eighths white, to board the East Louisiana Railroad and refuse to leave the white car even though officials had been notified earlier of his status as a black. He was arrested, and his case tried in Louisiana in late 1892. "The roads are not in favor of the separate car law, owing to the expense entailed," a lawyer looking into the matter reported, "but they fear to array themselves against it." It took four more years for the United States Supreme Court to hear the Plessy case, by which time segregation had been written into the laws of every Southern state except the Carolinas and Virginia. The years in between saw the political map of the South redrawn.[24]

The timing of the first wave of segregation law is explained, then, by the growing ambition, attainments, and assertiveness of blacks, by the striking expansion and importance of the railroad system in the 1880s, by a widespread distrust and dislike for the railroad corporations, by the course of legal cases at the state and circuit level, and by the example each state set for others. Most white officials who held power in these years played their role in the creation of statewide segregation; it was the product of no particular class, of no wave of hysteria or displaced frustration, no rising tide of abstract racism, no new ideas about race. Like everything else in the New South, segregation grew out of concrete situations, out of technological, demographic, economic, and political changes that had unforeseen and often unintended social consequences.[25]

Railroad segregation was not a throwback to old-fashioned racism; indeed, segregation became, to whites, a badge of sophisticated, modern, managed race relations. John Andrew Rice recalled an incident from his youth in South Carolina in 1892. He visited Columbia, then "an awkward overgrown village, like a country boy come to town all dressed up on a Saturday night." Despite the rawness of the state capital, "the main entrance to the town was the depot, and here was something new, something that marked the town as different from the country and the country depots at Lynchburg and Darlington and Varnville: two doors to two waiting rooms and on these two doors arresting signs, 'White' and 'Colored.'" Soon those signs *would* be in Lynchburg, Darlington, and Varnville as well, for state law would demand it. The railroads took a piece of the city with them wherever they went. The railroad cars and waiting rooms were marked by the same anonymity that was coming to characterize the towns and cities of the South, the same diversity within confined spaces, the same display of class by clothing and demeanor, the same crowding of men and women, the same crowding of different races. In fact, the railroads were even more "modern" than cities themselves, detached from their settings, transitory, volatile.[26]

Segregation laws, of course, could not contain all the conflicts generated by these new social relations. Blacks refused to be satisfied with the "compromise" of segregation, partly because its very existence was insulting and partly because of the way it was implemented. Two black men wrote a furious letter in the wake of Tennessee's 1891 law, charging that the black "first-class" area was in fact merely separated by a partition from the smoking area of the second-class car. As a result, they and their families had to wade through the smoke, tobacco juice, and jeers of white men to get to their section. The black men boldly warned the white South that "the signs of the times unmistakably show that unless public sentiment will cry down such injustice, the future of the two races will be (let us put it mildly) anything but peaceful." Jim Crow cars quickly became known as "universally filthy and uncomfortable," a symbol of "indignity, disgrace, and shame." Lawmakers and railroads merely clamped down more tightly. In Florida, for example, legislators empowered passengers to help conductors carry out their duties, codifying the sort of violence and bullying the segregation laws had been designed to stop in the first place. From Arkansas came word that municipalities, after the passage of the railroad law, began to implement racial restrictions far more than in the past.[27]

After 1891, only Virginia and the Carolinas did not have railroad segregation laws. The same forces working in the rest of the South worked in those states as well, of course, but having failed to put railroad segregation laws on the books in the late eighties and early nineties, they found that the political events of the next few years prevented them from joining their neighboring states. It was not until the late nineties that these states could implement their version of the law, just when the other Southern states began to enact even more kinds of segregation designed to enclose yet more of the machinery of the new age.[28]

Notes

1. Howard N. Rabinowitz, *Race Relations in the Urban South, 1865–1890* (New York: Oxford Univ. Press, 1978), 127–225, passim; *Memphis Commercial Appeal,* Jan. 6, 1885, quoted in Thomas H. Baker, *The Memphis "Commercial Appeal": The History of a Southern Newspaper* (Baton Rouge: Louisiana State University Press, 1971), 140. The timing of segregation has been a topic of prolonged debate in Southern history ever since the publication of C. Vann Woodward's classic, *The Strange Career of Jim Crow* (New York: Oxford Univ. Press, 1955). For a thorough overview of the debate, see Howard N. Rabinowitz, "More Than the Woodward Thesis: Assessing *The Strange Career of Jim Crow," Journal of American History* 75 (Dec. 1988): 842–56.

2. Woodward stressed the flux of the eighties in *Strange Career,* and subsequent studies have proven him correct. For the most thorough and systematic portrayals of race relations in the decade, see Joel Williamson, *The Crucible of Race: Black-White Relations in the American South Since Emancipation* (New York: Oxford Univ. Press, 1984); Joseph H. Cartwright, *The Triumph of Jim Crow: Tennessee Race Relations in the 1880s* (Knoxville: Univ. of Tennessee Press, 1976); George C. Wright, *Life Behind a Veil: Blacks in Louisville, Kentucky, 1865–1930* (Baton Rouge, Louisiana State University Press, 1985), 54; David Paul Bennetts, "Black and White Workers: New Orleans, 1880–1900" (Ph.D. diss., Univ. of Illinois at Urbana-Champaign, 1972), 211; Rabinowitz, *Race Relations.*

Some historians, focusing on law, emphasize the instrumental uses of racial prejudice for whites. From such a perspective, ravings about the black menace appear mainly as campaign rhetoric, smokescreens thrown up to hide more tangible motives of greed and lust for power. Segregation laws look like campaign ploys, ways to win the votes of ignorant voters back home. Some have seen similar desires behind the chilling racial violence of the New South, portraying lynchings as political maneuvers orchestrated to cow black opposition. An instrumental view is usually associated with the tradition of progressive history best embodied in the work of C. Vann Woodward, especially *Tom Watson: Agrarian Rebel* (New York: Macmillan, 1938) and *Origins of the New South, 1877–1913* (Baton Rouge: Louisiana State University Press, 1951). Woodward, while painfully aware of the power of race, has seen class and economic divisions as more fundamental; indeed, a considerable part of the power of his interpretations grows from his indignation at the uses of race by those who dominated the South. J. Morgan Kousser employs this perspective in a more insistent fashion in his *The Shaping of Southern Politics: Suffrage Restriction and the Establishment of the One-Party South, 1880–1910* (New Haven: Yale Univ. Press, 1974) and in "Progressivism—For Middle Class Whites Only: North Carolina Education, 1880–1910," *Journal of Southern History* 46 (May 1980): 169–94. For lynching, see James M. Inveriarity, "Populism and Lynching in Louisiana, 1889–1896: A Test of Erikson's Theory of the Relationship Between Boundary Crises and Repressive Justice," *American Sociological Review* 41 (April 1976): 262–80.

Others have seen racial prejudice in general as false consciousness, an illusion bred by the powerful. John W. Cell argues that "unlike class relations, which have their ultimate origins in contradictions that emerge within and between a society's basic modes of production and exchange, race relations are essentially extrinsic. Their origins are not in production, but in power. They are not inevitable or natural. They must therefore be imposed. In the evolution of history, however, race can and has become so embedded in fundamental institutions that it is virtually inseparable except by means of decisive overthrow or wholesale reordering of the political and social system. Racism is indeed what Lenin called false consciousness. It is nonetheless real and powerful." See *The Highest Stage of White Supremacy: The Origins of Segregation in South Africa and the American South* (New York: Cambridge Univ. Press, 1982), 117.

At the other pole of interpretation are those who focus on racism as a set of motivations that enveloped, subsumed, others. From such a perspective, the manifestations of racial conflict in the New South, whether segregation, disfranchisement, or lynching, were driven by ideas and notions promulgated by influential whites. This racism, in turn, grew out of those whites' personal experiences and conflicts, often intellectual, psychological, or sexual. Events appear caught in tides of irrational fear and resentment. A perspective that explores "the development of intellectualized racist theory and ideology as it was applied directly and programmatically to the 'problem' posed in the white mind by the presence of millions of blacks in the United States" is given its most sophisticated statement in George M. Fredrickson, *The Black Image in the White Mind: The Debate on Afro-American Character and Destiny, 1817–1914* (New York: Harper and Row, 1971); a bold psychological interpretation has been put forward in Joel Williamson's *The Crucible of Race*. As with the historians discussed in the preceding paragraph, both Fredrickson and Williamson portray race and racism in complex ways that cannot be reduced to easy characterization. While many less skilled historians merely invoke racism, Fredrickson and Williamson have explored it.

The present account seeks to show that relations among blacks and whites were so volatile precisely because they were inseparable from class, political, psychological, generational, and gender relations. I have been influenced by Barbara Jeanne Fields, "Ideology and Race in American History," in J. Morgan Kousser and James M. McPherson, eds., *Region, Race, and Reconstruction: Essays in Honor of C. Vann Woodward* (New York: Oxford Univ. Press, 1982), 143–77, and Judith Stein, " 'Of Mr. Booker T. Washington and Others': The Political Economy of Racism in the United States," *Science and Society* 38 (Winter 1974–75): 422–53.

3. On the uniqueness of travel, see Stephen J. Riegel, "The Persistent Career of Jim Crow: Lower Federal Courts and the 'Separate but Equal' Doctrine,

1865–1896," *American Journal of Legal History* 28 (Jan. 1984): 25, and Charles A. Lofgren, *The Plessy Case: A Legal-Historical Interpretation* (New York: Oxford Univ. Press, 1987), 17; Rabinowitz, "More Than the Woodward Thesis," 847.

4. "Papa" [J. C. Carpenter] to "My dear boy," Nov. 14, 1891, Carpenter Papers, LSU; Lofgren, *Plessy*, 9–17; also see Annie Perry [Jester] to "Dear Mother," Sept. 29, 1896, Annie Perry Jester Papers, SCa.

5. Ellen Glasgow, *The Voice of the People* (New York: Doubleday, Page, 1900), 309.

6. Sutton E. Griggs, *Imperium in Imperio* (1899; rpt., New York: Arno Press, 1969), 142–44.

7. Andrew W. Springs to Charles N. Hunter, Sept. 26, 1891, Hunter Papers, Duke.

8. James Melvin Washington, "The Origins and Emergence of Black Baptist Separation, 1863–1897" (Ph.D. diss., Yale Univ., 1979), 177–78.

9. Chattanooga *Times* in Nashville *American*, March 19, 1889, in John E. Buser, "After Half a Generation: The South of the 1880s" (Ph.D. diss., Univ. of Texas, 1968), 205–6.

10. New Orleans *Times-Democrat*, July 9, 1890, quoted in Otto Olsen, ed., *The Thin Disguise: Turning Point in Negro History—Plessy v. Ferguson: A Documentary Presentation (1864–1896)* (New York: Humanities Press, 1967), 53.

11. Buser, "After Half a Generation," 67; for a fascinating account of Southern race relations in this period that puts sexuality at the heart of conflict, though in a way that focuses more on changes in white psychology and less on evolving kinds of social interaction, see Williamson, *Crucible of Race*.

12. Quoted in John William Graves, "Town and Country: Race Relations and Urban Development in Arkansas, 1874–1905" (Ph.D. diss., Univ. of Virginia, 1978), 285.

13. A newspaper from Columbia had already suggested part of the answer; when the railroad voluntarily offered to run segregated trains to the state fair, the paper had warmly noted "a very obliging spirit on the part of the railroad authorities, and no doubt many ladies will in consequence come to the Fair who would not otherwise have attended." The governor accepted the offer because race mixing in the cars was often "attended by unpleasant incidents." All quotes from James Hammond Moore, introduction to Isaac DuBose Seabrook, *Before and After: or, The Relations of the Races of the South* (1895; rpt., Baton Rouge: Louisiana State University Press, 1967), 14–16.

14. "Studies in the South," *Atlantic Monthly* 50 (Nov. 1882): 627; Savannah *Tribune*, May 7, 1887, in Horace Calvin Wingo, "Race Relations in Georgia, 1872–1908" (Ph.D. diss., Univ. of Georgia, 1969), 130.

15. Mary Church Terrell, *A Colored Woman in a White World* (1940; rpt., New York: Arno, 1980), 296–98.

16. Riegel, "Persistent Career of Jim Crow," 25–27.

17. Lofgren, *Plessy*, 145–47; Henry M. Field, *Bright Skies and Dark Shadows* (New York: C. Scribner's Sons, 1890), 152; Buser, "After Half a Generation," 163–64, 203–4; Catherine A. Barnes, *Journey from Jim Crow: The Desegregation of Southern Transit* (New York: Columbia Univ. Press, 1983), 6–7.

18. Mobile *Register*, April 18, 1882, in Buser, "After Half a Generation," 56; Wright, *Life Behind a Veil*, 63–64. Also see John Hammond Moore, "Jim Crow in

Georgia," *South Atlantic Quarterly* 66 (Autumn 1967), 554–65; Henry C. Dethloff and Robert R. Jones, "Race Relations in Louisiana, 1877–1898," *Louisiana History* 9 (Fall 1968): 322; Wingo, "Race Relations in Georgia," 125–27.

19. Milton Smith, quoted in Maury Klein, *History of the Louisville and Nashville Railroad* (New York: Macmillan, 1972), 331.

20. Cartwright, *Triumph of Jim Crow,* 104–7; Roger L. Hart, *Redeemers, Bourbons, and Populists: Tennessee, 1870–1896* (Baton Rouge: Louisiana State University Press, 1975), 28–55; Franklin Johnson, *The Development of State Legislation Concerning the Free Negro* (1918; rpt., Westport: Greenwood, 1979), 184. Stanley Folmsbee, in a 1949 article, argued that this law was "a concession to Negroes," but Cartwright sees the law instead as "an effort by the legislature to sanction racial discrimination on the state's railroads in a more systematic basis than before." The law, it seems, was both an attempt to forestall further black agitation on the issue and an attempt to force the railroads to make more of an effort to appease blacks. See Folmsbee, "The Origins of the First 'Jim Crow' Law," *Journal of Southern History* 15 (May 1949): 235–47, and Cartwright, *The Triumph of Jim Crow,* 107.

21. Grady quoted in Dana White, "The Old South Under New Conditions," in Dana F. White and Victor A. Kramer, eds., *Olmsted South: Old South Critic/New South Planner* (Westport: Greenwood Press, 1979), 162; Paul M. Gaston, *The New South Creed: A Study in Southern Mythmaking* (New York: Alfred Knopf, 1970), 148–49; Cell, *Highest Stage of White Supremacy,* 181–83; Buser, "After Half a Generation," 204–5; Lofgren, *Plessy,* 24–25; Florida law in Johnson, *State Legislation,* 86.

22. Johnson, *State Legislation,* 133, 189.

23. Lofgren, *Plessy,* 24–25; Olsen, *The Thin Disguise,* 10–21.

24. Olsen, *The Thin Disguise,* 10–21; Lofgren, *Plessy,* 32.

25. Two very useful works that argue along similar lines are Riegel, "Persistent Career of Jim Crow," and Lofgren, *Plessy.* Rabinowitz's *Race Relations in the Urban South* has played an important role by calling attention to the generational differences among blacks and the growing militancy of the younger blacks. See pp. 334–35. For the role of example, a letter to the governor of South Carolina from a salesman who regularly traveled from Baltimore to Texas pointed out that "I cannot but see the great comfort and advantage to the White people of a state overcrowded with darkies in passing a Law of this Kind. . . . The passage of such a law during your administration would be greatly appreciated by all South Carolinians except RailRoad Lawyers and would be double valued by ladies." George F. Pringle to John Gary Evans, Aug. 21, 1894, Evans Papers, SCa.

26. John Andrew Rice, *I Came Out of the Eighteenth Century* (New York, London: Harper & Bros., 1942), 41–42. An exciting and innovative work on this topic is Cell's *Highest Stage of White Supremacy.* While I find his critique of extant scholarship and his emphasis on the "modernity" of segregation well taken, it seems to me that Cell does not take the context in which power was exercised—the state legislatures—as seriously as he should. Cell emphasizes the capitalist nature of the New South, only to turn to a rather mechanical reliance on a "power elite" in which planters play a large role to explain segregation. Of course men with power wrote the laws, but they possessed a temporary and quite circumscribed kind of power, thoroughly caught in the contingencies of electoral politics. Jeffrey Richards and John M. MacKenzie, *The Railway Station: A Social History* (Oxford: Clarendon, 1986), 137, point out that throughout the world the railroad station "was an

extraordinary agent of social mixing. . . . But the stations were in many respects designed to avoid these encounters across class and racial boundaries as much as possible."

27. Nashville *Banner,* June 12, 1891, quoted in Hart, *Redeemers, Bourbons, and Populists,* 164–65; "Jim Crow on Wheels," Chicago *Defender,* Nov. 3, 1917, quoted in Neil R. McMillen, *Dark Journey: Black Mississippians in the Age of Jim Crow* (Urbana: Univ. of Illinois Press, 1989), 293; Wali Rashash Kharif, "Refinement of Racial Segregation in Florida" (Ph.D. diss., Florida State Univ., 1983), 146–47; Willard B. Gatewood, Jr., "Arkansas Negroes in the 1890s: Documents," *Arkansas Historical Quarterly* 33 (1974): 296–97.

28. Virginia's railroad commissioner did propose a segregation law in 1891, but no action was taken. Charles Wynes argues that "by the end of the nineteenth century it was customary for the races to ride together on most of the railroads in Virginia without confinement to either a Jim Crow or the smoking car." This would mean that Virginia was quite different from the surrounding Southern states. See Wynes, *Race Relations in Virginia, 1870–1902* (Charlottesville: Univ. of Virginia Press, 1961), 73–74. A law was suggested in 1893 in North Carolina, but a black delegation won assurances from the speaker of the house that he would never allow such a law to pass while he held his office. Frenise Logan documents conflicts and black assertion in North Carolina that resembled those of states that did implement Jim Crow. See Frenise A. Logan, *The Negro in North Carolina, 1876–1894* (Chapel Hill: Univ. of North Carolina Press, 1964), 176–80. South Carolina saw railroad segregation laws "introduced and defeated by every legislature in the early 1890s. . . . Economic motives lay behind the opposition, which came largely from businessmen and pro-railroad men." Linda M. Matthews, "Keeping Down Jim Crow: The Railroads and the Separate Coach Bills in South Carolina," *South Atlantic Quarterly* 73 (1974): 121. The forthcoming dissertation by Patricia Minter of the University of Virginia promises to shed new light on the evolution of transportation and segregation law.

4. What did segregation replace?

Howard N. Rabinowitz

"From Exclusion to Segregation: Southern Race Relations, 1865–1890"

Howard N. Rabinowitz (1942–1998) was professor of history at the University of New Mexico, where he specialized in African American, southern, and urban history. A self-described "nuts and bolts kind of guy . . . suspicious of big, all-encompassing theories," as well as an indefatigable researcher, Rabinowitz emphasized heterogeneity in the past and treated the persons he wrote about "as subjects rather than mere objects of history, actors and not merely passive victims." His books include *Race Relations in the Urban South, 1865–1890* (1978), *The First New South, 1865–1920* (1992), and *Race, Ethnicity, and Urbanization: Selected Essays* (1994). In *Race Relations in the Urban South,* Rabinowitz agreed with Williamson that segregation appeared far earlier than Woodward had maintained. But Rabinowitz added a vital new component to the debate over the rise of segregation. In such areas as health and welfare services, education, public accommodations, and cultural life, he asserted, segregation replaced exclusion, not integration, and thus was more of an improvement than a setback for black southerners. Because they assumed that separate treatment would be equal treatment, blacks and their white allies generally supported de facto segregation as a progressive step over exclusion. In the 1890s, however, whites, obsessed with racial control, legalized the informal practices that had evolved since Reconstruction. As a result, for much of the next century Jim Crow ruled in the South, guaranteeing separate and unequal lives for African Americans.[1]

Questions for a Closer Reading

1. Before the Civil War, to what extent did slaves and free blacks have access to social services and public accommodations?

2. Once the war was over, to what extent were the freedpeople integrated into public places?

3. When and where were the first postwar separate facilities established for blacks?

4. Was Reconstruction-era segregation de jure or de facto?

5. In what specific services did segregation replace exclusion?

6. What tended to be the most integrated facility in the postwar South?

7. According to Rabinowitz, why did African Americans accept segregated facilities?

Note

1. Howard N. Rabinowitz, *Race, Ethnicity, and Urbanization: Selected Essays* (Columbia: University of Missouri Press, 1994), 15, 18.

"From Exclusion to Segregation: Southern Race Relations, 1865–1890"

Since the appearance in 1955 of C. Vann Woodward's *Strange Career of Jim Crow,* extensive research has been devoted to uncovering the origins of racial segregation in the South. Woodward challenges the traditional view that the restrictive Jim Crow codes were the product of the immediate post-Reconstruction period. Emphasizing the legal side of segregation, he argues that the separation of the races grew out of forces

Howard N. Rabinowitz, "From Exclusion to Segregation: Southern Race Relations, 1865–1890," from *Race, Ethnicity, and Urbanization: Selected Essays* (Columbia: University of Missouri Press, 1994), 137–63.

operating in the last decade of the nineteenth and the first years of the twentieth centuries. He has modified his original position, but the existence of a law enforcing segregation remains the key variable in evaluating the nature of race relations. Because of the alleged absence of these statutes, Woodward contends that "forgotten alternatives" existed in the period between Redemption and the full-scale arrival of Jim Crow.[1]

Although George Tindall had in part anticipated Woodward's arguments, it is the "Woodward thesis" over which historians have chosen sides. Charles E. Wynes, Frenise A. Logan, and Henry C. Dethloff and Robert P. Jones explicitly declare their support for Woodward (even though much of their evidence seems to point in the opposite direction); and the same is true of the more recent implicit endorsements by John W. Blassingame and Dale A. Somers. In his study of South Carolina blacks, however, Joel Williamson, unlike Woodward, emphasizes customs rather than laws and sees segregation so entrenched in the state by the end of Reconstruction that he refers to the early appearance of a "duochromatic order." Vernon Lane Wharton's account of Mississippi blacks reaches a similar conclusion, and it has been used to support the arguments of Woodward's critics. Richard C. Wade's work on slavery in antebellum southern cities, Roger A. Fischer's studies of antebellum and postbellum New Orleans, and Ira Berlin's treatment of antebellum free Negroes also question Woodward's conclusions.[2]

The debate has been fruitful, shedding light on race relations in the postbellum South. But the emphasis on the alternatives of segregation or integration has obscured the obvious "forgotten alternative"—exclusion. The issue is not merely when segregation first appeared, but what it replaced. Before the Civil War, blacks were excluded from militia companies and schools, as well as most hospitals, asylums, and public accommodations. The first postwar governments during Presidential Reconstruction generally sought to continue the antebellum policy of exclusion. Nevertheless, by 1890—before the resort to widespread de jure segregation—de facto segregation had replaced exclusion as the norm in southern race relations. In the process the integration stage had been largely bypassed. This shift occurred because of the efforts of white Republicans who initiated it, blacks who supported and at times requested it, and Redeemers who accepted and expanded the new policy once they came to power.[3]

The first postwar governments, composed of Confederate veterans and elected by white male suffrage, saw little need to alter the prewar pattern of exclusion of blacks from most sectors of southern life.

During the period from 1865 to 1867 southern whites sought to limit admission to poorhouses, orphanages, insane asylums, and institutions for the blind, deaf, and dumb to whites. The states that established systems of public education, such as Georgia, Arkansas, and Texas, opened the schools to whites only. The North Carolina public school system, which dated from antebellum years, was initially closed because of fears that it would be forced to admit blacks. Savannah officials made the same decision about their city's parks.[4] Meanwhile, hotels, restaurants, and many theaters continued to exclude blacks.

Nevertheless, the policy of segregation rather than exclusion was already being forced upon the South. In Richmond and Nashville, for example, the United States Army and the Freedmen's Bureau made the local Conservative governments provide poorhouse facilities to indigent blacks. In both cases blacks were placed in quarters separate from whites. The Nashville Board of Education, fearing that it would be forced to integrate its newly opened school system, voluntarily set up separate schools for blacks in 1867. A year earlier the new Nashville Street Railway, which previously had excluded blacks, began running a separate car for them. On the state level, Alabama Conservatives admitted blacks for the first time on a segregated basis to the state insane asylum.[5]

Further undermining the policy of exclusion were the practices in those facilities that had experienced the shift from exclusion to segregation during earlier years. The use of separate streetcars for blacks in New Orleans, for example, superseded exclusion during the antebellum and war years. Steamboats and railroads had for many years segregated those few blacks who traveled as paying passengers. This practice continued, and Texas, Mississippi, and Florida strengthened it through the passage of laws. Whatever exclusion there had been on boats and trains had not been forced; it had resulted from the absence of a large black clientele. Cemeteries suffered no such shortage. While most private cemeteries excluded all blacks except faithful servants, public cemeteries had by law or custom assigned blacks to special sections. This procedure continued after the war. Some places of amusement continued to exclude blacks; others retained their earlier pattern of segregated seating; still others, as in Nashville, opened their doors to freedmen for the first time, although on a segregated basis. Traveling circuses, especially popular with blacks, went so far in Montgomery as to establish separate entrances for the races. The Georgia Infirmary in Savannah and the Charity Hospital in New Orleans similarly continued as they had before the war to provide blacks with segregated medical care at city expense.[6]

Most white southerners remained committed to exclusion as the best racial policy. They were thwarted by the imposition of Congressional Reconstruction in March 1867 and thereafter were forced by military and civilian authorities to grant new privileges and services to blacks. Nonetheless, the net effect of the Radical measures on race relations in the southern states was to institutionalize the shift from exclusion to segregation.

The difference between the Republicans and their Conservative predecessors was particularly clear-cut in three areas: militia service, education, and welfare facilities. The former Confederates feared the arming of the freedmen and their enlistment in military companies; the Republicans quickly established black militia units, partly in the hopes that they would serve to support the governments. The Republicans, however, did not wish to antagonize local residents and so provided for segregated units under black officers. In a related area Radicals in Raleigh, North Carolina, and Nashville, Tennessee, established separate black fire companies.[7]

The public schools followed a similar policy. Under the Republicans, schools were opened to blacks for the first time. With the notable exceptions of South Carolina and Louisiana it was expected that there would be separate schools for each race. Only in New Orleans did a significant degree of integration take place, even during the height of Reconstruction.[8]

Much attention has been given to the Republicans' stand regarding the militia and public schools. This is not true of Republican welfare policy. It is commonly acknowledged that the Radical governments expanded the range of welfare services available to white and black southerners, but their private or public welfare facilities were rarely integrated. Blacks were provided for, but on a segregated basis. Republicans in Mississippi, North Carolina, and Virginia established either segregated quarters or entirely separate institutions for the Negro insane of their states. Facilities for the care of the Negro blind, deaf, and dumb in Mississippi and North Carolina were also segregated; the same would have been the case at the South Carolina Institution for the Deaf and Blind except that whites withdrew when blacks were admitted, thus forcing it to close. Segregated provision was also made for South Carolina's Negro orphans, although in most other states publicly supported orphanages remained for whites only. Montgomery, Alabama, Richmond, Virginia, Vicksburg and Natchez, Mississippi, and New Orleans, Louisiana, were among the many cities that provided new segregated dispensaries and hospitals for the Negro indigent.[9] But the poorhouses in Richmond and Nashville remained segregated, and in cities such as New Orleans, Raleigh, Richmond, and Nashville blacks were buried in segregated sections of the municipal cemeteries.

The Republican-controlled legislature in North Carolina was so averse to the idea of forced integration that in 1870 it defeated a proposal to assure Negroes the same facilities as whites on steamboats and railroads. Even the spate of antidiscrimination laws passed elsewhere often over the objections of some white Republicans seem to have had little effect on the pattern of segregation in public conveyances. If they accomplished any-thing, the laws encouraged the railroad and steamboat companies to pro-vide supposedly equal though separate accommodations for blacks. Despite the passage of the 1866 Civil Rights Act, a British traveler who toured the South during 1867–1868 concluded, "There are 'nigger cars' open, of course to white people, and often used as smoking cars, but to which all coloured passengers have to confine themselves." Wharton con-cluded about Mississippi's antidiscrimination railroad act passed in 1870: "In spite of its stringent provisions, the law had almost no effect." As demonstrated by the numerous suits by blacks against southern railroad companies, the best that blacks could hope for were segregated accommo-dations that equaled those provided the whites.[10]

The new governments had greater impact on traveling arrangements in streetcars. It is generally agreed that de jure segregation was a product of the 1890s.[11] The extent of prior de facto segregation remains uncertain, however, partly because of the character of the streetcar system itself. It would be a simple matter to determine if there had been different cars for the two races, either run separately or in tandem, but the presence of one car without racial designation might still mean that either blacks had been excluded or had been segregated within that car.

Another difficulty in considering streetcars arises from their staggered appearance in southern cities. The New Orleans system, for example, dates from the antebellum period, while Richmond's began operating in 1865, Atlanta's in 1871, and Raleigh's in 1886. Each line might have been segre-gated from its inception, and thus it cannot be assumed that because Louisville or New Orleans apparently desegregated their cars before 1870, subsequent lines in other cities followed their example. The same is true within each city—because segregation was discontinued on one line does not necessarily mean that it was not resumed until the appearance of Jim Crow legislation. Nor does it mean that other companies in the city might not have initiated de facto segregation.

What is clear is that in many cities the initial Republican contribution was to force streetcar companies to admit black riders. Richmond, Vir-ginia, provides an early example of the change in streetcar policy. Prior to May 1867, Richmond initially excluded Negroes from the cars and then permitted them to ride on the outside. In April 1867, four blacks staged a sit-in and were forcibly ejected from a car by a policeman. City officials ruled that as a private concern the railway company could establish its own regulations, but they were overruled by federal military authorities who directed that the cars must carry all passengers able to pay the fare. Never-theless, General John Schofield permitted the substitution of segregation for exclusion. Sources differ as to whether there were alternate cars for each race with the Negro car distinguished by a black ball on its roof or whether those cars with a white ball were solely for white women and their escorts.[12]

This transition from exclusion to segregation with perhaps an intermediary stage of riding on the platforms of the cars was repeated in other cities. Negroes in Nashville, Charleston, and Mobile were among the many who won the right to ride in the streetcars under civilian Republican or military authorities. Maria Waterbury, however, a northern teacher, found that as late as 1871 a Mobile streetcar contained an iron latticework dividing the car racially. When a woman took her servant into the wrong end of the car, the conductor stopped the vehicle and moved the black woman into her "proper place." In cities such as New Orleans the question remains as to the presence of segregation when blacks finally rode in the same cars as whites.[13]

In a variety of public accommodations the Reconstruction governments proved unable or unwilling to push for integration. Exclusion remained the rule in the best restaurants and hotels as well as in many theaters. Judging from the recurring use in newspaper advertisements of "gentlemen" and "ladies" to describe the patrons of skating rinks, this new craze was another form of recreation initially denied blacks.[14]

Nevertheless, blacks did enjoy many forms of segregated recreation. Newspapers were filled with advertisements or news accounts about "negro barrooms," "negro brothels," and "negro billiard parlors." Montgomery boasted a "colored skating rink," Nashville had a "colored fairgrounds," and New Orleans and Nashville had Negro grandstands at the local racetracks. Negroes in Montgomery went to picnics at Lambert Springs and the Cypress Pond while whites went to Oak Grove and Pickett Springs. And most of the theaters, including many previously closed to blacks, provided segregated seating in the galleries.[15]

There is also evidence that Republican politicians observed the color line in official functions. At the 1868 Constitutional Convention in South Carolina, white delegates occupied the front rows while the blacks filled in the seats at the rear of the hall; in the courtroom of the Radical circuit court judge in Richmond, whites sat on the west side and blacks on the east; and in 1868, North Carolina Republicans divided the gallery of the senate into three sections: one for whites, one for blacks, and one for both races.[16] Republican governor Robert K. Scott of South Carolina sought to make amends to that state's blacks because none had been invited to the annual ball of the governor in 1869. He held open house every Thursday, but "only Negro politicians called at that time."[17]

It would seem, therefore, that the Republicans had little desire to "Africanize" the South. Indeed, with the exception of a few egalitarians, southern Republicans, whether during or after Reconstruction, did not seek to force integration on unwilling southern whites. Whether because of their own racial prejudice, the need to attract white voters to the party, or the belief that legislated integration was unconstitutional or simply could not succeed, the Negroes' white allies sought to replace exclusion with segregation. Ascribing motivation is always risky, but perhaps it was hoped that such a policy would appease blacks, while at the same time not frighten prospective white voters with the specter of miscegenation.

The Republicans stood for more than segregation. They called for separate but equal treatment for blacks. During debates on congressional civil rights legislation, for example, Senator Joshua Hill of Georgia and Representative Alexander White of Alabama argued that separate provisions for blacks in public carriers, places of amusement, or hotels and restaurants was not a violation of civil rights if the accommodations were equal to those of whites.[18] The Alabama Republican party in its 1874 platform declared, "The republican party does not desire mixed schools or accommodations for colored people, but they ask that in all these advantages they shall be equal. We want no social equality enforced by law." Tennessee's Republican governor signed a separate but equal accommodations measure in 1881, and a Georgia Republican legislature passed a similar bill in 1870. Alabama Republicans pushed for such a measure and congratulated those railroads that voluntarily provided separate but equal accommodations.[19] The Republican legacy to the Redeemers therefore consisted of the seemingly mutually exclusive policies of segregation and equality.

Given the opposition of southern whites it seems unlikely that the Republicans could have forced integration on the South. Conditions in the South at the end of Reconstruction were revealed in the reaction to the civil rights agitation that culminated in the Civil Rights Act of 1875. The *Atlanta Constitution,* though thankful for omission of cemeteries and schools from the final version of the law, concluded, "Its other provisions are all that the most revolutionary white villain or the densest negro brain could desire." After passage of the act, the *Raleigh Daily Sentinel* argued, "If the principles of the Republicans succeed, the negro will be forced upon . . . [the white man's] wife, and his daughter, on the cars, steamboats, in public inns, at hotel tables, and in theatres and other places of amusement."[20]

Once passions cooled the southern press reassured its readers that either the law quickly would be declared unconstitutional or else the Democrats would repeal it when they won their expected victories in the 1876 presidential and congressional elections. Referring to the statute as a "dead letter," the *Atlanta Constitution* pointed out, "It gets a judicial cuff whenever it appears in the courts, no matter whether the judge be a republican or democrat."[21] The paper was correct. Federal courts in Atlanta, Richmond, and Savannah upheld the right of railroads and steamboats to provide separate accommodations for the races just as they could for members of the two sexes.[22]

Bothered little by the 1875 Civil Rights Act even before its official demise in 1883, the Redeemers occasionally returned to exclusion or instituted segregation in those few cases where there had been integration. For example, the Montgomery city hospital, which was operated on a segregated basis under a Radical Republican administration, was closed by the Redeemer mayor; alternative provision was made for white patients but not for black. And although Hamilton Park and Angelo's Hall in Jackson, Mississippi, had been used by whites and blacks on separate occasions under the Republicans, by 1890 both facilities were closed to blacks. The basic response of the Redeemers, however, was to continue already existing segregation. Frequently they sought to strengthen the barriers that had separated the races under the Republicans. Educational segregation previously enforced by school acts in Georgia, Tennessee, and North Carolina was now written into the new Redeemer constitutions.[23] Blacks in North Carolina and Alabama had been cared for in separate wards of white insane asylums; they were now moved into their own separate institutions. And in Raleigh, where the Radicals had given blacks the choice of being buried in the segregated portion of the old municipal cemetery or in a new cemetery built exclusively for them, the Redeemers prohibited the burial of blacks in the old cemetery.[24]

White opinion was not unified, but most Redeemers also adopted the rhetoric of the Republicans' separate but equal commitment. Despite the failure to honor this commitment, in several instances the Redeemers actually moved beyond their predecessors to provide segregated, if unequal, facilities in areas previously characterized by exclusion. Some whites distinguished between segregation and discrimination. Thus Tennessee law prohibited "discrimination" in any place of public amusement that charged a fee but nevertheless maintained that this provision did not outlaw "separate accommodations and seats for colored and white persons."[25]

Additional public institutions opened their doors to blacks for the first time under the Redeemers. Among those states making initial provision for Negro blind, deaf, and dumb were Texas, Georgia, Alabama, Tennessee, and South Carolina; and in 1887, the same year that Tennessee provided a Negro department for the previously all-white and privately run Tennessee Industrial School, North Carolina opened its Colored Orphan Asylum.[26]

Segregation may have also replaced exclusion in other areas of southern life after Reconstruction rather than integration. As early as 1872,

Atlanta's Union Passenger Depot had a "Freedmen's Saloon," and at least by 1885 Nashville's Union Depot had "a colored passenger room." In 1885 Austin, Texas, was among the Texas cities required by city ordinance to have separate waiting rooms for both races.[27] It is not known what facilities existed for blacks before the appearance of these Negro waiting rooms. The experiences of Montgomery, Alabama, and Raleigh, North Carolina, however, are instructive. The new Union Depot in Montgomery was described in 1877 as having "a ladies waiting room" and a "gents' waiting room"; the original plans for the Raleigh Union Depot in 1890 included a "ladies waiting room" and a "gentlemen's waiting room." Although there was no reference to a Negro waiting room, the use of the words *gents, gentlemen,* and *ladies* rather than *men* and *women* suggests the exclusion of blacks. The mention of three waiting rooms at the Montgomery Depot in 1885—one each for "ladies," "gentlemen," and "colored people"—and the revised plans for the Raleigh Depot that contained a separate waiting room for blacks suggest further evidence of the shift from exclusion to segregation.[28]

Segregation persisted or replaced exclusion in theaters. For the most part blacks were confined to separate galleries. In Richmond, however, because of the 1875 Civil Rights Act blacks won access to a segregated portion of the once exclusively white dress circle.[29] Most restaurants and hotels continued to exclude blacks, as did the better barrooms. Some bars catering to whites charged blacks outrageous prices or provided poor service; less subtle was the sign over the bar of a Nashville saloon in 1884—No Drinks Sold to Colored Persons. In 1888 the *Atlanta Constitution* reported that of Atlanta's sixty-eight saloons, five served only blacks and only two catered to both blacks and whites.[30] On those instances when blacks were admitted to primarily white restaurants, bars, and hotels, the races were carefully segregated. A restaurant in the rear of a Nashville saloon served food to "responsible and well behaved colored people" in its kitchen; the Planters Hotel in Augusta, Georgia, seated blacks at separate tables in the dining room; the St. Charles, the only Richmond hotel to accept a black delegate to the 1886 Knights of Labor Convention, gave him second-class quarters and seated him at a table in the dining room farthest from the door and behind a screen; and in answer to the Civil Rights Act, Montgomery's Ruby Saloon set up "a small counter" apart from the main bar for black customers.[31] Such examples probably marked only a transitory stage on the way to total segregation.

With the exception of New Orleans, athletic events in the South were rigidly segregated. Most cities had at least two black baseball teams. Militia companies similarly engaged in racially separated competition. Segregated places in parades and observances, usually in the rear, were provided for blacks as well.[32]

Prostitution also suffered the effects of segregation. Even in New Orleans, houses of prostitution offering white and black women to a mixed clientele had become a rarity by 1880. White and black prostitutes resided on separate blocks in Atlanta. When two well-dressed mulattoes sought admission to a brothel on Collins Street that served only whites, they were driven off by gunfire.[33] If taken to court, the prostitutes would likely have found the spectators racially separated, and perhaps, like the procedure in Savannah's mayor's court in 1876, they would have sworn on a Bible set aside for their particular race.[34]

The situation in parks was more complex. There were few formal parks and pleasure grounds in antebellum cities, and blacks were excluded from those that existed.[35] Indeed, it was not until the mid-1870s, in most cases after Republicans had relinquished control of local governments, that the park movement began to affect southern urban life. Most of these new parks were privately owned, often by streetcar companies that used them to encourage traffic on their lines, but municipally owned parks became common by the 1880s.

Increasingly blacks were barred from many parks. Sometimes this can be surmised only from the language of the local press.[36] In other cases speculation is unnecessary. Blacks taking the street railway to Atlanta's Ponce de Leon Springs in 1887 were informed "politely but forcibly" by policemen that they would not be admitted. Three years later blacks were excluded from the city's Inman Park. Already Atlanta blacks had begun to gravitate to the grounds and woods around Clark University, leading the *Atlanta Constitution* to call for construction of a park for them in that area.[37] Then, too, in most southern cities blacks and whites continued to frequent separate picnic groves while the large all-white cemeteries served as parks for whites.

Nevertheless, the existence of separate parks for whites and blacks as a general phenomenon seems to have been the product of the post-1890 period. As of 1882, Nashville's Watkins Park was visited by "persons of all shades and sizes." As late as 1890, blacks and whites were invited to watch a Negro militia company drill in Atlanta's Piedmont Park, and on Independence Day, blacks were among the mostly white crowd that enjoyed the facilities at the city's Grant Park. Montgomery's Highland and Raleigh's Pullen parks were apparently open to blacks and whites as well.[38]

In the absence of separate parks, segregation within the grounds became the norm. Although blacks enjoyed access to Atlanta's Ponce de Leon Springs until the late 1880s, the two races entertained themselves at separate dance halls and refreshment stands. Blacks attending the two free concerts given at Nashville's Glendale Park were barred from the new pavilion, while those visiting Raleigh's Brookside Park could not use the swimming pool. When a new zoo opened in Atlanta's Grant Park, it contained eight cages occupying the center of the building and stretching from end to end. An aisle was railed off on each side of the row of cages: one was for blacks, the other for whites. "There is no communication between them," the *Atlanta Constitution* observed, "and two large double doors at each end of the building serve as entrance and exit to the aisles."[39]

Segregation also seems to have been the rule at expositions and fairs. Nashville Negroes had fairgrounds purchased by a black organization. Blacks could attend certain functions at the white fairgrounds but specifically which functions and when is not always clear. Negroes were barred, for example, from the interstate drill competition held in 1883. But again admittance of both races went hand in hand with segregation. There was a special gate provided for blacks in the exposition building at a Nashville fair in 1875; there was a "colored people's saloon" in addition to the main grandstand saloon at the 1871 Georgia State Fair in Macon; and at the Southern Exposition held in Montgomery in 1890 the two races ate in separate restaurants.[40]

Southern whites did not have the option of providing or not providing accommodations for Negro lawbreakers. Yet confinement of blacks in penitentiaries and local jails was largely a postwar development. In the antebellum years Negro criminals were more likely to be whipped than incarcerated.[41] As a result of the influx of black prisoners, racial contact became as much of a problem within the correctional institutions as in the outside world. As in the society at large, segregation was seen as the ideal solution for regulating contact between the races once exclusion became unfeasible.[42] A committee of the Georgia legislature recommended in 1866 that Negro and white convicts receive equal punishment, but hastened to add that "under no circumstances would a social equality be recognized—not even in the worst cases of felony." Nevertheless, segregation was possible only if there were sufficient space. When room was limited, blacks and whites were confined together despite the desires of law enforcement officials.[43]

One way to prevent the mixture of the races at small penitentiaries was to lease out black prisoners. This plan had the added advantages of providing favored employers with a source of cheap labor and the state government with extra revenue. Although some whites were leased, blacks suffered most from this inhumane and corrupt system.[44]

The need for segregation remained uppermost in the minds of Georgia officials who sought alternatives to the lease system. In 1876 the keeper of the penitentiary proposed substituting the islands off Savannah as penal colonies. "It would be my policy," he averred, "to separate the whites and blacks, working them on distinct farms." The lease system was kept, however, and after a trip to one of the camps, the keeper reported approvingly that in the barracks "the white men sleep to themselves on one side of the building." Most of the camps were in fact composed exclusively of Negroes so that intra-camp segregation was usually unnecessary. Laws passed in 1888 and 1890 decreed that white and black prisoners were not to work or be confined together, adding legal sanction to customs and attitudes already governing behavior.[45]

Although males were segregated in the Alabama prison camps by 1882, because of overcrowding, white women convicted of adultery with blacks occupied the same cells as Negro women. The warden complained, calling for the complete segregation of prisoners in one large prison. The two main prison camps for leased convicts had separate quarters for the races by 1884; in at least one of the camps two rows of tubs stood in the newly erected bathhouse—one side for blacks and the other for whites. Six years later Wetumpka Prison, where nonleased convicts were confined, had a different building for each race.[46]

Integration was probably more often present in local jails and work-houses. Chain gangs were instituted mainly for Negroes, but all prisoners had to be kept inside at night. Whether or not segregation existed depended mainly on the size of the facility; whether or not segregation appeared in descriptions of jails depended on the observer. In Richmond to 1890, for example, neither the city council minutes nor the yearly reports of the various city departments concerning the jail mention racial separation, yet an inspection committee appointed by the Hustings Court in 1882 reported that the races occupied cells on the opposite sides of the building. Accounts for subsequent years continued to note this arrangement as well as the existence of Jim Crow bathtubs by 1889.[47] Questions remain about the nature of pre-1882 policy.

No matter how great the desire for segregated quarters, integration in small jails was often unavoidable. Not until the end of the period, for example, did the construction of larger jails in Atlanta and Nashville assure racial segregation.[48] In Montgomery, Alabama, where segregated quarters were assigned as early as 1865 and retained by a Radical jailer, racial mixing among convicts sometimes resulted from overcrowding. Even after the passage of a state law prohibiting the confining together of black and white prisoners, the *Montgomery Advertiser* complained in 1885 that at the county jail "the arrangements for keeping the races separate are far from what they should be." The shift from exclusion to segregation finally became complete that summer as plans were announced for a new jail, one that had solitary cells "for both male and female—whites and blacks separate."[49]

The situation in public conveyances is less discernible, and there seems to have been a greater divergence in practice. As under the Republicans, steamboats remained the most segregated form of travel. Although Virginia did not pass a law requiring the racial separation of passengers on steamboats until 1900, the *City of Richmond,* in service to Norfolk since 1880, had from its inception "a neat and comfortable dining room for colored passengers in the lower cabin." George Washington Cable discovered in 1887 that Louisiana Negroes had to confine themselves to a separate quarter of the boats called the "Freedman's bureau." And to Frederick Douglass it seemed ironic that the Negro had more freedom on steamboats as a slave since "he could ride anywhere, side by side with his white master. . . . [A]s a freeman, he was not allowed a cabin abaft the wheel."[50]

Although there was greater integration in train travel, blacks were generally confined to the smoking and second-class cars. Occasionally they were provided with separate first-class accommodations equal to those given to white passengers. During her trip through the United States in 1883, Iza Duffus Hardy was especially struck by the variety of methods used on trains to keep Negroes "in their place." On the train leaving Charleston, Negroes were in a separate second-class car although they did pay a lower fare than whites. At Savannah on the Florida Express, the Negroes rode in the forward part of the smoking car nearest the engine. Somewhat farther south Hardy found a car labeled For Coloured [*sic*] Passengers, which she discovered "was in every respect exactly like the car reserved for us 'white folk,' the same velvet seats, ice water tank; every comfort the same—and of course, the same fare." As opposed to this rare instance of a first-class car, the car assigned to Negroes in Charleston was described by her traveling companion, Lady Duffus Hardy, as "seedy looking." The association of Negroes with smoking cars was pronounced. While traveling on the Central Railroad in Georgia, Alexander Stephens and two other noted white Georgians were ejected from a first-class Negro car because they had seen blacks in it and had assumed it was a second-class car where they could smoke.[51]

The first-class cars for Negroes on the Central Railroad reflected an effort by certain railroads and sympathetic whites to provide separate but equal accommodations for blacks able to afford first-class rates. Noting the noncompliance with the 1881 statute requiring separate but equal accommodations for the races on Tennessee's railroads, the *Nashville American* observed in 1885:

> The blacks are forced into the smoking cars where they are subjected not only to all the annoyance of smoke and dirt, but often to the additional hardship of association with the roughest and most quarrelsome class of whites. . . . Now these things *should not be.* They are bad for the black race and they are equally bad for the white race. The law which provides for separate cars and equal accommodations is right. It is the only law which can be just to both of these classes of citizens, and at the same time prevent race conflicts, which would disturb the peace of the community.[52]

As early as 1870, the Orange Railroad passenger trains in Virginia had a special car exclusively for Negroes where smoking was prohibited. A regular smoking car was to be used by both blacks and whites. The Houston and Texas Central agreed in 1883 to provide "separate, exclusive, equal accommodations for colored patrons." Two years later a Louisville and Nashville train running between Montgomery and Mobile had a first-class coach "specially provided for colored people." In the opinion of the *Atlanta Constitution,* it "was as good in every sense as the [white] car. . . . There was no smoking or disorder permitted." In a case involving alleged discrimination on an Alabama railroad in 1887, the Interstate Commerce Commission held that different cars for the races could indeed be used provided that the accommodations were equal and that Negroes paying first-class fare received first-class facilities.[53]

In only one area of southern life was the shift to segregation relatively incomplete by 1890. Most southern streetcar systems initially excluded blacks; separate cars for the races followed. Once blacks gained entrance to the white cars, documenting the existence of segregation becomes difficult. August Meier and Elliott Rudwick argue that segregation "declined after being instituted in many places prior to and just after the Civil War." There is evidence to support the contention that streetcars were the most integrated southern facility. Referring to the color line, the *Nashville American* observed in 1880, "In Tennessee there is such a line, as every man, white and black, well knows, but on our street cars the races ride together without thought of it, or offensive exhibition, or attempt to isolate the colored passenger." Ten years later, when there was a rumor that the president of one of Richmond's street railways had been asked to provide separate cars for black passengers, the *Richmond Planet,* a Negro newspaper, expressed surprise and counseled against the plan since "we do not know of a city in the south in which discrimination is made on the street cars." In 1908 Ray Stannard Baker sadly concluded that "a few years ago the Negro came and went in the street cars in most cities and sat where he pleased, but gradually Jim Crow laws or local regulations were passed forcing him into certain seats at the back of the car."[54]

Segregation, however, may have been more prevalent than these accounts indicate. In Richmond and Savannah segregated streetcars persisted at least until the mid-1870s.[55] But segregation on horsecars could be inconvenient and expensive to maintain. Because the horses could pull only one rather small car at a time, the segregation of passengers required either the use of an entirely separate car and horse for blacks or limited them to a portion of the already crowded cars open to whites. This problem was remedied by the appearance on southern streets at the end of the 1880s of the dummy streetcar and the later electrification of the lines. The steam-driven dummy derived its name from the attempt to disguise the engine as a passenger car in order to cut down on noise and to avoid frightening horses. Since it had two cars or else a single car larger than that pulled by horses, segregation of the races was easier.

Montgomery initiated dummy service in 1886 with the forward cars reserved for whites and the rear cars for blacks. Two years later the dummy also made possible the first clear indication of segregation in Atlanta. The dummy service, begun by the Metropolitan Street Railway Company in September 1888, included two cars plus the engine—one painted yellow for whites, the other red for blacks. Likewise, the first documented case of segregation in a Nashville streetcar after 1867 was contained in an 1888 report about a Negro minister's sermon. It simply noted, "In a sermon Sunday night, [the minister] attacked the management of the dummy line for insisting that he should move to another car or get off." During the following two years, however, the newspapers reported additional instances of blacks being told to go to separate cars.[56]

The period of seeming flexibility came to an end with the passage of statutes enforcing segregation. Both blacks and the streetcar companies often objected to Jim Crow measures. But what were they protesting? Was it segregation or legal segregation that blacks were against? Did the streetcar owners object to any form of racial separation or simply to one that made them supply additional cars, usually an unprofitable venture? The fact that many Nashville blacks would have settled for separate cars in 1905 as long as there were black fare collectors suggests that the boycotts were not simply against segregation. The twentieth-century practice of dividing streetcars into black and white sections lends credence to the view that white owners objected less to the initiation of segregation than to the law requiring more cars. As the *Richmond Planet* noted, southern managers realized that "separate cars would not pay and what was worse there would be more trouble on account of it."[57] Thanks to the cooperation of local officials the managers could handle the "trouble"; financial aspects were another matter.

Then, too, why would streetcars be immune from segregation, given its prevalence in most other areas of southern life? One answer would seem to rest less with the absence of white hostility than in the circumstances in which streetcars operated. The resistance of white managers might be a reason, but as important was the greater leverage blacks exercised over streetcar policy as compared, for example, to railroad policy. Clearly boycotts presented a more serious threat to local streetcar lines than they did to a railroad that drew passengers from many communities. In addition, boycotts could be better organized because of the existence of alternative means of transportation. Whether by using hacks, private carriages, or by simply walking, Negroes could go about their business without the streetcars.

This essay has been primarily concerned with the pervasiveness of segregation in the postbellum South as it came to replace exclusion as the dominant characteristic of race relations. It has been argued that both white Republicans and Redeemers came to embrace this new policy, though often for different reasons. But what helped to assure this shift was the attitude of the blacks themselves.

Blacks on occasion did challenge segregation. During Richmond's celebration of the passage of the Fifteenth Amendment, a Negro minister was accused by the *Richmond Dispatch* of saying, "The negroes must claim the right to sit with the whites in theatres, churches, and other public buildings, to ride with them on the cars, and to stay at the same hotels with them." Similarly after Tennessee passed its Jim Crow law in 1881, a minister from Nashville argued, "No man of color [should] ride in a car simply because it is set apart and *labeled* 'exclusively for negroes,' but rather let every individual choose of the regular coaches the one in which to ride." And six years later when Charles Dudley Warner asked a group of leading black Nashville businessmen, "What do you want here in the way of civil rights that you have not?" the answer was, "We want to be treated like men, like anybody else regardless of color. . . . We want public conveyances open to us according to the fare we pay; we want the privilege to go to hotels and to theatres, operas and places of amusement. . . . [We] cannot go to the places assigned us in concerts and theatres without loss of self respect."[58]

Negroes opposed segregation by deeds as well as by words. By 1870, Charleston, New Orleans, Richmond, Mobile, and Nashville were among the cities to experience challenges to exclusion or segregation on their streetcars. Suits were brought also against offending railroad companies. Challenges to segregation were most pronounced after passage of the

1875 Civil Rights Act. For the most part, blacks failed to break down the racial barriers in theaters, hotels, restaurants, public conveyances, and bars. More isolated and equally unsuccessful attempts occurred with decreasing frequency in subsequent years.[59]

Despite this opposition to segregation, the majority of blacks, including their leaders, focused their attention elsewhere. The failure of a sustained attack on segregation perhaps resulted from the lack of support from white allies and the courts. There were other reasons as well. Five prominent Nashville blacks, for example, argued that Negroes would not use passage of the Civil Rights Act "to make themselves obnoxious" since they "had too much self respect to go where they were not wanted." Besides, they said, such actions would lead only to disturbances, and "colored people wanted peace and as little agitation as possible." Bishop Henry M. Turner echoed this view in 1889, telling a reporter that "I don't find much trouble in traveling at [*sic*] the south on account of my color, for the simple reason that I am not in the habit of pushing myself where I am not wanted." A similar attitude might have governed the response of "several really respectable colored persons" in Charleston to the attempt of a Negro to buy a ticket for the orchestra or dress circle of the Academy of Music in 1870. Calling the move a cheap political trick, they "avowed their willingness to sit in the places provided for their own race when they visited the Academy."[60]

Economic pressures also led blacks to accept segregation. Negroes who relied on a white clientele were especially reluctant to serve members of both races. Shortly after the passage of the Civil Rights Act two Negro barbers in Edgefield, across the river from Nashville, refused to serve black customers. The previous year a Negro delegation had been ejected when it demanded shaves at the shop of a black barber in Chattanooga. Asked if their money were not as good as a white man's, the barber, fearful of the loss of his white customers, answered, "Yes just as good, but there is not enough of it." Both whites and blacks understood the locus of economic power. In 1875 the *Nashville Union and American* listed twelve blacks who had been testing compliance to the Civil Rights Act. The fact that "most of them got their reward by losing their situations" helps explain why there were not more protestors.[61]

Other blacks sought to work out an equitable arrangement within the confines of a segregated order. They accepted segregation because it was seen as an improvement over exclusion and because they believed, or at least hoped, that separate facilities could be equal. A rider in 1866 on the Nashville streetcar set apart for blacks did not complain about the segregation, but threatened a boycott unless the company protected black passengers from abusive whites who forced their way into the car and used obscene language in front of black women. A Norfolk, Virginia, Negro observing that the city was building a new opera house, suggested that "colored theatregoers . . . petition the managers to give them a respectable place to sit, apart from those of a lewd character." To one Atlanta citizen, writing during a period of racial tension in his city, it seemed that whites and blacks should "travel each in their own distinct paths, steering clear of debatable ground, never forgetting to render one to the other that which equality and good conscience demands." And when the Negro principal of the Alabama State Normal School brought suit against the Western and Atlantic Railroad on the ground that despite his possession of a first-class ticket he was ejected from the first-class car and removed to the Negro car, he admitted the right of the company to classify passengers by race, but maintained it was the duty of the railroad to furnish equal facilities and conveniences for both races. This belief in the need to guarantee separate but equal treatment was expressed in a resolution offered in the Virginia senate by a Negro legislator in 1870. It provided that whites would be forbidden from traveling in portions of boats, trains, and streetcars reserved for blacks. In a letter to the *Richmond Dispatch,* the legislator attributed his action to the fact that there was little possibility of blacks being allowed to ride wherever they wanted and this would protect them, especially the women, from the intrusion of undesirable whites.[62]

In other areas, acceptance of segregation did not necessarily mean passivity on the part of blacks. Again, the targets of protest were exclusion and unequal treatment rather than segregation. For example, blacks placed more emphasis on securing better schools and welfare institutions that on achieving integrated institutions. Blacks went even further. They called for black control of separate facilities through the use of black staff or black directors of public institutions, such as penitentiaries and institutions for the blind, deaf, and dumb. The increase in the number of black colleges, like Tuskegee and Morris Brown, founded and run by blacks was another manifestation of this desire for control over separate institutions.[63]

When the white community persisted in its policy of exclusion, blacks responded by opening their own hospitals, orphanages, hotels, ice cream parlors, and skating rinks.[64] Part of this response was an accommodation to white prejudice; but it was also related to the development of a group identity among blacks. Though it cannot be equated with the racism of whites, by moving in this direction blacks themselves contributed to the emergence of the separate black and white worlds that characterized southern life by 1890.

Although the sanction of law underwrote much of the system of parallel facilities, the separation of the races was accomplished largely without the aid of statutes for as long as both races accepted its existence. As early as

1866, an English traveler, William Hepworth Dixon, noted that the Negro in Richmond, Virginia, regardless of his legal rights, knew "how far he may go, and where he must stop." He knew also that "[h]abits are not changed by paper law." In 1880 two of the Negro witnesses testifying before a congressional committee pointed to this difference between the power of law and the power of custom. When asked if there were any laws in Alabama applied solely to one race, James T. Rapier answered: "Custom is law in our country now, and was before the war." Asked again if there were any discriminatory provisions in the constitution or state statutes, he replied: "None that I know of; but what we complain of is the administration of the law—the custom of the country." James O'Hara of North Carolina made a similar statement: "These are matters [segregation in public accommodations] that are and must be regulated purely by prejudice and feeling, and that the law cannot regulate."[65]

Though prejudice persisted during the quarter century after 1865, a profound change occurred in southern race relations. The policy of exclusion was largely discarded. Instead, by 1890 segregation had been extended to every major area of southern life. Doubts remained, however, as to the possibility of keeping Negroes fully "in their place" without resort to laws. During the last decade of the nineteenth and the first decade of the twentieth centuries, these doubts resulted in the legalization of practices in effect since the end of the war. As Gilbert Stephenson pointed out for train travel, "The 'Jim Crow' laws . . . coming later, did scarcely more than to legalize an existing and wide-spread custom."[66] For whether under Radical Reconstruction or Redemption, the best that blacks could hope for in southern racial policy was separate but equal access. In fact, they usually met with either exclusion or separate but unequal treatment. Integration was rarely permitted. When it did occur, it was only at the initiation of whites and was confined as a rule to the least desirable facilities—cheap bars, inferior restaurants, second-class and smoking cars on trains. Whites were there because they chose to be; blacks were there because they had no choice.

Notes

1. *The Strange Career of Jim Crow*, 3d rev. ed. (New York: Oxford University Press, 1974), 65, 7, 3–109.

2. Tindall, *South Carolina Negroes, 1877–1900* (Columbia: University of South Carolina Press, 1952; reprint ed., Baton Rouge: Louisiana State University Press, 1966); Wynes, *Race Relations in Virginia, 1870–1902* (Charlottesville: University Press of Virginia, 1961); Logan, *The Negro in North Carolina, 1876–1894* (Chapel Hill: University of North Carolina Press, 1964); Dethloff and Jones, "Race Relations

in Louisiana, 1877–1898," *Louisiana History* 9 (Fall 1968): 301–23; Blassingame, *Black New Orleans, 1860–1880* (Chicago: University of Chicago Press, 1973); Somers, "Black and White in New Orleans: A Study in Urban Race Relations, 1865–1900," *Journal of Southern History* 40 (February 1974): 19–42; Williamson, *After Slavery: The Negro in South Carolina during Reconstruction, 1861–1877* (Chapel Hill: University of North Carolina Press, 1965); Wharton, *The Negro in Mississippi, 1865–1890* (Chapel Hill: University of North Carolina Press, 1947); Wade, *Slavery in the Cities: The South, 1820–1860* (New York: Oxford University Press, 1964); Fischer, "Racial Segregation in Ante Bellum New Orleans," *American Historical Review* 74 (February 1969): 926–37; Fischer, "The Post–Civil War Segregation Struggle," in *The Past as Prelude: New Orleans, 1718–1968,* ed. Hodding Carter et al. (New Orleans: Pelican Publishing House, 1968), 288–304; Fischer, *The Segregation Struggle in Louisiana, 1862–1877* (Urbana: University of Illinois Press, 1974); Berlin, *Slaves without Masters: The Free Negro in the Antebellum South* (New York: Pantheon, 1974).

3. Throughout this study *exclusion* refers to the policy by which blacks were not permitted to enjoy or benefit from the kinds of facilities available to whites. If, for example, only one insane asylum existed in a state and it barred blacks, this would constitute exclusion. But if provisions were made for blacks either in a separate wing of that asylum or in an entirely separate asylum, this would constitute segregation. By forming their own institutions after being excluded from comparable white ones, blacks contributed to the shift from exclusion to segregation.

4. Howard N. Rabinowitz, "From Exclusion to Segregation: Health and Welfare Services for Southern Blacks, 1865–1890"; Georgia, *Acts,* 1866, 59; Arkansas, *Laws,* 1866–1867, 416; Texas, *General Laws,* 1866, 195. Tennessee was an exception. Because it was already in Republican hands, provision was made for the education of Negroes, though on a segregated basis. Tennessee, *Laws,* 1865–1866, 65; North Carolina, *Public Laws,* 1866, 87. In February 1867 a new system of public education was established in North Carolina for whites only. Ibid., 1866–1867, 117–20; Robert E. Perdue, *The Negro in Savannah, 1865–1900* (New York: Exposition Press, 1973), 22.

5. Richmond City Council Minutes, November 27, 1865; May 14, 1866; August 17, 1867; March 31, July 1, 14, November 20, Dec. 1, 1868, Archives Division of the Virginia State Library, Richmond; after 1866 the minutes are located in the Office of the City Clerk, Richmond City Hall; *Nashville Press and Times,* August 6, 1866; *Nashville Press and Times,* June 4, 1867; Letter of "A Colored Man" to the editor, ibid., June 26, 1866; Alabama, *Seventh Annual Report of the Officers of the Alabama Insane Hospital for the Year 1867* (Tuscaloosa, 1867), 9. Texas Conservatives appropriated ten thousand dollars to set up an asylum for Negroes, but evidently took no further action. Texas, *General Laws,* 1866, 207.

6. Roger A. Fischer, "A Pioneer Protest: The New Orleans Street-Car Controversy of 1867," *Journal of Negro History* 53 (July 1968): 219–33; Texas, *General Laws,* 1866, 97; *Mississippi, Laws,* 1865, 231–32; Florida, *Laws,* 1865, 24; Raleigh, *Charters Including Amendments Together with the Ordinances of the City for 1854* (Raleigh, 1854), 75; ibid., 1873, 31–32; Nashville, *A Digest of the Charter, Amendments and Acts of the General Assembly Pertaining to the City of Nashville with the Ordinances of the City in Force, June 1868* (Nashville, 1868), 60; Richmond, *Charter and Ordinances,* 1867 (Richmond, 1867), 91–92; Blassingame, *Black New Orleans,* 197; Fischer, "Post–Civil War Segregation Struggle," 296; Somers, "Black and White in New Orleans," 25; *Nashville Press and Times,* April 21, 1866; Whitelaw Reid, *After the War: A Southern*

Tour, May 1, 1865, to May 1, 1866 (London, 1866), 377; *Montgomery Ledger,* November 20, 1865. See also *Raleigh Standard,* March 3, 1866; *Richmond Dispatch,* October 6, November 7, 1866; *Nashville Press and Times,* April 3, 1865; Perdue, *Negro in Savannah,* 22; Blassingame, *Black New Orleans,* 197.

7. Otis A. Singletary, *Negro Militia and Reconstruction* (Austin: University of Texas Press, 1957), 5, 11–15, 21; L. Branson, ed., *The North Carolina Business Directory,* 1869 (Raleigh, 1869), 152; *Nashville Union and Dispatch,* October 22–25, 1867.

8. North Carolina, *Public Laws,* 1868–1869, 471; Georgia, *Acts and Resolutions,* 1870, 57; Alabama, *Acts,* 1868, 148; Joe M. Richardson, *The Negro in the Reconstruction of Florida* (Tallahassee: Florida State University Press, 1965), 113–14; Wharton, *Negro in Mississippi,* 244; Williamson, *After Slavery,* 219–22; Louis R. Harlan, "Desegregation in New Orleans Public Schools during Reconstruction," *American Historical Review* 67 (April 1962): 663–75.

9. Wharton, *Negro in Mississippi,* 267; Williamson, *After Slavery,* 281; L. L. Polk, comp., *Handbook of North Carolina Embracing Historical and Physiographical Sketches of the State with Statistical and Other Information Relating to Its Industries, Resources, and Political Conditions* (Raleigh, 1879), 181–82; Dr. William Francis Drewy, *Historical Sketch of the Central State Hospital and the Care of the Colored Insane of Virginia* (Richmond: Everett Waddey, 1905); Wharton, *Negro in Mississippi,* 268; Polk, *Handbook of North Carolina,* 182; Tindall, *South Carolina Negroes,* 280–81, 278; Montgomery City Council Minutes, October 5, 1868, March 18, 1872, Alabama Department of Archives and History, Montgomery; Richmond, *Charter and Ordinances,* 1867, 130; Wharton, *Negro in Mississippi,* 266; Blassingame, *Black New Orleans,* 166.

10. "A Bill to Protect the Rights of Citizens Traveling in Public Conveyances," February 21, 1870, Legislative Papers no. 836, North Carolina Department of Archives and History, Raleigh; Williamson, *After Slavery,* 279–80, 357; Wharton, *Negro in Mississippi,* 230–31; *Cong. Globe,* 42d Congress, 2d session, 429–34 (January 17, 1872); David Macrae, *The Americans at Home: Pen-and-Ink Sketches of American Men, Manners, and Institutions,* 2 vols. (Edinburgh, 1870), 2:219. See also, Two Englishmen [Alexander Rivington and Harris Rivington], *Reminiscences of America in 1869* (London, 1870), 220; Wharton, *Negro in Mississippi,* 231. Louisiana's law was equally ineffective with regard to steamboats and railroads. Significant integration in trains, however, may have been secured through the use during the chartering process of written and verbal pledges to provide "equal accommodations" to members of both races. Blassingame, *Black New Orleans,* 190–94; for suits by blacks, see *Atlanta Constitution,* April 12, May 19, 1871; January 28, 1876; *Richmond Dispatch,* May 24, 1876; *Nashville American,* May 16, 1879; letter to the editor, *Montgomery Advertiser,* November 8, 1871.

11. Fischer, "A Pioneer Protest," 232–33; Marjorie M. Norris, "An Early Instance of Non-Violence: The Louisville Demonstrations of 1870–1871," *Journal of Southern History* 32 (November 1966): 487–504; August Meier and Elliott Rudwick, "A Strange Chapter in the Career of 'Jim Crow,'" in *The Black Community in Modern America,* 14–19, vol. 2 of *The Making of Black America: Essays in Negro Life & History,* 2 vols., ed. Meier and Rudwick (New York: Atheneum, 1969); August Meier and Elliott Rudwick, "Negro Boycotts of Jim Crow Street Cars in Tennessee," *American Quarterly* 21 (Winter 1969), 755–63; August Meier and Elliott Rudwick, "The Boycott Movement against Jim Crow Streetcars in the South, 1900–1906," *Journal of American History* 55 (March 1969), 756–75.

12. Writers Program of the Works Progress Administration in the State of Virginia, comp., *The Negro in Virginia* (New York: Hastings House, 1940), 241–42; Alexander Wilbourne Weddell, *Richmond, Virginia, in Old Prints 1737–1887* (Richmond: Johnson Publishing Co., 1932), 234; *Richmond Dispatch,* May 9, 1867; January 29, 1870.

13. *Nashville Press and Times,* June 26, 1866; June 18, 25, 28, 1867; *Mobile Nationalist,* May 9, July 25, 1867; April 29, 1870; Waterbury, *Seven Years among the Freedmen* (Chicago, 1891), 115–16; see Fischer, "A Pioneer Protest," 219–33. Fischer never confronts the basic distinction between exclusion and segregation.

14. Charles Dudley Warner, *Studies in the South and West with Comments on Canada* (New York, 1889), 14–15; *Montgomery Advertiser,* February 26, 1873; *Montgomery Alabama State Journal,* March 7, 1873; *Atlanta Constitution,* October 7, 1868; *Montgomery Advertiser,* March 12, 1870; *Montgomery Alabama State Journal,* April 9, 1872; *Atlanta Constitution,* December 21, 1869; October 18, 1871; *Nashville Union and American,* June 7, 1870.

15. *Atlanta Intelligencer,* July 14, 1870; *Nashville Press and Times,* February 1, 1868; *Montgomery State Sentinel,* July 3, 1867; *Montgomery Advertiser,* March 9, 1871; *Montgomery Republican Sentinel,* October 31, 1872; *Montgomery Alabama State Journal,* April 6, 1873; *Nashville Republican Banner,* March 2, 8, April 13, 1871; Blassingame, *Black New Orleans,* 185; *Montgomery Advertiser,* May 4, 29, June 3, July 6, 1869; May 28, 1870; *Montgomery Alabama State Journal,* July 5, 31, 1869; May 8, 17, June 11, 1872; for examples of seating in galleries, see advertisements in *Atlanta Constitution,* January 21, 1871; *Raleigh Standard,* October 15, 1869; *Richmond Dispatch,* May 3, 1869; *Nashville Union and American,* January 25, 1871; *Montgomery Advertiser,* January 30, 1872.

16. Williamson, *After Slavery,* 293–94; *Richmond Dispatch,* May 9, 1867; North Carolina, *Senate Journal* (July 1868), 41. Democrats also practiced segregation at their rallies. For the presence of separate speakers' stands and dinner tables at a Democratic barbecue, see *Montgomery Advertiser,* August 16, 1868.

17. Williamson, *After Slavery,* 294.

18. *Congressional Globe,* 42d Congress, 2d session, 241 (December 20, 1871); *Congressional Record,* 43d Congress, 2d session, Appendix, 15 (February 4, 1875). For the opposition of Tennessee white Republicans to national civil rights legislation, see *Nashville Republican Banner,* May 8, September 10, October 1, 1874. For further support of the contention that, with the exception of a few Radicals, congressional Republicans sought to end exclusion and unequal treatment of blacks rather than segregation per se, see Alfred Avins, "Racial Segregation in Public Accommodations: Some Reflected Light on the Fourteenth Amendment From the Civil Rights Act of 1875," *Western Reserve Law Review* 18 (May 1967): 125–83.

19. *Montgomery Alabama State Journal,* August 23, 1874; Georgia, *Laws,* 1870, 398; Stanley J. Folmsbee, "The Origin of the First 'Jim Crow' Law," *Journal of Southern History* 15 (May 1949): 235–47; for the attempt to pass state civil rights legislation, see *Montgomery Alabama State Journal,* February 25, March 1, 7, 9, 10, April 8, August 14, 1873. For Republican support of separate but equal treatment, see ibid., January 27, 1872; May 29, June 6, 14, 30, July 11, 1874; *Alabama Weekly State Journal,* December 11, 1869; March 18, 1870; *Mobile Nationalist,* April 18, 1867.

20. For earlier opposition to prospective state civil rights acts, see *Montgomery Advertiser,* August 13, 1868; December 7, 1869; July 4, 1873; Blassingame, *Black New*

Orleans, 183–84, 190–91; Williamson, *After Slavery,* 280; *Atlanta Constitution,* February 6, 1875; *Raleigh Daily Sentinel,* August 2, 1875.

21. *Atlanta Constitution,* April 3, 1876; March 27, 1875; *Richmond Dispatch,* March 10, 1875; *Nashville Republican Banner,* March 2, 1875; *Nashville Banner,* October 18, 1883; *Montgomery Advertiser,* October 23, 1883. Even if the law did not alter southern life, the potential for more rigid enforcement always existed and whites therefore rejoiced when the United States Supreme Court declared it unconstitutional in 1883. *Richmond Dispatch,* October 14–21, 1883; *Atlanta Constitution,* October 16, 21, 1883.

22. *Atlanta Constitution,* January 28, 1876; *Richmond Dispatch,* May 24, 1876; *Nashville American,* May 16, 1879.

23. Montgomery, *Annual Message of the Mayor of Montgomery and Reports of the Various City Officers and Standing Committees of the City Council for the Year Ending April 30, 1877,* (Montgomery, 1877), 14; ibid., 1885, 55–56; C. J. Allardt, comp., *Montgomery City Directory for 1888* (Montgomery: R. L. Polk and Co., 1888), 19; Wharton, *Negro in Mississippi,* 232; Georgia Constitution (1877), art. 8, sec. 1; Tennessee Constitution (1870), art. 11, sec. 12; North Carolina Constitution (1875), art. 9, sec. 2.

24. Polk, *Handbook of North Carolina,* 181–82; *Raleigh Daily Sentinel,* March 18, November 3, December 8, 1875; North Carolina, *Annual Report of the Board of Directors and the Superintendent of the North Carolina Insane Asylum for 1877* (Raleigh, 1877), 30; Alabama, *Annual Report of Alabama Insane Hospital,* 1878, 45–46; ibid., 1880, 18; ibid., 1888, 24; Raleigh, *Charters and Ordinances,* 1876, 96–97. See also Wharton, *Negro in Mississippi,* 232.

25. For the Redeemers' failure to honor separate but equal treatment, see my essays "Health and Welfare Services for Southern Blacks" and "Half a Loaf: The Shift from White to Black Teachers in the Negro Schools of the Urban South, 1865–1890"; Tennessee, *Laws,* 1885, 124–25. See also Henry W. Grady, *The New South* (New York, 1889), 246.

26. Lawrence D. Rice, *The Negro In Texas, 1874–1900* (Baton Rouge: Louisiana State University Press, 1971), 237–38; Georgia, *Report of the Institution for the Deaf and Dumb,* 1876 (Rome, Ga., 1876), 6; ibid., 1882, 7; Georgia, *Report of the Board of Trustees of the Georgia Academy for the Blind for 1883* (Macon, Ga., 1883), 11; Alabama, *Annual Reports of the Alabama Institution for the Education of the Deaf and Dumb and Blind for 1889 and 1890* (Montgomery, 1890), 7–8; 1891–1892, 11; Tennessee, *Acts,* 1881, 139; Tennessee, *Twenty-First Biennial Report of the Trustees and Superintendent of the Tennessee School of the Blind for 1885* (Nashville, 1885), 10; Tindall, *South Carolina Negroes,* 281; Tennessee, *First Biennial Report of the Tennessee Industrial School for the Period 1887–1888* (Nashville, 1888), 22; North Carolina, *Report of the Board of Public Charities of North Carolina for 1891* (Raleigh, 1891), 12–14. By 1887 the Arkansas Insane Asylum had separate wings for the races. In Kentucky, a southern but non-Confederate state, the legislature did not provide for the education of the Negro blind until 1884. Three years later the inmates of the Institution for the Blind were living in segregated quarters as was the case at the Industrial School of Reform. Warner, *Studies in the South and West,* 286.

27. *Atlanta Constitution,* January 25, 1872; *Nashville Banner,* December 15, 1885; Rice, *Negro in Texas,* 147. Segregation in Nashville waiting rooms was probably in force much earlier than 1885. The fact that in 1873 the city's Louisville Depot had a "gentlemen's sitting room" rather than a "men's" waiting room suggests the exis-

tence of a Negro waiting room or the absence of any provision for black passengers. *Nashville Republican Banner,* November 14, 1873.

28. *Montgomery Advertiser,* February 14, 1877; October 17, 1885; *Raleigh News and Observer,* April 24, October 31, 1890.

29. *Atlanta Weekly Defiance,* October 8, 1881; *Atlanta Constitution,* September 23, 1874; *Nashville Republican Banner,* November 8, 1873; *Raleigh News and Observer,* January 11, 1891; *Richmond Dispatch,* December 9, 11, 1875. John Blassingame reports that after being confined to the Jim Crow section of the St. Charles Theatre following the war, New Orleans blacks finally gained the right to sit in the dress circle as a result of the Civil Rights Act of 1875. He does not mention if they were segregated as in Richmond. He also points out that after vacillating between segregation and integration, the New Orleans Opera House was finally forced to accept integration. There is no indication as to how long this policy persisted, but, whatever the length, it clearly departed from the provisions elsewhere in the South. Blassingame, *Black New Orleans,* 186–87.

30. *Nashville Union and American,* March 16, 1875; *Nashville Banner,* November 3, 1884; *Atlanta Constitution,* February 18, 1888. Under fear that the Civil Rights Act of 1875 would force black guests upon them, white hotels in Augusta, Georgia, and Chattanooga, Tennessee, gave up their public licenses and became private boarding houses. *Atlanta Constitution,* March 7, 9, 1875. A black who sought lodging at a Nashville boarding house was told by the proprietor, "I don't board your kind." *Nashville Union and American,* March 11, 1875. Blassingame concluded that even in New Orleans white hotel and restaurant owners were among the staunchest foes of the civil rights act. *Black New Orleans,* 196. See also Fischer, "Post–Civil War Segregation Struggle," 296–97; Wynes, *Race Relations in Virginia,* 76.

31. *Nashville American,* June 13, 1883; *Atlanta Constitution,* March 9, 1875; *Richmond Dispatch,* October 7, 1886; *Montgomery Advertiser,* May 12, 1875. The situation in New Orleans again seems to have been atypical in that a number of the leading restaurants were integrated. Even so, by 1874 former lieutenant governor P. B. S. Pinchback was refused service at Redwitz's Saloon. Blassingame, *Black New Orleans,* 188–89. White teachers at Negro colleges were severely criticized for eating at the same tables with their students. *American Missionary* 20 (February 1876): 36.

32. *Atlanta Constitution,* May 31, 1886; August 11, 1887; *Nashville Press and Times,* March 24, 1868; *Nashville Banner,* July 6, 1881; September 2, 1887; Sarah McCulloh Lemmon, "Entertainment in Raleigh in 1890," *North Carolina Historical Review* 40 (October 1963): 334; *Atlanta Constitution,* July 6, 1884; Somers, "Black and White in New Orleans," 34–35, 39–41; *Richmond Dispatch,* October 17, 1885; *Atlanta Constitution,* August 23, 1883. White military companies from Atlanta, Savannah, and Montgomery withdrew from the national drill held in Washington, D.C., because black companies were to participate. *Savannah Tribune,* April 9, 1887. See also *Atlanta Constitution,* August 7, September 1, 1885; *Montgomery Alabama State Journal,* April 17–18, 1872; *Richmond Dispatch,* October 25, 1875; *Nashville Banner,* October 15, 1887.

33. Fischer, "Post–Civil War Segregation Struggle," 304; H. G. Saunders, comp., *Atlanta Directory,* 1891 (Atlanta, 1891), 150, 245; *Atlanta Constitution,* July 31, 1888. Nashville's Lone Star brothel had its ground and upper floors occupied by white prostitutes and its basement by blacks. It is not known whether or not the clientele was also mixed. *Nashville American,* March 28, 1877.

34. *Savannah Colored Tribune,* July 15, 1876. Jim Crow Bibles were present by 1868 in some courts in Virginia. Macrae, *Americans at Home* 1:146–47.

35. Wade, *Slavery in the Cities,* 267.

36. See, for example, *Nashville Banner,* June 16, July 7, 1883.

37. Letter to the editor, *Atlanta Constitution,* July 19, 1887; July 1, 1890; March 24, 1889.

38. *Nashville Banner,* October 16, 1882; *Atlanta Constitution,* July 5, 10, 1890; *Montgomery Advertiser,* June 3, 1890; *Raleigh News and Observer,* July 21, 1889. Highland Park had its name changed to Oak Park during the 1890s and was one of those affected by the trend toward separate parks for the races. A local Negro resident remembered that the only blacks admitted by that time were nurses with white children. Bertha Thomas McClain, *Montgomery Then and Now as I Remember* (Montgomery: Walker Printing Co., 1960), 23.

39. *Atlanta Constitution,* July 19, 1874; *Nashville Banner,* May 22, 1888; *Raleigh News and Observer,* May 4, June 13, 1890; *Atlanta Constitution,* April 4, 1890. It is not known if Negroes had been permitted in the old building and if so, under what conditions.

40. *Nashville Republican Banner,* March 2, 1871; *Nashville Banner,* May 25, 1883; *Nashville Republican Banner,* May 20, 1875; *Atlanta Constitution,* October 16, 19, 1871; *Montgomery Advertiser,* November 5, 1890.

41. Tennessee, *Message of John C. Brown, Governor of Tennessee, to the Thirty-ninth General Assembly of the State of Tennessee, January 4, 1875* (Nashville, 1875), 19; Georgia, *Reports of the Principal Keeper and Officers of the Georgia Penitentiary from April, 1872, to December 31, 1873* (Atlanta, 1874), 22.

42. This had been tried before the Civil War. Berlin, *Slaves without Masters,* 324.

43. *Atlanta New Era,* November 20, 1866. See also Williamson, *After Slavery,* 281; this was true during the post-1890 period when penal segregation is generally acknowledged to have become pervasive. The Code of Laws and Regulations for the Penitentiary System of Tennessee in 1896, for example, called for the separation of white and black convicts, but added that this should be done "only as far as practicable." Tennessee, *Report of the Warden, Superintendent, and Other Officers of the Tennessee Penitentiary for the Year Ending December 31, 1896* (Nashville, 1897), 13. See also Frank William Hoffer, Delbert Martin Mann, and Floyd Nelson House, *The Jails of Virginia: A Study of the Local Penal System* (New York: D. Appleton-Century, Co., 1933), 112.

44. Virginia used the system as early as 1858 as a substitute for exclusion. Berlin, *Slaves without Masters,* 323–24. See also Georgia, *Reports of the Penitentiary* (1888–1890), 3; North Carolina, *Biennial Report of the Board of Directors, Architect and Warden, Steward and Physician of the North Carolina State Penitentiary for the Two Years Ending November 30, 1890* (Raleigh, 1890), 40; Wharton, *Negro in Mississippi,* 239–40.

45. Georgia, *Reports of the Penitentiary* (1876), 10–12; ibid. (1878–1880), 4; Amanda Johnson, *Georgia as Colony and State* (Atlanta: Walter W. Brown, 1938), 668; Gilbert Thomas Stephenson, *Race Distinctions in American Law* (London: D. Appleton and Company, 1910), 146.

46. Alabama, *Biennial Report of the Inspectors of the Alabama Penitentiary for the Two Years Ending September 30, 1882* (Montgomery, 1882), 19–21; ibid., 1882–1884, 22, 27, 201, 264; Alabama, *First Biennial Report of the Inspectors of Convicts from October 1, 1888 to October 1, 1890* (Montgomery, 1890), 5. For a call for the use of entirely separate prisons to prevent any contact between the races, see ibid., 1884–1886, 17.

For segregated cells, hospitals, and prayer meetings in other state prisons, see North Carolina, *Reports of the Penitentiary*, 1878–1880, 46; ibid., 1882–1884, 17; Tennessee, *Reports of the Penitentiary*, 1878–1880, 15, 30; *Nashville Union and American*, December 15, 1870; *Nashville Banner*, April 3, 1885; Fischer, *Segregation Struggle*, 84.

47. Hustings Court Order Books, no. 13, 60, 367, Richmond City Hall; ibid., no. 16, 241: ibid., no. 24, 163.

48. Atlanta, *Annual Report of the Officers of the City of Atlanta for the Year Ending December 31, 1889* (Atlanta, 1889), 159; *Nashville Banner*, August 30, 1890. For complaints about the confining together of some black and white prisoners due to a lack of room, see *Nashville American*, October 13, 1887. By 1889 the Fulton County Jail as well as the Atlanta City Jail were segregated. *Atlanta Constitution*, June 11, 1889. During 1889, four years before the passage of a law requiring separation of young offenders, a group of Atlanta citizens proposed building a segregated reformatory. Ibid., December 21, 1889. Plans drawn the following year for a new stockade for county chain gang convicts included separate bathtubs for whites and blacks. Ibid., February 9, 1890. Raleigh, North Carolina, also may have followed the Atlanta and Nashville pattern. By 1890 it had a segregated jail, workhouse, and chain gang. *Raleigh News and Observer*, March 29, 1890.

49. *Montgomery Ledger*, August 29, 1865; *Montgomery State Sentinel*, July 22, 1867; *Montgomery Advertiser*, February 26, 1885, September 26, 1871; Stephenson, *Race Distinctions in American Law*, 146; *Montgomery Advertiser*, July 11, 1885. A similar progression had perhaps taken place by 1875 in Orleans Parish Prison in New Orleans. Fischer, *Segregation Struggle*, 84.

50. Stephenson, *Race Distinctions in American Law*, 215; *Richmond Dispatch*, August 27, 1880; Cable, "The Negro Question," *The Negro Question: A Selection of Writings on Civil Rights in the South by George W. Cable*, ed. Arlin Turner (Garden City, N.Y.: Doubleday, 1958), 129; Douglass, "The Color Line," *North American Review* 132 (July 1881): 576. See also *Raleigh News and Observer*, May 4, 1890.

51. Iza Duffus Hardy, *Between Two Oceans or Sketches of American Travel* (London, 1884), 306–07; Lady Duffus Hardy [Mary McDowell], *Down South* (London, 1883), 85; *Nashville Republican Banner*, May 11, 1875. For further examples of the confinement of blacks to smoking cars, see *Nashville American*, March 23, 1879; W. H. Crogman, *Talks for the Times* (Atlanta, 1896), 191; *Atlanta Constitution*, April 10, 1889.

52. *Nashville American*, July 30, 1885. For additional examples of the concern shown by the Redeemer press for separate but equal accommodations, see *Montgomery Advertiser*, February 21, March 8, 1873; *Richmond Dispatch*, October 14, 1870; *Atlanta Constitution*, October 16, 1883; January 1, 1885; *Nashville American*, October 3, 1881.

53. *Lynchburg News*, quoted in *Richmond Dispatch*, April 8, 1870; *Houston Post*, quoted in David G. McComb, *Houston: The Bayou City* (Austin: University of Texas Press, 1969), 160; *Atlanta Constitution*, June 15, 1885; December 4, 1887.

54. Meier and Rudwick, "A Strange Chapter in the Career of 'Jim Crow,' " 15; *Nashville American*, April 11, 1880; *Richmond Planet*, December 27, 1890; Baker, *Following the Color Line: An Account of Negro Citizenship in the American Democracy* (New York: Doubleday, Page and Company, 1908), 30.

55. *Congressional Record*, 43d Congress, 2d session, 955, 957 (February 3, 1875); Meier and Rudwick, "A Strange Chapter in the Career of 'Jim Crow,' " 16. See also Perdue, *Negro in Savannah*, 34; Nordhoff, *The Cotton States*, 106.

56. *Atlanta Constitution*, July 28, 1889; Franklin M. Garrett, *Atlanta and Environs:*

A Chronicle of Its People and Events, 3 vols. (New York: Lewis Historical Publishing Company, 1954) 2:175; *Nashville Banner*, May 1, 1888; May 26, June 9, 1890. See also the statement by a white, W. F. Slaton, in which he remembered being ejected from the Negro car on the Nashville dummy even though there were only a few people in it while the white car was packed full." *Atlanta Constitution*, August 6, 1889.

57. Meier and Rudwick, "Boycott Movement Against Jim Crow Streetcars in the South," 757; "Negro Boycotts in Tennessee," 761; *Richmond Planet*, December 27, 1890.

58. *Richmond Dispatch*, April 22, 1870. See also *Savannah Colored Tribune*, March 25, 1876. Letter of W. A. Sinclair to the editor, *Nashville American*, October 4, 1881; Warner, *Studies in the South and West*, 116–17.

59. *Nashville Union and Dispatch*, December 19, 1867; *Atlanta Constitution*, April 12, May 19, 1871; Blassingame, *Black New Orleans*, 191–92, 185–86; *Nashville Republican Banner*, March 13–14, 1875; *Nashville Union and American*, March 13–14, 1875; *Atlanta Constitution*, March 6, 9, 10, 1875; *Raleigh Sentinel*, March 6, 1875; *Richmond Dispatch*, March 9, 10, 1875; *Montgomery Advertiser*, March 6, 13, 14, 1875. For "testing" on railroads, see *Nashville American*, October 2, 3, 5, 1881; *Nashville Banner*, September 30, October 7, 1881; *Atlanta Constitution*, August 9, 1889. For an attempt to buy soda water at a Nashville shop that served only whites, see *Nashville Banner*, October 3, 1881. For attempts to sit in white sections of theaters, see *Atlanta Constitution*, September 28, 1881; *Nashville Republican Banner*, April 17, 1887. For an attempt to integrate a Nashville streetcar, see *Nashville American*, July 20, 1889.

60. Quoted in *Atlanta Constitution*, March 6, 1875; January 7, 1889; *Charleston News*, January 10, 1870. Implicit here is support for Fischer's contention that many blacks accepted segregation out of a belief that the ultimate reward was not worth the effort needed to secure it. Fischer, "Post–Civil War Segregation Struggle," 297.

61. *Nashville Union and American*, March 9, 1875; *Cincinnati Commercial*, quoted in the *Nashville Republican Banner*, June 17, 1874; *Nashville Union and American*, March 11, 1875. For the threat of economic retaliation against protesters, see *Nashville Republican Banner*, March 11, 1875; *Montgomery Alabama State Journal*, March 13, 14, 1875; *Montgomery Advertiser*, March 24, 1875. The fear of economic retaliation led Elias Napier, a prosperous livery stable owner in Nashville, to announce publicly that he was not one of a group of Negroes who had sought admission to a white restaurant. "I do not wish myself on any man," he wrote, "and as for civil rights, I want all to know that I was opposed to the passage of the civil rights bill from the first." *Nashville Republican Banner*, March 11, 1875.

62. *Nashville Press and Times*, June 26, 1866; *Richmond Virginia Star*, March 27, 1880; *Atlanta Constitution*, August 15, 1889; July 24, 1887; *Richmond Dispatch*, July 1, 4, 1870. For additional evidence of black interest in separate but equal accommodations in public conveyances, see *Montgomery Alabama State Journal*, July 26, 1869; *Alabama State Journal*, December 16, 1870; *Montgomery Advertiser*, June 2, 1885; Avins, "Racial Segregation," 1280.

63. See "Half a Loaf" and "Health and Welfare Services for Southern Blacks." See also James M. McPherson, "White Liberals and Black Power in Negro Education, 1865–1915," *American Historical Review* 75 (June 1970): 1357–86; for the successful attempt of Morris Brown officials to secure the appropriation from the

Georgia legislature that had previously gone to Atlanta University, see *Atlanta Constitution,* June 11, 12, July 19, 21, 1887; November 28, 1889.

64. Rabinowitz, "Health and Welfare Services for Southern Blacks"; Blassingame, *Black New Orleans,* 166–71; *Montgomery Advertiser,* August 16, 1885; J. H. Chataigne, comp., *Chataigne's Directory of Richmond for 1891* (Richmond, 1891), 1031; *Richmond Virginia Star,* December 14, 1878; December 9, 23, 1882; *Richmond Planet,* June 12, 1886; *Atlanta Constitution,* March 10, 1882; *Nashville Union and American,* September 14, 1873; *Montgomery Citizen,* August 2, 1884; J. H. Chataigne, comp., *Raleigh City Directory,* 1875, 133; *Montgomery Herald,* July 23, 1887; *Fisk Herald* 7 (May 1890): 16; *Atlanta Defiance,* October 8, 1881; *Atlanta Constitution,* April 23, 1885; *Montgomery Alabama State Journal,* April 6, 1873.

65. William Hepworth Dixon, *New America,* 2 vols. (London, 1867), 2:332–33; U.S. Senate, *Report and Testimony of the Select Committee of the United States Senate to Investigate the Causes of the Removal of the Negroes from the Southern States to the Northern States* (Washington, 1880), part 2, 476–77; ibid., part 1, 57.

66. Part of the uncertainty as to the efficacy of de facto segregation may have been due to a more aggressive attitude on the part of younger educated blacks. Howard N. Rabinowitz, "Search for Social Control: Race Relations in the Urban South, 1865–1890," 2 vols. (Ph.D. diss., University of Chicago, 1973), 1:534–38, 2:887–90; Stephenson, *Race Distinctions in American Law,* 214. See also John Snyder, "Prejudice Against the Negro," *Forum* 8 (October 1889), 222.

┌───┐
│ **5. What role did gender play**   │
│   **in railroad segregation?**   │
└───┘

Barbara Y. Welke

From *"When All the Women Were White, and All the Blacks Were Men: Gender, Class, Race, and the Road to* Plessy, *1855–1914"*

Barbara Y. Welke (b. 1958) is assistant professor of history at the University of Minnesota and specializes in U.S. legal and constitutional history. She received her J.D. from the University of Michigan Law School in 1983 and her Ph.D. in history from the University of Chicago in 1995. Welke's dissertation, "Gendered Journeys: A History of Injury, Public Transport, and American Law, 1865–1920," received the Lerner-Scott Prize for the best doctoral dissertation in women's history from the Organization of American Historians in 1996. In addition to articles in *Law & Social Inquiry* (1994), *Law and History Review* (1995), and *Utah Law Review* (2000), Welke has published *Recasting American Liberty: Gender, Race, Law and the Railroad Revolution, 1865–1920* (2001). In her article "When All the Women Were White, and All the Blacks Were Men: Gender, Class, Race, and the Road to *Plessy,* 1855–1914," Welke challenged Woodward's argument for the fluidity of post-emancipation race relations. Based on her examination of forty-seven civil court cases challenging racial segregation (thirty-one initiated by black women), Welke documented that southern railroad companies systematically attempted to exclude black women from first-class ("ladies'") railroad cars. Emphasizing their rights as women and relying on common law, women received favorable trial verdicts in seventeen of the cases. Determined to protect white women from contact with blacks, southern state legislatures in the late 1880s and 1890s passed statutes formalizing racial separation, requiring that railroads provide separate but equal accommodations for white and black passengers. The move to statutory Jim Crow, Welke concludes, resulted from the obsession of white southerners to protect southern "white womanhood" from black men, "but also to force common carriers and Southern courts into line."[1]

Questions for a Closer Reading

1. Did African American women travel on first-class ("ladies") railroad cars before emancipation?

2. Following the Civil War, why did whites seek to exclude black women from first-class cars?

3. Why did women of color protest against riding in smoking cars?

4. How did black women challenge the railroads? Were they successful? Why?

5. How did southern railroad companies define black women — by gender, race, or class?

6. How did black women define themselves — by gender, race, or class?

7. What role did class play in determining whether or not black women filed lawsuits?

8. What does Welke mean by the "gendering of race"?

9. According to Welke, what role did gender play in the timing of statutory Jim Crow?

Note

1. Barbara Y. Welke, "When All the Women Were White, and All the Blacks Were Men: Gender, Class, Race, and the Road to *Plessy*, 1855–1914," *Law and History Review*, 13 (Fall 1995): 295–313, 312.

From "When All the Women Were White, and All the Blacks Were Men: Gender, Class, Race, and the Road to Plessy, 1855–1914"

Crafting a Law of Racial Segregation

It was C. Vann Woodward who reminded Americans that statutory racial segregation did not follow in the immediate wake of Reconstruction. Woodward claimed that the years from 1865 to roughly 1890 were fluid ones in terms of race relations. His argument is in part directed toward suggesting that race relations might have taken a different path from the one they did. The argument presented here strongly disputes that claim. As other scholars have argued, one can only see these interim years as fluid by largely ignoring the role of custom and private carrier regulations in guarding white supremacy. While a small minority of women of color succeeded for a time in demanding the right to enjoy first-class accommodations, they succeeded because of the privileges traditionally extended to women traveling first-class and ultimately failed because of the commitment of white society to preserving white hegemony embodied in the ideal of white womanhood.

This argument substantially revises the telling of why Southern states began in the late 1880s to mandate racial separation by statute. In *The Strange Career of Jim Crow*, Woodward argued that the South's embrace of statutory racial segregation stemmed from three related political factors: first, eroding Northern opposition to racial segregation; second, weakened white conservative determination to ensure fair treatment of blacks; and third, the end of white radical hopes for a biracial coalition.[1] Other historians have argued that this view is incomplete and treats Southern blacks as

Barbara Y. Welke, from "When All the Women Were White, and All the Blacks Were Men: Gender, Class, Race, and the Road to *Plessy*, 1855–1914," *Law and History Review*, 13 (Fall 1995): 295–313.

objects rather than as subjects of history. Howard Rabinowitz argues that to Woodward's argument a fourth factor must be added: the pressure created by a new generation of largely urban Southern blacks who had little or no memory of slavery and refused to abide by the old standards of behavior.[2] Others have agreed with Rabinowitz. For example, Charles Lofgren notes, "the most direct trigger for the initial wave of Jim Crow legislation was increasing black unwillingness to defer to whites."[3]

Both explanations are clearly right, but they are seriously incomplete. They suffer from a blindness common to much of history and particularly true of the history of race relations in the post-emancipation South: premised on a historical narrative focusing on political and civil rights, they largely ignore or treat as peripheral women, white and black. Yet women, white and black, were absolutely central. Ladies' accommodations had embedded in public travel an accepted system of unequal accommodation. In the wake of the Civil War, these special accommodations became the frontline for defending white womanhood, and hence the ideology of white supremacy. Yet in the end, ladies' accommodations would prove a double-edged sword.

Only recently have historians begun to recognize that the principle of separate but substantially equal accommodations was part of the common law well before statutory Jim Crow and the United States Supreme Court's decision in *Plessy v. Ferguson*.[4] State supreme courts on the eve of and in the immediate wake of the Civil War held that common carriers' broad right to adopt reasonable regulations included the right to segregate, though not to exclude, passengers by race.[5] Indeed, every court to reach the issue held that regulations separating black and white passengers were "reasonable under the circumstances," even though the circumstances were largely a matter of white prejudice.

From the first post–Civil War case, segregation by gender served as a legal analogy justifying regulations segregating passengers by race. But while gender seemed a fruitful analogy for race, in practice it created a tension best described by the question of whether a woman of color should be defined by her gender or by her race. In the eyes of most whites, the reference "black lady" was an oxymoron. Indeed, the term "lady" had always included the unstated racial modifier "white." In the climate of the post–Civil War South refusing to recognize black women as ladies was an essential component of retaining the purity and superiority of white womanhood. From the beginning, carriers pressed arguments that would protect the enclave of white women without imposing on carriers the obligation to provide the same quality of accommodations for people of color. Yet women of color, by virtue of their gender and class, pushed courts to measure equality based on the standard of accommodations provided for white women. Gradually, carriers replaced gendered terms of travel (ladies' car/smoking car), with facially neutral terms (front car/rear car). In doing so, carriers were attempting to take the privileges of white women out of the debate over race. Carriers were in a socially and financially impossible position. White prejudice required that the enclave of white ladies be protected. Yet as state and federal courts interpreted the common law, it required carriers to provide for women of color paying first-class fare substantially equal accommodations to those provided to white women. Law and their own financial interest led carriers to stray from the fold. The compromise they reached was most obvious on railroads: they directed all blacks to the smoking car, but then allowed respectable black women—women who might or did object—to ride in the ladies' car.[6] But in the ideology of white supremacy, the defense of white womanhood, there was no margin for compromise. Social norms, white womanhood, women of color, carriers, and courts, together pushed Southern legislatures beginning in the late 1880s and early 1890s to mandate racial separation by statute.

While it is natural in retrospect to see Jim Crow as a monolithic law of racial segregation, in the years after the Civil War the legal legitimacy of segregation had to be worked out in each separate legal context in which it arose. Common carriers were one context and were governed by a distinct, well-established common law. Unlike other privately owned public places such as restaurants, theaters, and cemeteries, which had long excluded and would continue after the war to exclude blacks,[7] common carriers were considered by law to be exercising a public trust.[8] The common law of common carriers legally required carriers to carry all passengers paying the required fare, with only a limited number of exceptions. Race was not among them. The common law did allow carriers to adopt reasonable regulations for the convenience and comfort of other passengers, as well as to protect their private business interests. Yet most of these regulations related to issues such as requiring passengers to purchase tickets at designated offices or barring passengers from riding on the platforms of coaches. Regulations setting aside accommodations for ladies from which men were excluded, in contrast, were based on an immutable characteristic (sex) and reflected social norms of public contact between two groups (men and women). Most important, they had long been accepted as reasonable regulations.[9]

Segregation by sex provided a natural analogy for segregation by race under the common law of common carriers. Black was to white, as male was to female. From the first post-war decisions of a state supreme court and of the United States Supreme Court addressing racial segregation, judges and advocates recognized the compelling analogy that segregation by gender on common carriers provided for segregation by race. "The simple question," wrote Justice Daniel Agnew of the Pennsylvania Supreme Court in *West Chester and Philadelphia R.R. v. Miles,* in 1867, "is whether a public carrier may, in the exercise of his private right of property, and in the due performance of his public duty, separate passengers by any other well-defined characteristic than that of sex." His unqualified answer was "yes." Gender as an existing, accepted ground for separating passengers paying the same fare provided a legal, socially unrefutable analogy for separating passengers by race.[10]

In *Hall v. Decuir,* the first post–Civil War case challenging racial segregation on common carriers before the United States Supreme Court, R. H. Marr, the defendant's lawyer, argued, "A male passenger, basing his right on the laws of the United States, might have complained that he was not allowed a stateroom in the ladies' cabin, with as much force and propriety as a colored passenger could have complained that he was furnished apartments and accommodations not inferior to, but different in locality, from those furnished to white passengers."[11]

As Marr argued, "Passengers on steamboats are not huddled together, male and female, in the same apartments; separation on the basis of sex is a requirement of common decency." "No one pretends," he insisted, "that this uniform separation violates the law of equality; nor can it be tortured into an assertion of the superiority of one sex or the other."[12] Through the post-emancipation years and into the twentieth century, the ladies' car/ladies' cabin analogy remained fundamental to the legal justification of racial segregation on common carriers.[13]

Yet what the Pennsylvania Supreme Court in *Miles,* the defendant's lawyer in *Decuir,* and others who relied on the analogy provided by gender ignored was precisely the gender of the plaintiffs before them. Mary Miles and Josephine Decuir, and the majority of other plaintiffs in suits challenging racial segregation on carriers, however inconveniently for the defendants, were women. The very existence of regulations providing special accommodations to ladies on public transit meant that women of color would seek the privilege of their gender. With the common law right of carriers to segregate passengers by race established, and the common law right to segregate passengers by gender affirmed, state and federal courts between 1870 and 1890 struggled to achieve a balance between the two.

As a practical matter, so long as a carrier only had one or the other regulation there was no conflict. No distinction based on sex existed on the train on which Mary Miles was riding. The train had only one passenger car. The railroad had adopted a regulation requiring colored persons to sit at one end of the car.[14] In Anna Williams's 1870 suit against the Chicago & Northwestern Railroad the reverse was true. The railroad had no formal regulation barring people of color from the ladies' car, but it did have a regulation establishing a ladies' car for the exclusive use of ladies traveling alone or with an escort.

As Anna Williams's lawyer before the Illinois Supreme Court argued, the defendant railroad "had established a rule discriminating between the sexes." "[H]aving made such discrimination, and thereby rendered some cars less fit and less desirable for the use of ladies than would have been the case had no such distinction been made, the company had no right to exclude the plaintiff from the ladies' car." Moreover by excluding her from the ladies' car on account of her color, the defendant had virtually excluded Anna Williams from its train. She was a lady traveling alone who had purchased her ticket assuming that, as a lady, she would enjoy the protections afforded by the ladies' car. In a sense, by relegating her to the smoking car, the defendant had proclaimed that Anna Williams was not a lady and was "not a fit person to sit even in the presence of ladies, on a railroad train."[15] The Illinois Supreme Court essentially agreed with Williams's argument.[16] Under the circumstances, the railroad could not require Williams to "go forward to the car set apart for and occupied mostly by men." The court continued, "It is a sufficient answer to say, that that car was not provided by any rule of the company for the use of women, and that another one was. This fact was known to the appellee at that time. She may have undertaken the journey alone, in view of that very fact, as women often do."[17] The law to which the Illinois Supreme Court, and most courts thereafter, referred was not statutory or constitutional law, but the common law of carriers.

Yet if gender provided a useful analogy for race under the common law, there was a stumbling block: a person of color in the shape of a lady. What result was a court to reach where the two regulations stood counterpoised? So long as segregation was a matter of company regulation and the vocabulary of ladies' car and smoker held, state and federal courts, particularly trial courts, demanded that women of color paying first-class fare enjoy the same privileges that white women paying first-class fare enjoyed.[18] In 1877, in *United States v. Dodge,* Judge Duval, a federal trial judge in Texas, instructed the jury that "every citizen of the United States, male or female, native born or naturalized, white or black, who pays to the carrier the fare demanded for the best accommodations, is entitled to the best provided for the different sexes." If the train had only one car appropriate for the accommodation of ladies, then Milly Anderson was entitled to a seat there.

Only if the evidence showed that both cars on the train were equally used by gentlemen and ladies, without distinction of race, would the conductor have not been guilty for directing Anderson to one car rather than the other. But, the judge insisted, the jury must be convinced that the car to which the conductor had directed Anderson "was in fact, in all respects, equal to the other, and was as fit and appropriate at that time for white female citizens as for colored female citizens." In fact, they should consider the evidence as though the woman had been a "white female citizen, instead of a colored one."[19]

When Selina Gray and her husband, William, brought suit against the Cincinnati Railroad Company in federal district court in Ohio in 1882, Judge Swing strongly directed the jury that the common law of common carriers and the United States Constitution required that what a carrier provided for white ladies traveling first class must be provided for ladies of color traveling first class. Railroads "may have the right to make a regulation that the gentlemen shall ride in one car, and the ladies shall ride in another car," Judge Swing explained, and "[t]hey perhaps have a right (which it is not now necessary to determine) that the colored people shall ride in another car." But, he continued, if "this lady," Selina Gray, bought a first-class ticket and presented herself for admission to the ladies' car and there was room in that car, the agents of the company were obligated to open the door and furnish her a seat. If they refused to do so and agreed to carry her only so long as she would ride in the smoking car "where none but gentlemen were, and where they were smoking, she had a right, under the law, to say that she would not go into it." The law required this company "to provide for this colored woman precisely such accommodation, in every respect, as were provided upon their trains for white women." "Not every man likes smoke; not every man likes tobacco," he explained to the jury. "It is bad enough for them to force a gentleman who does not use tobacco, and who sickens at the scent of smoke or tobacco, into a car of that character, let alone forcing a lady there with a sick child."[20] Three years later, in 1885, Judge E. S. Hammond, a federal district judge in Tennessee, echoed this conclusion in *Logwood v. Memphis & Charleston R.R.* Judge Hammond instructed the jury that although carriers may segregate passengers by race, they must nonetheless "furnish substantially the same accommodations to all." "If a railroad company furnishes for white ladies a car with special privileges of seclusion and other comforts, the same must be substantially furnished for colored ladies."[21]

From the beginning, the balance courts struck between race and gender was a fragile one. It had long been accepted that men did not need, deserve, or desire the creature comforts essential to ladies.[22] The language of equality, however, had assumed a place in the vocabulary it had not had before. In 1882, Judge Swing, in *Gray v. Cincinnati S. R.R.*, had spoken deploringly, but resignedly of the practice of requiring all men, even those who sickened from or detested smoke to ride in the smoker if they were not accompanying a lady. He had insisted that "the gentlemen's money is just as good as the lady's, in the eye of the law and they are bound to provide for him such reasonable accommodation as he has paid and contracted for."[23] In 1885, Judge D. M. Key, a federal district judge in Tennessee, suggested to the jury that a white man ejected from the ladies' car and ordered into the smoker would have had as much right to object as a man of color.[24] Judge Key pointedly told the jury:

> A train with but two cars in which passengers could go, as in this case, and in which the ladies and their friends had one exclusively, the other car being used for smoking and for gentlemen without lady friends, does not give like accommodations to all. The passenger from the rear car may go into the forward car and smoke, but the passenger in the forward car cannot go into the rear car for any purpose. He cannot go into it to smoke or to escape the smoke, however offensive to him.[25]

With these words, Judge Key became the first to hold that accommodations provided for men and women, black and white, must be substantially equal.

Two years after *Murphy*, the Interstate Commerce Commission echoed Judge Key's language in its first decision interpreting Section 1 of the Interstate Commerce Act as applied to racial segregation in accommodations on railroads for interstate passengers. In *Councill v. Western & Atlantic R.R.*, the commission exhorted, "[b]ut the right of the carrier to assign a white man to another car than the ladies' car, or a colored man to a car for his own race, takes nothing from the right of either to have accommodations substantially equal to those of other passengers paying the same fare." The car to which William Councill had been removed did not meet this standard. "This was a half car, half lighted," excoriated the commission, "in which men and women were huddled together, and where men, white and black, smoked at pleasure."[26] The smoke-filled air and general filth of the car to which railroad employees had directed a man of color, as well as the drinking, cursing, and other crude conduct tolerated there, became as important an ingredient in men's suits as it had always been in suits brought by women of color.[27] This did not mean though, that large numbers of men, white or black, suddenly began challenging the gender line. Until statutes formalized racial segregation, most men of color, even men of standing in the black community, continued to ride in the smoker when necessary. Nonetheless, these cases were an essential component of the shift from the language of gender to the language of race.

Defendant carriers were anxious to preserve their rights to segregate passengers according to their own designs. The most obvious method—establishing certain classes of carriage for which people of color were refused tickets—did not have the sanction of law, but was probably common in practice.[28] After the war, courts consistently interpreted the common law of carriers to require that a carrier could not exclude passengers from accommodations for which they were willing to pay the required fare unless the carrier provided substantially equal, separate accommodations.[29] In *McCabe v. Atchison, Topeka & Santa Fe Ry.,* decided in 1914, the United States Supreme Court noted in dicta that the same standard applied under the Equal Protection Clause of the Fourteenth Amendment.[30] The Court flatly rejected the argument that a state statute (the Oklahoma Separate Coach Law) mandating separate but equal accommodations for white and black passengers could constitutionally except certain luxury cars (sleeping, dining, and club cars), and allow carriers to provide these cars for white passengers but not persons of color because it was uneconomical to provide them for the latter. Writing for the Court Justice Hughes explained,

> This argument with respect to volume of traffic seems to us to be without merit. It makes the constitutional right depend upon the number of persons who may be discriminated against, whereas the essence of the constitutional right is that it is a personal one. Whether or not particular facilities shall be provided may doubtless be conditioned upon there being a reasonable demand therefore, but, if facilities are provided, substantial equality of treatment of persons traveling under like conditions cannot be refused. It is the individual who is entitled to the equal protection of the laws, and if he is denied by a common carrier, acting in the matter under the authority of a state law, a facility or convenience in the course of his journey which under substantially the same circumstances is furnished to another traveler, he may properly complain that his constitutional privilege has been invaded.[31]

If carriers could not legally refuse first-class accommodations to people of color, they nonetheless employed a series of overlapping strategies to protect the domain of white women from incursion by women and men of color.

From the outset, defendants sought to "gender race." In the years following the Civil War and before the formalization of statutory Jim Crow, carriers regularly, and often successfully, made immorality and sexual threat code words for color. If social assumptions about white ladies and white men made it imperative to provide white ladies separate traveling facilities from white men, an even more persuasive case for separating all people of color from white ladies could be made if carriers could resort to popular racist assumptions. In ejecting Jane Brown from a ladies' car in Corinth, Tennessee, in 1880 on the Memphis & C. Railroad, the railroad claimed Brown was a "notorious courtesan, addicted to lascivious and profane conversation and immodest deportment in public places." In other words, Jane Brown was a prostitute and therefore could not be permitted to ride among ladies. "[N]othing could be more repulsive and annoying to ladies, and their fathers, husbands and brothers," argued the defendant's lawyer, "than to know that whores will be entitled to be seated by them in railroad cars." "Why establish or maintain a 'ladies' car' at all," he asked, "if whores and all other classes of improper characters, can get admittance there, and their exclusion therefrom can only be justified from bad conduct at the time?"[32]

In Jane Brown's case, the ploy failed. Judge Hammond, the Tennessee federal district judge trying the case, instructed the jury to treat the case exactly as though Jane Brown "were a white woman excluded under similar circumstances." He pointedly denied the right of a carrier to adopt a regulation which excluded women from the ladies' car on the basis of their character for chastity. Such a regulation, he explained, "would put every woman purchasing a railroad ticket on trial for her virtue before the conductor as her judge, and in case of mistake, would lead to breaches of the peace. It would practically exclude all sensible and sensitive women from traveling at all, no matter how virtuous, for fear they might be put into or unconsciously occupy the wrong car." The jury obviously agreed, for they awarded Jane Brown a verdict of three thousand dollars.[33]

One suspects that most women were not as fortunate as Brown. As William Randolph would argue, unsuccessfully, on behalf of Sallie Robinson before the United States Supreme Court in *Robinson v. Memphis & Charleston R.R.*, one of the cases consolidated before the Court in *The Civil Rights Cases*, "What is the difference between denying her 'the full and equal enjoyment' because of her color, and denying the same thing to her because of a belief, that she being colored and her traveling companion white, therefore, she must necessarily be a woman wanting in virtue? In either case the substantiate ground of the denial was because of Mrs. Robinson's color, which must be regarded as the proximate cause of her exclusion." If Mrs. Robinson were not a woman of color, but were the wife of some distinguished white citizen, could such a pretext be used to exclude her? "In such a case," Randolph argued, "is there a court in the country that would listen with patience to such an absurdity? And is there any difference between the case supposed and Mrs. Robinson's case, except in the fact that she is colored?"[34] Unfortunately, the facts all too clearly showed that most whites did not assume that women of color as a class were virtuous, or entitled to the same assumptions of respectability which white women enjoyed.

Although there are fewer cases involving men, it is clear that the same process was at work. Justice Agnew's opinion for the Pennsylvania Supreme Court in *Miles* in 1867 deliberately played to the white fear of the sexual threat of black men to white women as a ground for requiring separating blacks from whites. "If a negro take his seat beside a white man or his wife or daughter," he explained, "the law cannot repress the anger, or conquer the aversion which some will feel." Justice Agnew's opinion is dotted with references to "illicit intercourse," "intermarriage," and "promiscuous sitting." Despite the fact that the plaintiff, Mary Miles, was a woman, Justice Agnew's opinion portrayed a world in which there were white men protecting white ladies from black men.[35] The fear to which Justice Agnew played was real enough in the minds of many Southern white men and women: Southern judges repeated Justice Agnew's words in their opinions; southern white men violently ejected black men from ladies' accommodations to make them safe for white women; and southern editors trumpeted the warning against the dangers of black men sitting next to a white man's wife or daughter on trains and steamboats.[36]

In each of these instances, and one imagines in many others that never became lawsuits, what might be called the "gendering of race" served at least three potential functions. First, under circumstances where law forbade discrimination on the basis of race, or where the custom of racial exclusion had not been formalized in regulations, the gendering of race provided an alternative basis for excluding or ejecting a person of color from first-class ladies' accommodations. If a woman of color was not a lady, it followed that she had no right to ride in the ladies' car. Second, the portrayal of women and men of color as immoral justified regulations excluding persons of color in general from facilities set aside for white ladies. Finally, the image of women of color as low class and immoral explained why most whites saw no injustice in requiring women of color to ride in smoking cars with white and black men or in colored bureaus with minimal privacy, while white women enjoyed segregated facilities.

At the same time that defendant-carriers were gendering race, they sought to take the language of gender, at least the privileges of white ladies, out of the debate over race. They did so in three ways: first, by minimizing the significance of gendered accommodations; second, by focusing on the bare physical accommodations; and third, by substituting ungendered terms for the traditional gendered terms of carriage.

To minimize the significance of gender as a basis for distinguishing among passengers, railroads downplayed actual practice. The lawyer for the Chicago & Northwestern Railroad in Anna Williams's 1867 suit insisted that gentlemen regularly traveled in the ladies' car and that ladies "habitually and constantly ride" in the car that Williams had referred to as the "gentlemen's car."[37] Over and over in suits brought by women of color challenging railroad attempts to force them to ride in smoking cars, the railroads controverted the women's testimony that no women were riding in the smoker at the time. In Mary Jane Chilton's 1870 suit against St. Louis & Iron Mountain Railway, the conductor insisted that "all classes, both male and female" rode in the smoker.[38] In Lola Houck's 1887 suit against the Southern Pacific Railway, the brakeman insisted that there was another colored woman, "very nearly white," with a small child already in the car.[39]

They also ignored gender altogether. By ignoring or treating as insignificant the conduct and sex of the passengers who occupied the accommodations and by focusing instead on the bare physical accommodations, defendants could wean sympathetic courts away from the realization that no white lady would ever be directed to the smoker. In Mary Jane Chilton's 1870 suit against the St. Louis and Iron Mountain Railway, the lawyer for the railway carefully focused the court's attention on the trifling differences in the bare physical accommodations between the two cars of the train. "Surely," the railroad's lawyer contemptuously begged the Missouri Supreme Court to reflect, "the difference between seats covered with enameled cloth and seats covered with plush, is not so great, as that one should consider himself greatly wronged, if not allowed to chose between them."[40] He ignored, of course, that Mary Jane Chilton was a woman, that she was traveling with two children in her care, that night was falling, that the car to which the brakeman and conductor ordered her was a smoking car occupied by white men who were strangers to her, and that she was afraid, under these circumstances, to ride in the smoker.

In fact, witnesses for defendant carriers, in cases involving women of color, were unable to provide examples of ever having directed a white woman to the smoking car.[41] A 1901 Georgia Supreme Court decision suggests how sternly courts would view such an action. In *Southern Railway v. Wood*, the plaintiff, a white woman, had herself asked for the cheapest fare. The railroad sold her a second-class ticket and seated her in the smoker. When she subsequently brought suit against the railroad, a Georgia trial court, affirmed by the Georgia Supreme Court, awarded her a judgment against the railroad. As the Georgia Supreme Court noted, the car in which she was forced to ride was a "dingy, dirty, smoking car, occupied by men only, many of whom were smoking." It was a car "in which no other ladies were riding, the only female besides herself being a negro."[42] The court's pointed reservation of the label "lady" for white females, its emphasis on the sex of those riding in the car and their conduct is a telling reminder that gender and conduct retained their sanctity for white Southerners discussing the rights of white southern women.

In cases involving women of color, railroads blunted arguments of inequality, in part by avoiding gendered names of carriage. In *Chilton v. St. Louis & Iron Mountain Ry.*, for example, the railroad couched its argument in partially ungendered terms. In its pleadings and briefs, the defendant referred to the ladies' car, from which the conductor and brakeman had excluded Chilton, and "another car equally safe, comfortable, commodious, and convenient," to which they had directed her. The trial court and, in turn, the Missouri Supreme Court adopted the defendant's labels. By substituting a conclusory label for what was, in fact, the smoker, the defendant and the courts could ignore that white passengers were segregated by sex to provide white ladies with a car free from the vices of men. Having semantically eradicated the inequality between the two cars, the courts could go on to conclude that there were no differences between the two cars which mattered. "We think," Justice George B. MacFarlane wrote for the Missouri Supreme Court, "that the car in which she was requested to ride was equal in these accommodations to the one in which she insisted on riding, and whether the instructions required less in the way of accommodations than the law entitled her to it is not necessary to inquire."[43]

As a practical matter, the transition from gender to race was largely a matter of switching the labels on the doors of the existing unequal accommodations. It was no coincidence that, over time, the smoker became the "colored" or "Jim Crow" car, or that the ladies' car became the car for white ladies and gentlemen. Or in other cases, that the smoker was the car partitioned to create a segregated place for passengers of color on trains. These cases both generated the change and froze it in time as a fossil might be left in the rock in a sudden, dramatic, and devastating climatic shift.

No case more epitomized this process than Rebecca Smith's 1891 suit against the South Carolina Railway Company. Smith brought suit against the receiver of the railway company for being forcibly ejected from the ladies' room of the station house at Graniteville, South Carolina, and ordered to go into the room for male passengers. The depot agent, Fishburne, testified that the room Smith was in was not the ladies' room, but one for the use of whites, and the other room to which he directed her, was not for males, but for blacks of both sexes. The trial judge interpreted the evidence for the jury:

It is true, that some testimony has been brought out in the hearing, tending to show a discrimination against the plaintiff on account of color—she being a colored woman. This testimony was admitted without objection; but I do not think it was responsive to any allegation in the complaint, or any issue raised by the pleadings. The plaintiff, in her complaint, does not complain that she was discriminated against on account of color. Her cause of action, as set forth in her complaint, grows out of the alleged fact that she was forcibly and unlawfully ejected from the ladies' waiting room, where she had gone to purchase a ticket, for the purpose of becoming a passenger on the railway of said company.

Was the room from which Rebecca Smith was ejected a waiting room for white passengers or a ladies' room? Smith's lawyer argued that at the least the court should instruct the jury that if smoking and chewing were allowed in one room but not in the other, the two would not be equal. The judge limited the charge, telling the jury that the room would not be equal only if the smoking, chewing or cursing were going on at the time that Rebecca Smith was ordered into the room and that it was up to them to decide whether any had been going on at that time. The court left to the jury of white men to choose between the testimony of other white men and a woman of color. The jury reached a verdict for the defendant and the South Carolina Supreme Court affirmed.[44]

The social construction of gender and class had set in motion a complex chain of causation. In origin, the special accommodations assigned to ladies, the inferior ones assigned to men, had nothing to do with race. But in the wake of the Civil War in the American South they came to have everything to do with race. Women of color demanded access to first-class ladies' accommodations as a matter of physical safety and personal respectability.

State and federal courts failed to block their path. As long as racial segregation on common carriers remained largely a matter of state and federal common law, all passengers paying the same fare had the right to substantially equal accommodations. Women of color, by virtue of their sex, drew on the rights granted to white women. As courts held, if carriers provided to white women traveling first-class accommodations with special privileges of exclusion and other comforts, the common law required that they provide substantially equal accommodations to women of color paying first-class fare. The legal risk carriers faced proved real enough: when carriers assigned respectable women of color paying first-class fare to second-class accommodations, courts applying the common law of common carriers often found in the women's favor.

Custom and private regulation had proved inadequate to the task. Women of color riding in the ladies' car or enjoying other ladies' accommodations, where they did not do so clearly in the status as servant or nurse to white women or children, threatened the superior, almost sacred status of white womanhood. It is in this context, that the move to statutory Jim Crow must be placed. By 1893, when the South Carolina Supreme Court issued its opinion in *Smith v. Chamberlain,* eight southern states (Florida, Mississippi, Texas, Louisiana, Alabama, Arkansas, Georgia, and Kentucky) had adopted statutes requiring that railroads provide equal but separate accommodations for white and black passengers traveling within the state. By 1900, every state in the South would have such a statute.[45] By 1915, the requirement would have been extended as well to streetcars and from there quickly spread to virtually every aspect of Southern life.

Those in power in the South adopted statutory Jim Crow beginning in the 1890s because the political climate North and South made it possible; because they faced a growing class among people of color who could afford and would demand first-class carriage and other privileges of white society; because courts applying the common law of common carriers required that if carriers separated passengers by race, they had to provide for women of color substantially equal accommodations as those provided to white women; and because carriers in allowing respectable black women to ride in first-class ladies' accommodations were themselves failing to protect the purity of white womanhood. Seen in this light, the shift to statutory Jim Crow not only was necessary to control Southern blacks, but also to force common carriers and Southern courts into line.

Statutory Jim Crow provided an absolute protection of white womanhood and thus of white supremacy in the South by protecting the enclave of white women from encroachment by women and men of color. State statutes mandating separate accommodations for black and white passengers made the color line supreme in intrastate travel and effectively had the same result for interstate travel.[46] These statutes eliminated the conflict that had resulted from imposing a system of racial segregation on top of the existing system of sexual segregation.

It is no coincidence that the move to statutory Jim Crow in the late 1880s and early 1890s occurred at the same time that Southern states moved to disenfranchise black men. In one sense, the demand of women of color to ladies' accommodations was the gender equivalent of the political and economic power men of color had gained with freedom, the passage of the Civil Rights Act of 1866, and the ratification of the Fifteenth Amendment. Statutory Jim Crow was for women, the gender equivalent of disenfranchisement of black men. Given the importance of a woman's status for determining the status of the men related to her, denying respectable women of color status as ladies barred all blacks—men and women—from the world of white respectability. Both processes—the denial of political and social rights to blacks—were essential to re-establishing the pre–Civil War racial and social status quo in the American South.

Notes

1. C. Vann Woodward, *The Strange Career of Jim Crow,* 3rd rev. ed. (New York: Oxford University Press, 1974), 69.

2. Howard N. Rabinowitz, *Race Relations in the Urban South, 1865–1890* (New York: Oxford University Press, 1978), 333–39.

3. Charles A. Lofgren, *The Plessy Case: A Legal-Historical Interpretation* (New York: Oxford University Press, 1987), 25.

4. See ibid., 116–47; Stephen J. Riegel, "The Persistent Career of Jim Crow: Lower Federal Courts and the 'Separate but Equal' Doctrine, 1865–1896," *American Journal of Legal History* 28 (January 1984): 17, 20.

5. *Day v. Owen,* 5 Mich. 527 (1859); *The West Chester and Philadelphia R.R. v. Miles,* 55 Pa. 209, 215 (1867).

6. For example, on every railroad journey before and after her trip on September 21, 1886, the railway's employees had allowed Lola Houck to ride in the ladies' car without objection. Testimony of Lola Houck (plaintiff), Transcript of Testimony, pp. 1–2, 6, Record in *Houck v. Southern Pacific Ry.*

7. See Rabinowitz, *Race Relations,* passim.

8. See *Inhabitants of Worcester v. The Western R.R.,* 4 Met. 564, 566 (1842); Joseph Story, *Commentaries on the Law of Bailments* (Boston: Little, Brown, 1870, 8th ed.), 581.

9. It is critical to bear in mind that the social norms relating to gender and embodied in ladies' and gentlemen's accommodations resulted in a physical structure of travel that lent itself to segregation.

10. 55 Pa. 209, 211.

11. Brief & Argument for Plaintiff in Error (John G. Benson, defendant), December 1876, p. 10, Record in *Hall v. Decuir.* The Court in *Decuir* struck down an 1869 Louisiana statute barring racial discrimination on common carriers. The Court held that in regulating interstate as well as intrastate passengers the law violated the Commerce Clause of the U.S. Constitution.

12. Brief and Argument for Plaintiff in Error (John G. Benson, defendant), p. 33, Record in *Hall v. Decuir.*

13. See, e.g., *Council v. Western & Atlantic R.R.,* 1 I.C.C. 638, 641 (1887); *Chiles v. Chesapeake & Ohio Ry.,* 125 Ky. 299, 305 (1907).

14. The *West Chester and Philadelphia R.R. v. Miles,* 55 Pa. 209, 210 (1867).

15. Appellee's Brief (Anna Williams, plaintiff), pp. 1–4, Record in *Chicago & Northwestern Ry. v. Williams.*

16. While many of the cases, including *Williams,* sound like breach of contract cases, the courts never treated them as such. Rather, courts uniformly applied the common law of common carriers and state and, when the plaintiff raised them, federal constitutional provisions. Many of the cases, moreover, included a claim for physical assault. These claims depended upon the court's finding as to whether the carrier's servants removed or forcibly excluded the passenger pursuant to a regulation. Under the common law of carriers, a carrier was allowed to use reasonable force to remove passengers violating reasonable regulations. Finally, the damages awarded included not only actual damages (which in many

cases would have been nominal) but also damages for any indignity, vexation, or disgrace which the individual had suffered, which was consistent with the distinctive legal status of these claims. See, e.g., *Chicago & Northwestern Ry. v. Williams,* 55 Ill. 185, 188, 190 (1870).

17. *Chicago & Northwestern R.R. v. Williams,* 55 Ill. 185, 189 (1870).

18. The references to first-class fare can be confusing. On many trains, as on the Chicago & Northwestern R.R. train on which Anna Williams had sought passage, there was a single fare which applied to all the coaches. In these cases, the railroads uniformly referred to the single fare as first-class fare.

19. *U.S. v. Dodge,* 25 F. Cas. 882 (D.C.W.D. Tex. 1877) (No. 14,976) (charge to jury). *Dodge* was a criminal prosecution against the president, vice-president, superintendent, and conductor on the Houston & Texas Central Railway under the Civil Rights Act of 1875, but the Court stressed in its jury charge that the right to equal carriage was protected by the common law.

20. *Gray v. Cincinnati S. R.R.,* 11 F. 686–87.

21. *Logwood v. Memphis & Charleston R.R.,* 23 F. 319. Despite this favorable instruction, other aspects of the case explain why the jury reached a verdict for the defendant railroad. The conductor had testified that although "colored people" were generally required to ride in the front car, "proper persons" who objected to sitting there were allowed to take a seat in the ladies' car. He noted as well that the Logwoods had always been permitted to ride in the ladies' car and insisted that he had told Mrs. Logwood to take a seat in the forward car and when he finished he would find her a seat in the ladies' car. Judge Hammond told the jury that "[a]ll the travelers have to submit to some discomforts and inconveniences, and should not be too exacting, but are entitled to polite treatment, free from any kind of indignity." He then instructed the jury that if they believed the conductor and "there was no unreasonable delay" the Logwoods could not recover.

22. The fact that automobile makers at the turn of the twentieth century designed and marketed automobiles relying on these same assumptions suggests that the assumptions themselves retained their social currency. As historian Virginia Scharff describes, "manufacturers tended to associate the qualities of comfort, convenience, and aesthetic appeal with women, while linking power, range, economy and thrift with men. Women were presumed to be too weak, timid, and fastidious to want to drive noisy, smelly gasoline-powered cars." As she explains these assumptions led manufacturers to devise "a kind of 'separate spheres' ideology about automobiles: gas cars were for men, electric cars were for women." Scharff, *Taking the Wheel,* 36–37.

23. *Gray v. Cincinnati S. R.R.,* 11 F. 683, 686.

24. It is important to recall that when Murphy entered the ladies' car several white men were already riding there unmolested by the conductor.

25. *Murphy v. Western & Atlantic R.R.,* 23 F. 637, 640 (C.C.E.D. Tenn. 1885).

26. *Council v. Western & Atlantic R.R.,* 1 I.C.C. 638, 641 (1887).

27. See, e.g., Letter from Winfield Cozart to E. A. Mosely, Informal Complaint, July 6, 1908, Record in *Cozart v. Southern Ry.;* Petition, February 25, 1908, Record in *Williams v. Jacksonville, Tampa & Key West Ry.*

28. For example, in her testimony in The *Sue,* Martha Stewart noted that she and her sisters had not even bothered to seek a stateroom, because steamers absolutely refused to sell them to people of color. The general manager for the steamboat line admitted this point. Nevertheless, the Stewart sisters had not chal-

lenged this practice and Judge Murphy did not touch on it in his opinion in favor of the Stewart sisters. Testimony of Martha Stewart (libellant), Jan. 29, 1885, Transcript of Testimony, p. 8, Testimony of Reuben Foster (general manager of the Chesapeake & Richmond Steamboat Co., witness for defendant), Jan. 30, 1885, Transcript of Testimony, p. 45, Record in The *Sue*, 22 F. 843 (D. Md. 1885). Similarly, during the testimony in William H. Heard's case before the Interstate Commerce Commission in 1887, against the Georgia Railroad, one conductor explained that he would find any way he could around selling a sleeping car ticket to a person of color. The general counsel for the railroad warned that if the Commission required the railroad to give people of color access to sleeping accommodations when that issue came before the Commission, the railroad would stop providing sleeping cars to all passengers rather than grant access to people of color or provide separate cars for them. Deposition of Mr. Harris (conductor, witness for defendant), Argument of Joseph B. Cumming (general counsel, the Georgia Railroad), Dec. 15, 1887, Transcript of Hearing, pp. 10–11, 34–35, Record in *Heard v. Georgia R.R.*

29. In the early cases this issue was presented and addressed indirectly. See, e.g., *United States v. Dodge*, 25 F. Cas. 882 (D.C.W.D. Tex. 1877) (No. 14,976). See also *Gaines v. Seaboard Air Line Ry.*, 16 I.C.C. 471 (1909), interpreting the Interstate Commerce Act to require carriers who offer Pullman sleeping accommodations and dining accommodations to white passengers to provide the same to passengers of color.

30. *McCabe v. Atchison, Topeka & Santa Fe Ry.*, 235 U.S. 151 (1914). Despite the Court's favorable position on this point, it nevertheless refused to grant the injunction the plaintiffs sought against enforcement of the statute because they had not met the legal standard for injunctive relief.

31. *McCabe v. Atchison, Topeka & Santa Fe Ry.*, 235 U.S. 151, 161–62 (1914).

32. *Brown v. Memphis & C. R.R.*, 7 F 58. Significantly, the defendant railroad in *Brown* had also initially claimed to eject Brown on the basis of a regulation barring colored persons from riding in the ladies' car. The railroad later withdrew the argument because, in fact, it did not have a formal regulation.

33. *Brown v. Memphis & C. R.R.*, 5 F. 499, 500, 502 (C.C.W.D. Tenn. 1880).

34. Brief for Plaintiffs in Error (Richard A. & Sallie J. Robinson), p. 17, *Robinson v. Memphis & Charleston R.R.* The Civil Rights Act of 1875 provided that all persons "shall be entitled to the full and equal enjoyment of the accommodations, advantages, facilities and privileges of inns, public conveyances on land or water, theatres, and other public places of amusement, subject only to the conditions and limitations established by law, and applicable alike to citizens of every race and color, regardless of any previous condition of servitude." The Civil Rights Act of 1875, 18 (Part 3) Stat. 335, 336 (1875). The Court held the act unconstitutional insofar as it attempted to regulate intrastate accommodations. 109 U.S. 3 (1883).

35. The *West Chester and Philadelphia R.R. v. Miles*, 55 Pa. 211–12.

36. *Bowie v. Birmingham Ry. & Electric Co.*, 125 Ala. 397, 405–10 (1899); *Murphy v. Western & Atlantic R.R.*, 23 F. 637, 638–41 (C.C.E.D. Tenn. 1885). After passage of the Civil Rights Act of 1875, which forbade discrimination on the basis of race in public accommodations, an editorial in a North Carolina paper warned "if the principles of the Republicans succeed, the negro will be forced upon . . . [the white man's] wife, and his daughter, on the cars, steamboats, in public inns, at hotel tables, and in theatres and other places of amusement." *Raleigh Daily Sentinel*, Aug. 2, 1875, quoted in Rabinowitz, *Race Relations*, 186.

37. Appellant's [Defendant Chicago & Northwestern Railroad] Oral Argument, pp. 4–5, Record in *Chicago & Northwestern Ry. v. Williams.*

38. Testimony of Charles H. Dorr (conductor, witness for defendant), December 11, 1872, Transcript of Testimony p. 37, Record in *Chilton v. St. Louis & Iron Mountain Ry.*

39. Testimony of Charles Oaks (brakeman, witness for defendant), Transcript of Testimony, p. 31, Record in *Houck v. Southern Pacific Ry.*

40. Statement and Brief of the Respondent, p. 22, Record in *Chilton v. St. Louis & Iron Mountain Ry.*

41. See, e.g., Testimony of F. Farnsworth (conductor, witness for defendant Southern Pacific Railway), Transcript of Testimony, p. 44, Record in *Houck v. Southern Pacific Ry.*

42. *Southern Ry. v. Wood,* 114 Ga. 159 (1901).

43. Amended Answer (St. Louis & Iron Mountain Ry.), November 1, 1871, Statement and Brief of the Respondent, p. 22, *Chilton v. St. Louis & Iron Mountain Ry.,* 114 Mo. 94.

44. 38 S.C. 529, 532, 539, 546 (1892).

45. Tennessee was the first state in the wake of Reconstruction to adopt a law relating to race and accommodations on railroads. But the Tennessee statute (prior to its amendment in the early 1890s) was not a Jim Crow measure as we would later come to understand that term. Its specific purpose was to end the widespread railroad practice of forcing first-class passengers of color to ride in smoking cars and to guarantee them equal, though not racially integrated, first-class accommodations. See Lofgren, *Plessy,* 21–22.

46. It is too often forgotten that in the wake of *Plessy,* only carriers had the right to regulate the conditions of passage for interstate, as opposed to intrastate, passengers. By 1910, even the Supreme Court, it seemed, was willing to ignore exactly what ground—company regulation or state statute—was the basis for excluding a person of color from the first-class white car. See *Chiles v. Chesapeake & Ohio Ry.,* 218 U.S. 71, 75, 77 (1910); Testimony of J. Alexander Chiles (plaintiff), Testimony of W. Ridgeway (conductor, witness for defendant), Transcript of Record, pp. 20, 32, Record in *Chiles v. Chesapeake & Ohio Ry.* From its first pronouncements on race after the Civil War, the United States Supreme Court played an important role in allowing Southern states to decide the terms on which blacks would enjoy access to accommodations in public transit. In 1876, in *Hall v. Decuir,* the United States Supreme Court struck down a Louisiana statute which forbade racial discrimination on common carriers. In *The Civil Rights Cases,* decided in 1883, the Court struck down most of The Civil Rights Act of 1875, including the restriction against racial discrimination on common carriers.

6. How did segregation enforce racial subordination?

Leon F. Litwack

From *Trouble in Mind: Black Southerners in the Age of Jim Crow*

One of the foremost specialists in African American history, Leon F. Litwack (b. 1929) is Alexander F. and May T. Morrison Professor of American History at the University of California, Berkeley. Litwack's pathbreaking *North of Slavery: The Negro in the Free States, 1790–1860* (1961) revealed the breadth of discrimination, including all manner of segregation, that limited the freedom of "free" blacks in the antebellum North. His *Been in the Storm So Long: The Aftermath of Slavery* (1979), which won both the Pulitzer and Francis Parkman prizes, uncovered extensive patterns of de facto segregation during Reconstruction. In the book's sequel, *Trouble in Mind: Black Southerners in the Age of Jim Crow* (1998), Litwack carefully examined how African Americans responded not only to de jure and de facto segregation, but also to rampant racial violence, brutality, and intimidation in the aftermath of Reconstruction. Longing for the loyal and contented mythical "old Negro" of slavery times, late-nineteenth-century white southerners viewed the new generation of "uppity" blacks with disdain and fear. Disfranchisement and segregation lay at the heart of white southerners' commitment to control them. "When the white South acted on its racial creed," Litwack explains, "it sought to impress on black men and women their political and economic powerlessness and vulnerability—and, most critically, to diminish both their self-esteem and their social aspirations." In this selection, Litwack details the lengths to which whites went to restrict interracial contact once disfranchisement was in place.[1]

Questions for a Closer Reading

1. According to Litwack, what characterized southern race relations between Reconstruction and Redemption?
2. What, in Sam Gadsden's opinion, was the cause of the new segregation of the 1890s?
3. Why were railroads, in Litwack's words, special "arenas of confrontation" for interracial conflict?
4. Why did whites sometimes substitute the term *colored* for *black* in Jim Crow signs?
5. What, in your mind, was the most remarkable or unsettling expression of Jim Crow as described by Litwack?
6. How did the new segregation of the 1890s differ from the segregation of the Old South and Reconstruction?

Note

1. Leon F. Litwack, *Trouble in Mind: Black Southerners in the Age of Jim Crow* (New York: Alfred A. Knopf, 1998), 219.

From *Trouble in Mind: Black Southerners in the Age of Jim Crow*

Racial segregation was hardly a new phenomenon. Before the Civil War, when slavery had fixed the status of most blacks, no need was felt for statutory measures segregating the races. The restrictive Black Codes, along with the few segregation laws passed by the first postwar governments, did not survive Reconstruction. What replaced them, however, was not racial integration but an informal code of exclusion and discrimination. Even the Radical legislatures in which blacks played a prominent role made no concerted effort to force integration on unwilling and resisting whites, especially in the public schools; constitutional or legislative provisions mandating integration were almost impossible to enforce. The

Leon F. Litwack, from *Trouble in Mind: Black Southerners in the Age of Jim Crow* (New York: Alfred A. Knopf, 1998), 229–37.

determination of blacks to improve their position during and after Reconstruction revolved largely around efforts to secure accommodations that equaled those afforded whites. Custom, habit, and etiquette, then, defined the social relations between the races and enforced separation in many areas of southern life. Whatever the Negro's legal rights, an English traveler noted in Richmond in 1866, he knows "how far he may go, and where he must stop" and that "habits are not changed by paper laws."[1]

But in the 1890s whites perceived in the behavior of "uppity" (and invariably younger) blacks a growing threat or indifference to the prevailing customs, habits, and etiquette. Over the next two decades, white Southerners would construct in response an imposing and extensive system of legal mechanisms designed to institutionalize the already familiar and customary subordination of black men and women. Between 1890 and 1915, state after state wrote the prevailing racial customs and habits into the statute books. Jim Crow came to the South in an expanded and more rigid form, partly in response to fears of a new generation of blacks unschooled in racial etiquette and to growing doubts that this generation could be trusted to stay in its place without legal force. If the old Negro knew his "place," the New Negro evidently did not. "The white people began to begrudge these niggers their running around and doing just as they chose," recalled Sam Gadsden, a black South Carolinian born in 1882. "That's all there is to segregation, that caused the whole thing. The white people couldn't master these niggers any more so they took up the task of intimidating them."[2]

What made the laws increasingly urgent was the refusal of blacks to keep to their place. In the late nineteenth century, economic and social changes swept through the South, introducing new sites and sources of potential racial contact and conflict; at the same time, white women in increasing numbers moved into the public arena and workplace. Both races availed themselves of the expanding means of rail transportation, with middle-class blacks in particular asserting their independence and social position. Refusing to be confined to the second-class or "smoking" car, they purchased tickets in the first-class or "ladies" car, much to the consternation of whites who resented these "impudent" assertions of social equality. In response to white complaints, conductors expelled blacks from the first-class seats they had purchased, resulting in disruptive incidents and litigation.

Segregation, even more than disfranchisement, came to be linked to white fears of social equality. The railroad and the streetcar became early arenas of confrontation, precisely because in no other area of public life (except the polling place) did blacks and whites come together on such an equal footing. "In their homes and in ordinary employment," as one observer noted, "they meet as master and servant; but in the street cars they touch as free citizens, each paying for the right to ride, the white not in a place of command, the Negro without an obligation of servitude. Street car relationships are, therefore, symbolic of the new conditions." In daily travel, the proximity of the races was likely to be much closer, more intimate, more productive of evil, as a New Orleans newspaper suggested: "A man that would be horrified at the idea of his wife or daughter seated by the side of a burly negro in the parlor of a hotel or at a restaurant cannot see her occupying a crowded seat in a car next to a negro without the same feeling of disgust." An English visitor heard the Jim Crow car defended not only as a necessary means to keep the peace but "on the ground of the special aversion which . . . the negro male excites in the white woman."[3]

In South Carolina, where legislation segregating public transportation had been previously defeated, the question took on a new urgency in the late 1890s. Explaining that urgency and why it no longer opposed such legislation, a Columbia newspaper referred to the "many" and "constant" complaints over racial intermingling on the railway trains.

> The seeming humiliation put upon respectable colored people is to be regretted, but they suffer from the conduct of those of their race who have not appreciated the privileges which they were accorded on the railroads of this state. The obtrusiveness and hardly-veiled insolence of many negroes constantly offends ladies traveling and this settles it.

Legislators and editors voiced support of segregation while lamenting the passage of the "old Negro." The linkage seemed obvious. The new laws, explained a state senator, were not needed to protect whites from "good old farm hands and respectable negroes" but from "that insolent class who desired to force themselves into first class coaches."[4]

To resolve this growing problem, state after state, beginning in the 1880s, responded by designating cars for whites and blacks, in many instances making the "smoking" or second-class car the only car available to black passengers. The same assertiveness by blacks on the urban street-cars and trolleys, including the refusal to sit in separate sections or to give up seats to whites, prompted municipalities to take similar action. In Jacksonville, Florida, for example, the city council enacted a separate streetcar ordinance after reports of disturbances on the cars and growing complaints from whites about "the attitude" of black passengers.[5]

Some municipalities prescribed separate cars; most settled on partitions that separated the races on the same car, with blacks relegated to the rear seats. On boarding a streetcar in Atlanta, for example, the passenger would see over each door a sign reading

White People Will Seat From Front of Car Toward
the Back and Colored People from Rear Toward Front

With some exceptions, that became the standard arrangement. In Birmingham, blacks sat in the front section, and attempts to reverse the order clashed with custom. "After all," one white resident noted, "it is not important which end of the car is given to the nigger. The main point is that he must sit where he is told."[6]

Variations appeared in the way municipalities chose to define and enforce the restrictions. In the absence of clear demarcations within the car, it might be left to the discretion of the conductor. "Heh, you nigger, get back there," an Atlanta conductor shouted, and the black man, who had taken a seat too far forward, complied with the demand. But in most places, as in New Orleans, screens clearly defined where blacks could sit, and if whites filled their section, the screen could be moved farther to the rear. To listen to black passengers, the restrictions were often enforced arbitrarily, almost always to their discomfort and disadvantage. In responding to the complaint of a black woman, who objected to a white man smoking in a car assigned black passengers, the conductor placed the entire Jim Crow apparatus in its proper context: "The law was made to keep you in your place, not the white people."[7]

The new railway stations in Birmingham, Atlanta, Charleston, and Jacksonville impressed visitors with their spaciousness and impressive architecture. Each station also had its separate entrances, waiting rooms, and ticket offices marked "For White Passengers" and "For Colored Passengers." The rod separating the white section from the black section, unlike the screens in streetcars, as one visitor noted, was neither provisional nor movable "but fixed as the foundations of the building." Throughout the South, segregation was extended to waiting rooms, most often confining blacks to smaller and cramped quarters. In one station, the waiting rooms were designated "White Men," "White Women," "Black Men," and "Black Women," but some of the local whites became alarmed at the limited scope of the term "Black" and authorities substituted "Colored."[8]

Although blacks had previously experienced segregation in various forms, the thoroughness of Jim Crow made it strikingly different. What the white South did was to segregate the races by law and enforced custom in practically every conceivable situation in which whites and blacks might come into social contact: from public transportation to public parks, from the workplace to hospitals, asylums, and orphanages, from the homes for the aged, the blind, deaf, and dumb, to the prisons, from saloons to churches. Not only were the races to be kept apart in hospitals (including a special section for black infants requiring medical attention), but some denied admission to blacks altogether. Laws or custom also required that black and white nurses tend only the sick of their own race. By 1885, most states had already legally mandated separate schools. Where intermarriage and cohabitation had not been outlawed, states quickly moved to place such restrictions in law.

The signs "White Only" and "Colored" (or "Negroes") would henceforth punctuate the southern landscape, appearing over the entrances to parks, theaters, boardinghouses, waiting rooms, toilets, and water fountains. Movie houses were becoming increasingly popular, and Jim Crow demanded not only separate ticket windows and entrances but also separate seating, usually in the balcony—what came to be known as the "buzzard roost" or "nigger heaven." And blacks came to learn that in places where they were permitted to mix with whites—stores, post offices, and banks, for example—they would need to wait until all the whites had been served. Special rules also restricted blacks when shopping in white stores, forbidding women, for example, from trying on dresses, hats, and shoes before purchasing them.[9]

The rapid industrialization of the South introduced another set of problems, increasing racial tensions in places employing both races. Where whites and blacks worked in the same factories, the law would now mandate segregation wherever feasible. The code adopted in South Carolina, for example, prohibited textile factories from permitting black and white laborers to work together in the same room, or to use the same entrances, pay windows, exits, doorways, or stairways at the same time, or the same "lavatories, toilets, drinking water buckets, pails, cups, dippers or glasses" at any time. Under certain conditions, such as an emergency, the code permitted black firemen, floor scrubbers, and repairmen to associate with white laborers.[10]

Separation of the races often meant the total exclusion of black men and women from certain facilities. The expansion of recreation in the late nineteenth century mandated exclusion of blacks from most amusement parks, roller skating rinks, bowling alleys, swimming pools, and tennis courts. It was not uncommon to find a sign at the entrance to a public park reading "Negroes and Dogs Not Allowed." Excluding blacks from parks deprived them not only of a recreational area but of free public entertainment. "Think of it," a black visitor to Atlanta informed a friend in New York, "Negroes not allowed in some of the parks here, to listen to [a] band which plays here on Sundays." Some communities admitted blacks to parks on certain days, designated a portion for their use, or made arrangements for separate parks.[11]

With few exceptions, municipal libraries were reserved for the exclusive use of whites. Between 1900 and 1910, some public libraries extended limited service — that is, blacks were still denied access to the reading room or the privilege of browsing in the stacks, but they might in some instances borrow books for home use. Rather than make any such provisions in the main library, some cities chose to establish separate branches to serve black patrons.[12] But for whites who feared educated blacks, barring them from libraries altogether made eminently good sense. "[T]he libraries in the Southern States are closed to the low down negro eyes . . . because he is not worthy of an education," a Florida white man wrote to a northern critic. "All the mean crimes, that are done are committed by some educated negro. . . ." In one community, the librarian had a ready answer to a question about why blacks could not be permitted to check out books: "[T]he southern people do not believe in 'social equality.' "[13]

Although most business establishments welcomed black customers, there were exceptions and restrictions. Many laundries, for example, posted signs reading "We Wash For White People Only"; in Nashville, a laundry declared on the sides of its delivery wagons and on advertisements in streetcars "No Negro Washing Taken."[14] Where custom had largely governed which if any restaurants blacks could patronize, laws in some states mandated separate accommodations, often a small room with a separate entrance, and many restaurants barred blacks altogether.[15]

In the early twentieth century, the growing availability of automobiles to both races precipitated a variety of measures. While some communities limited the access of black motorists to the public streets, others placed restrictions on where they might park. In much of the South, racial etiquette dictated that black drivers should make no effort to overtake buggies and wagons driven by whites on unpaved roads. Not only could such behavior be construed as "impudence," but also the white passengers might be enveloped by a cloud of dust. "As a rule," Benjamin Mays recalled, "Negroes did not pass white people on either a dusty or a muddy road. . . . I have been with my father when he apologized for passing a white driver by saying, 'Excuse me, Boss, I'm in a hurry.' Did this mean that my father mentally accepted or emotionally approved this cringing behavior? I doubt it. . . . It was a technique of survival."[16]

If the use of roads could be legislated, so could a town's sidewalks, where custom had always dictated that blacks step aside to provide ample room for whites. In Danville, Virginia, after hearing complaints about black children occupying the entire sidewalk on their way to and from school, a new police rule limited their use of those sidewalks when white children were coming or going in the other direction.[17] Of course, whether by law or custom, blacks of any age were expected to step aside when white adults approached.

In the towns and cities, segregated residential patterns were now legally sanctioned, making it difficult for blacks of any class to move into a white block and accelerating the appearance or growth of a distinct district designated as "darktown" or "niggertown." Whether by custom or ordinance, the newer and most rapidly growing cities tended to be the most segregated; by the mid-1890s, for example, racially exclusive sections characterized Atlanta, Richmond, and Montgomery.[18] In some of the older antebellum communities, where house slaves and free blacks had lived near their white employers, black housing tended to be more widely scattered. Some whites thought laws or ordinances restricting where blacks could live were unnecessary, that public sentiment would expeditiously settle the issue. "[T]here is no use to make a law that says one set of men can do this or do that," a resident of Greensboro, North Carolina, argued. "In this white man's town when an African proposed to 'move into' a white section, he was given to understand that it wouldn't do. And if he had moved in he would have moved out a great deal quicker—and a pile of ashes would have marked the house. That is what the White Man will do, law or no law, and that is understood." In a small community south of Clinton, Mississippi, as in Forsyth County, Georgia, public sentiment and night riders imposed their own version of exclusivity by driving out all the black residents.[19]

The legislation of Jim Crow affected all classes and ages, and it tended to be thorough, far-reaching, even imaginative: from separate public school textbooks for black and white children and Jim Crow Bibles on which to swear in black witnesses in court, to separate telephone booths, separate windows in the banks for black and white depositors, and Jim Crow elevators in office buildings, one for whites and one for blacks and freight. New Orleans went so far as to adopt an ordinance segregating black and white prostitutes; Atlanta confined them to separate blocks, while a Nashville brothel settled for a plan by which black prostitutes were placed in the basement and white prostitutes on the ground and upper floors. In Atlanta, the art school that had used black models needed no law to dispense with their employment.[20]

Even as the laws decreed that black babies would enter the world in separate facilities, so blacks would occupy separate places at the end of their lives. The ways in which Jim Crow made its mark on the ritual of death could assume bizarre dimensions. Will Mathis, a convicted white felon, appealed to a judge that he be hanged at a different hour than Orlando

Lester, a black man, and from a different set of gallows. The same plea was made by a white Tennessean convicted of the brutal murder of his wife. After he objected to going to the gallows with three black men, the authorities agreed to hang them first.[21] Custom, if not ordinances, dictated that blacks and whites be buried in separate cemeteries. "If a colored person was to be buried among the whites," one observer noted sarcastically in Alabama, "the latter would all rise from their graves in indignation. How they tolerate the 'niggers' in heaven is a mystery, unless the mansions there are provided with kitchens and stables." On the edge of Little Rock, Arkansas, in still another unique expression of white supremacy, a section of the cemetery once reserved for blacks was converted into an exclusively white cemetery. "There are a lot of colored folks buried there and white folks on top of them," a black resident observed. "They didn't move the colored because there wasn't nobody to pay for moving. They just buried the whites on top of them."[22]

Enforcement of the Jim Crow laws could be as harsh and vigorous as the spirit and rhetoric that had demanded them. Had these laws not been adopted, an English visitor thought, "the South would have been a nation of saints, not of men. It is in the methods of its enforcement that they sometimes show themselves not only human but inhuman." The often savage beatings and expulsions on railroads and streetcars attested not only to white determination to enforce the law but also to black resistance to its implementation. Calling the Jim Crow car an "unmixed blessing," a Richmond newspaper noted that those "ill-advised" blacks who had protested it "only accentuated its need and its usefulness." Law and custom interacted to keep blacks in their place, and it would be the responsibility of blacks to learn how to adapt to these conditions as a way of life. That required a knowledge not only of local customs and laws but also of the way these might differ from place to place. "Every town had its own mores, its own unwritten restrictions," a black educator recalled. "The trick was to find out from local [black] people what the 'rules' were."[23]

Perhaps the most revealing aspects of Jim Crow were the exceptions made for black domestic workers. If a black servant, for example, accompanied a white child into a railroad coach or into a park reserved for whites, that was perfectly acceptable, since the association did not imply an equal relationship. "Everything was all right," a Georgia house servant revealed, "so long as I was in the white man's part of the street car or in the white man's coach as a servant—a slave—but as soon as I did not present myself as a menial, and the relationship of master and servant was abolished by my not having the white children with me, I would be forthwith assigned to the 'nigger' seats or the 'colored people's coach.' " The same exception applied to black servants overseeing white children in public parks that barred blacks. Some of the parks bore signs reading "No Negroes Allowed on These Grounds Except as Servants." A black teacher ventured into a restricted park in Charleston in the company of a white friend and fellow teacher and precipitated no objections. "Of course," she noted, "every one thought I was her maid."[24]

Whether in the exceptions made for black employees or in the quality of the facilities afforded blacks, the position of superior and inferior had to be absolutely clear. "The black nurse with a white baby in her arms, the black valet looking after the comfort of a white invalid," an Episcopal minister in Napoleonville, Louisiana, explained, "have the label of their inferiority conspicuously upon them; they understand themselves, and everybody understands them, to be servants, enjoying certain privileges for the sake of the person served. Almost anything the Negro may do in the South, and anywhere he may go, provided the manner of his doing and his going is that of an inferior. Such is the premium put upon his inferiority; such his inducement to maintain it."[25] On this basis, the poorest illiterate white could claim a standing in society denied to the wealthiest and most intelligent and educated black.

Notes

1. Howard N. Rabinowitz, "From Exclusion to Segregation: Southern Race Relations, 1865–1890," *Journal of American History*, 63 (Sept. 1976), 325–50, and *Race Relations in the Urban South, 1865–1890* (New York, 1978), 197.

2. Sam Gadsden, *An Oral History of Edisto Island: Sam Gadsden Tells the Story* (Goshen, Ind., 1974), 46.

3. Ray Stannard Baker, *Following the Colour Line: An Account of Negro Citizenship in the American Democracy* (New York, 1908), 30; Edward L. Ayers, *The Promise of the New South: Life After Reconstruction* (New York, 1992), 139; William Archer, *Through Afro-America: An English Reading of the Race Problem* (London, 1910), 70–71.

4. Linda Matthews, "Keeping Down Jim Crow: The Railroads and the Separate Coach Bills in South Carolina," *South Atlantic Quarterly*, 73:1 (1974), 127–28.

5. *New York Times*, Nov. 6, 1902.

6. Baker, *Following the Colour Line*, 31; Julian Street, *American Adventures* (New York, 1917), 422.

7. Baker, *Following the Colour Line*, 31; *Southwestern Christian Advocate*, Sept. 29, 1904. On "separate but equal" facilities on trains and streetcars, see also *Southwest Christian Advocate*, Nov. 6, 1902, Mar. 26, 1903, June 8, 1905; Archer, *Through Afro-America*, 93, 176; Baker, *Following the Colour Line*, 30–34; Dr. Sudhindra Bose, *Fifteen Years in America* (Calcutta, 1920), 358; W. L. George, *Hail Columbia! Random Impressions of a Conservative English Radical* (New York, 1921), 185.

8. Archer, *Through Afro-America*, 127; *Southwestern Christian Advocate*, June 22, 1905, April 20, 1899.

9. Bertram Doyle, *The Etiquette of Race Relations in the South: A Study in Social Control* (Chicago, 1937), 147; Richard R. Wright, Jr., *87 Years Behind the Black Cur-*

tain: An Autobiography (Philadelphia, 1965), 71; Ruth Hill, ed., *Black Women Oral History Project,* 10 vols. (Westport, Conn., 1991), X, 23.

10. C. Vann Woodward, *The Strange Career of Jim Crow,* 3d rev. ed. (New York, 1974), 98.

11. Doyle, *Etiquette of Race Relations,* 147; Rabinowitz, *Race Relations in the Urban South,* 189–90; *Crisis,* I (March 1911), 28, II (June 1911), 77; W. Owens King, Atlanta, Ga., to John E. Bruce, Aug. 26, 1891, John E. Bruce Papers, Schomburg Center for Research in Black Culture of the New York Public Library. The black visitor to Atlanta was an entertainer from the North on tour in the South.

12. Eliza A. Gleason, *The Southern Negro and the Public Library* (Chicago, 1941), 19–24; Archer, *Through Afro-America,* 40–41; Rabinowitz, *Race Relations in the Urban South,* 239.

13. Sm. Cowart, Newberry, Fla., to Oswald Villard, April 1, 1911, repr. *Crisis,* II (May 1911), 32; Lillie B. Chace Wyman, "A Southern Study," *New England Magazine,* IV (June 1891), 524.

14. Archer, *Through Afro-America,* 127; *Southwestern Christian Advocate,* April 14, 1898.

15. James A. Atkins, *The Age of Jim Crow* (New York, 1964), 95–96; *Crisis,* I (Nov. 1910), 8, (April 1911), 6.

16. Benjamin F. Mays, *Born to Rebel: An Autobiography* (New York, 1971), 26. On the etiquette associated with automobiles see also Neil R. McMillen, *Dark Journey: Black Mississippians in the Age of Jim Crow* (Urbana, 1989), 11.

17. *Chicago Defender,* March 6, 1915.

18. Ayers, *The Promise of the New South,* 67–68. See also *Crisis,* I (Nov. 1910), 6, 7, 11, (Dec. 1910), 9, (Jan. 1911), 12, (April 1911), 8–9, II (May 1911), 5 (Aug. 1911), 140; III (Nov. 1911), 27–30.

19. McMillen, *Dark Journey,* 12–13; *Norfolk Journal & Guide,* March 27, 1915, Hunter Scrapbooks, Box 13 (1871–1928), Charles N. Hunter Papers, Duke University Library; Thomas Bailey, *Race Orthodoxy in the South* (New York, 1914), 79; Donald L. Grant, *The Way It Was in the South: The Black Experience in Georgia* (New York, 1993), 170.

20. Woodward, *Strange Career of Jim Crow,* 86–87; *Southwestern Christian Advocate,* April 2, 1903; Rabinowitz, *Race Relations in the Urban South,* 189; Baker, *Following the Colour Line,* 36.

21. *Birmingham Age-Herald,* January 16, 1902, quoted in Sheldon Hackney, *Populism to Progressivism in Alabama* (Princeton, 1969), 182; *New York Star,* Jan. 7, 1890, quoted in W. Laird Clowes, *Black America: A Study of the Ex-Slave and His Late Master* (London, 1891), 96.

22. Clifton Johnson, *Highways and Byways of the South* (New York, 1904), 90; George P. Rawick, ed., *The American Slave: A Composite Autobiography,* Suppl., Ser. 2, 9 vols. (Westport, Conn., 1979), I: (Ala. Narr.), 91–92.

23. Archer, *Through Afro-America,* 72; *Richmond Leader,* quoted in *Crisis,* I (March 1911), 13; Ayers, *Promise of the New South,* 17; McMillen, *Dark Journey,* 12.

24. "More Slavery at the South" and "The Negro Problem," *The Independent,* LXXII (Jan. 25, 1912), 198–99 and LIV (Sep. 18, 1902), 2221; *Crisis,* I (Nov. 1910), 14.

25. Quincy Ewing, "The Heart of the Race Problem," *Atlantic Monthly,* 103 (March 1909), quoted in Charles E. Wynes, ed., *Forgotten Voices: Dissenting Southerners in an Age of Conformity* (Baton Rouge, La., 1967), p. 132.

Making Connections

The questions that precede each selection in this volume are intended to help students deal with that particular piece of writing. But all the selections here are in dialogue with one another around one large problem: that of dating segregation's beginnings and its subsequent implications for the history of American race relations. As the selections show, there are many possible solutions. They may be mutually exclusive, or they may complement one another. Certainly, these selections make much more sense if each is read as part of a discussion rather than as a stand-alone work. The questions that follow should help students realize that the discussion is not finished; everyone is free to join in.

1. Using the history of segregation as an example, which model—continuity or discontinuity—do you find more persuasive for explaining the history of race relations in the South?

2. Given America's two-hundred-year-long history of slavery, was segregation inevitable following the Civil War?

3. Woodward, an outspoken critic of segregation and a contributor to the NAACP's legal brief in *Brown v. Board of Education* (1954), published *Strange Career* the following year. As a result he has been criticized for "presentism"—that is, writing history with a purpose and creating a usable past. Is this a legitimate charge? Can—should—historians distance themselves from their social or political biases and agendas?

4. In framing the debate over segregation, why do you think that Woodward ignored Rabinowitz's favorite "forgotten alternative"—exclusion?

5. How, specifically, did Woodward define segregation? How have his critics defined it?

6. In determining degrees of physical or spatial separation, is it important to differentiate between racial etiquette (de facto segregation) and racial law (de jure segregation)? Or should all forms of segregation be considered of equal significance? Do they have equal force?

7. Do laws simplify or codify customary practice or compel social change?

8. Why has gender only recently entered into discussions of the origins of segregation?

9. Can separate facilities or accommodations be equal?

10. Why would any minority group consciously segregate itself?

11. Are racial distinctions always discriminatory?

12. Does white supremacy necessarily translate into segregation?

13. Given the relatively small percentage of African Americans (17.4 percent in the South Atlantic states in 1890) who lived in southern cities after the Civil War, can we apply urban patterns of racial separation to the entire South?

14. Which would you have found preferable: exclusion or segregation?

15. How did African Americans survive segregation?

16. To what extent was the triumph of Jim Crow a product of national, not necessarily sectional, forces?

17. Which force — class, gender, or race — do you consider to be the most powerful in leading to the implementation of de jure segregation?

18. Based on these readings, when would you date the origin of segregation in the American South?

Suggestions for Further Reading

This volume is not intended to provide a massive bibliography on the origins of segregation, but any interested student will want to delve into the subject more deeply. For a selection drawn from a book, the best way to start is to go to that book and place the selection within the author's larger argument. Each selection is produced with annotations in order to allow interested students to go to the author's original sources, study them, and compare their own readings with what the author has made of the same material. The following bibliographical essay does not repeat references to works cited in the Introduction.

Because of its complexity, the literature on the history of slavery, emancipation, and segregation is immense. Fortunately there are several reference tools to guide students. For bibliographical information on varied aspects of nineteenth-century race relations, see Charles B. Dew, "Critical Essay on Recent Works," in C. Vann Woodward, *Origins of the New South, 1877–1913* (1951; Baton Rouge: Louisiana State University Press, 1971), 517–628; John David Smith, comp., *Black Slavery in the Americas: An Interdisciplinary Bibliography, 1865–1980,* 2 vols. (Westport, Conn.: Greenwood Press, 1982); Joseph C. Miller, comp., *Slavery and Slaving in World History: A Bibliography,* 2 vols. (Armonk, N.Y.: M. E. Sharpe, 1999); and David A. Lincove, comp., *Reconstruction in the United States: An Annotated Bibliography* (Westport, Conn.: Greenwood Press, 2000).

Readers will find many useful articles relating to the transition from slavery to freedom to segregation in Randall M. Miller and John David Smith, eds., *Dictionary of Afro-American Slavery* (1988; Westport, Conn.: Praeger, 1997); Junius P. Rodriguez, ed., *The Historical Encyclopedia of World Slavery,* 2 vols. (Santa Barbara, Calif.: ABC-CLIO, 1997); Paul Finkelman and Joseph C. Miller, eds., *Macmillan Encyclopedia of World Slavery,* 2 vols. (New York: Macmillan Reference, 1998); and Seymour Drescher and Stanley L. Engerman, eds., *A Historical Guide to World Slavery* (New York: Oxford University Press, 1998). Other reference works with useful articles pertaining to the origins of segregation include David C. Roller and Robert W. Twyman, eds., *The Encyclopedia of Southern History* (Baton Rouge: Louisiana State

University Press, 1979); Charles Reagan Wilson and William Ferris, eds., *Encyclopedia of Southern Culture* (Chapel Hill: University of North Carolina Press, 1989); Hans L. Trefousse, ed., *Historical Dictionary of Reconstruction* (Westport, Conn.: Greenwood Press, 1991); Charles D. Lowery and John F. Marszalek, eds., *Encyclopedia of African-American Civil Rights: From Emancipation to the Present* (Westport, Conn.: Greenwood Press, 1992); and Arvarh E. Strickland and Robert E. Weems, Jr., eds., *The African American Experience: An Historiographical and Bibliographical Guide* (Westport, Conn.: Greenwood Press, 2001).

To sort out the historiographical debates over segregation's origins, students should consult the essays in Arthur S. Link and Rembert W. Patrick, eds., *Writing Southern History: Essays in Historiography in Honor of Fletcher M. Green* (Baton Rouge: Louisiana State University Press, 1965); Joel Williamson, ed., *The Origins of Segregation* (Boston: D. C. Heath, 1968); Peter J. Parish, ed., *Reader's Guide to American History* (London: Fitzroy Dearborn, 1997); and Claire Bond Potter, "The Problem of the Color Line: Segregation, Politics, and Historical Writing," *Cultural Critique*, 38 (Winter 1997–1998): 65–89. On C. Vann Woodward as historian, see John Herbert Roper, ed., *C. Vann Woodward: A Southern Historian and His Critics* (Athens: University of Georgia Press, 1997). On Howard N. Rabinowitz as historian, see Daniel Feller, comp., *Remembering Howard Rabinowitz* (Albuquerque: Department of History, University of New Mexico, 2000). On the ongoing debate over the significance of *The Strange Career of Jim Crow* following Woodward's death in 1999, see letters by Norman F. Cantor, David Bell, John Braeman, Peter Gay, and J. R. Pole, in the London *Times Literary Supplement*, May 12, 2000, p. 17; June 2, 2000, p. 17; June 9, 2000, p. 17; June 30, 2000, p. 17; and July 28, 2000, p. 15. For a review essay on current scholarship and "the recrudescence of the Woodwardian attention to 'forgotten alternatives,'" see Michael O'Brien, "Jim Crow was there," London *Times Literary Supplement*, May 25, 2001, pp. 13–14.

For background on slavery and racism as ideas, the essential starting place is Winthrop D. Jordan, *White over Black: American Attitudes Toward the Negro, 1550–1812* (Chapel Hill: University of North Carolina Press, 1968), followed by George Fredrickson, *The Black Image in the White Mind: The Debate on Afro-American Character and Destiny, 1817–1914* (New York: Harper & Row, 1971), and *White Supremacy: A Comparative Study in American & South African History* (New York: Oxford University Press, 1981); Barbara J. Fields, "Ideology and Race in American History," in J. Morgan Kousser and James M. McPherson, eds., *Region, Race, and Reconstruction: Essays in Honor of C. Vann Woodward* (New York: Oxford University Press, 1982), 143–78; and Mia Bay, *The White Image in the Black Mind: African-American Ideas about White People, 1830–1925* (New York: Oxford University Press, 2000).

Despite Ulrich Bonnell Phillips's racial and class bias, to understand slavery as a system of social and economic control, students still should consult his *American Negro Slavery: A Survey of the Supply, Employment and Control of Negro Labor as Determined by the Plantation Régime* (1918; reprint, Baton Rouge: Louisiana State University Press, 1966), and Phillips's essays in Eugene D. Genovese, ed., *The Slave Economy of the Old South* (Baton Rouge: Louisiana State University Press, 1968). Up-to-date, revisionist studies that emphasize the slaves' agency and resistance include John B. Boles, *Black Southerners, 1619–1869* (Lexington: University Press of Kentucky, 1983) and Peter Kolchin, *American Slavery, 1619–1877* (New York: Hill and Wang, 1993). The best treatment of free blacks in the Old South remains Ira Berlin's *Slaves without Masters: The Free Negro in the Antebellum South* (New York: Pantheon, 1974). On the lives of free blacks in the Old North, see James Oliver Horton and Lois E. Horton, *In Hope of Liberty: Culture, Community and Protest Among Northern Free Blacks, 1700–1860* (New York: Oxford University Press, 1997). On Jim Crow in antebellum Massachusetts, see Louis Ruchames, "Jim Crow Railroads in Massachusetts," *American Quarterly*, 8 (Spring 1956): 61–75.

The Freedmen and Southern Society Project has edited several volumes (all published by Cambridge University Press) that document the history of emancipation in the Civil War era. These include Ira Berlin and Leslie S. Rowland, eds., *The Black Military Experience* (1982); *The Destruction of Slavery* (1985); *The Wartime Genesis of Free Labor: The Lower South* (1990); and *The Wartime Genesis of Free Labor: The Upper South* (1993). Other works that explain the ambiguous meaning of freedom in the post–Civil War decades include David G. Sansing, ed., *What Was Freedom's Price?* (Jackson: University Press of Mississippi, 1978); Richard H. King, *Civil Rights and the Idea of Freedom* (New York: Oxford University Press, 1992); Michael Vorenberg, "Final Freedom: The Civil War, the End of Slavery, and the Thirteenth Amendment" (Ph.D. diss., Harvard University, 1995); Eric Foner, *The Story of American Freedom* (New York: W. W. Norton, 1998); Cecilia Elizabeth O'Leary, *To Die For: The Paradox of American Patriotism* (Princeton, N.J.: Princeton University Press, 1999); and David W. Blight, *Race and Reunion: The Civil War in American Memory* (Cambridge, Mass.: Harvard University Press, 2001).

Essential detailed surveys on the history of segregation include Charles S. Johnson, *Patterns of Negro Segregation* (New York: Harper & Brothers, 1943); Phineas Indritz, "Post Civil War Ordinances Prohibiting Racial Discrimination in the District of Columbia," *Georgetown Law Journal*, 42 (January 1954): 179–209; "A Note on the History of School Segregation," *Journal of Public Law*, 3 (Spring 1954): 167–70; Alfred H. Kelly, "The Fourteenth Amendment: The Segregation Question," *Michigan Law Review*, 54

(June 1956): 1049–86, and "The Congressional Controversy over School Segregation, 1867–1875," *American Historical Review*, 64 (April 1959): 537–63; John Hope Franklin, "History of Racial Segregation in the United States," *Annals of the American Academy of Political and Social Science*, 304 (March 1956): 1–9, and "Jim Crow Goes to School: The Genesis of Legal Segregation in Southern Schools," *South Atlantic Quarterly*, 58 (Spring 1959): 225–35; Louis R. Harlan, "Desegregation in New Orleans Public Schools During Reconstruction," *American Historical Review*, 67 (April 1962): 663–75; C. Vann Woodward, "The Birth of Jim Crow," *American Heritage*, 15 (April 1964): 52–55, 100–103; Roger A. Fischer, "Segregation," in Miller and Smith, eds., *The Dictionary of Afro-American Slavery*, 659–61; and Keith Weldon Medley, "The Sad Story of How 'Separate but Equal' Was Born," *Smithsonian*, 24 (February 1994): 104–17.

For the late nineteenth-century southern and national contexts, students should start with Woodward's still invaluable *Origins of the New South, 1877–1913* (1951) and also study Louis R. Harlan, *Separate and Unequal: Public School Campaigns and Racism in the Southern Seaboard States, 1901–1915* (Chapel Hill: University of North Carolina Press, 1958); Vincent P. De Santis, *Republicans Face the Southern Question — The New Departure Years, 1877–1897* (Baltimore: Johns Hopkins University Press, 1959); Stanley P. Hirshson, *Farewell to the Bloody Shirt: Northern Republicans & the Southern Negro, 1877–1893* (Bloomington: Indiana University Press, 1962); August Meier, *Negro Thought in America, 1880–1915: Racial Ideologies in the Age of Booker T. Washington* (Ann Arbor: University of Michigan Press, 1963); George B. Tindall, *The Emergence of the New South, 1912–1945* (Baton Rouge: Louisiana State University Press, 1967); Orville Vernon Burton and Robert C. McMath, Jr., eds., *Toward a New South: Studies in Post–Civil War Southern Communities* (Westport, Conn.: Greenwood Press, 1982); Dewey W. Grantham, *Southern Progressivism: The Reconciliation of Progress and Tradition* (Knoxville: University of Tennessee Press, 1983); William A. Link, *The Paradox of Southern Progressivism, 1880–1930* (Chapel Hill: University of North Carolina Press, 1992); Richard H. King and Helen Taylor, eds., *Dixie Debates: Perspectives on Southern Cultures* (London: Pluto Press, 1996); and Michael Perman, *Struggle for Mastery: Disfranchisement in the South, 1888–1908* (Chapel Hill: University of North Carolina Press, 2001). William S. McFeely compares the "First" and "Second" Reconstructions in "Two Reconstructions, Two Nations," *Massachusetts Review*, 32 (Spring 1991): 39–55.

Several works position segregationist ideas within broader patterns of anti-Negro thought and notions of white supremacy. See Idus A. Newby, *Jim Crow's Defense: Anti-Negro Thought in America, 1900–1930* (Baton Rouge: Louisiana State University Press, 1965); Lawrence J. Friedman, *The White*

Savage: Racial Fantasies in the Postbellum South (Englewood Cliffs, N.J.: Prentice-Hall, 1970); Bruce Clayton, *The Savage Ideal: Intolerance and Intellectual Leadership in the South, 1890–1914* (Baltimore: Johns Hopkins University Press, 1972); William L. Van Deburg, *Slavery & Race in American Popular Culture* (Madison: University of Wisconsin Press, 1984); John David Smith, *An Old Creed for the New South: Proslavery Ideology and Historiography, 1865–1918* (1985; reprint, Athens: University of Georgia Press, 1991); John H. Stanfield, *Philanthropy and Jim Crow in American Social Science* (Westport, Conn.: Greenwood Press, 1985); Ralph E. Luker, *The Social Gospel in Black & White: American Racial Reform, 1885–1912* (Chapel Hill: University of North Carolina Press, 1991); Lee D. Baker, *From Savage to Negro: Anthropology and the Construction of Race, 1896–1954* (Berkeley: University of California Press, 1998); and Stephen Kantrowitz, *Ben Tillman & the Reconstruction of White Supremacy* (Chapel Hill: University of North Carolina Press, 2000).

Students interested in the history of segregation in the twentieth century should consult Idus A. Newby, *Challenge to the Court: Social Scientists and the Defense of Segregation, 1954–1966* (Baton Rouge: Louisiana State University Press, 1967); Robert Haws, ed., *The Age of Segregation: Race Relations in the South, 1890–1945* (Jackson: University Press of Mississippi, 1978); Pete Daniel, *Standing at the Crossroads: Southern Life in the Twentieth Century* (New York: Hill and Wang, 1986), and *Lost Revolutions: The South in the 1950s* (Chapel Hill: University of North Carolina Press, 2000); Bruce Clayton and John A. Salmond, eds., *The South Is Another Land: Essays on the Twentieth-Century South* (Westport, Conn.: Greenwood Press, 1987); Dewey W. Grantham, *The Life and Death of the Solid South: A Political History* (Lexington: University Press of Kentucky, 1988); Numan V. Bartley, *The New South, 1945–1980* (Baton Rouge: Louisiana State University Press, 1995); Bruce Clayton and John A. Salmond, eds., *Debating Southern History: Ideas and Action in the Twentieth Century* (Lantham, Md.: Rowan & Littlefield, 1999); and Jane Dailey, Glenda Elizabeth Gilmore, and Bryant Simon, eds., *Jumpin' Jim Crow: Southern Politics from Civil War to Civil Rights* (Princeton, N.J.: Princeton University Press, 2000).

Scholars have contributed many specialized studies on the origins of segregation. On minstrelsy and Jim Crow, see Robert C. Toll, *Blacking Up: The Minstrel Show in Nineteenth-Century America* (New York: Oxford University Press, 1974), and Eric Lott, *Love and Theft: Blackface Minstrelsy and the American Working Class* (New York: Oxford University Press, 1993). On social issues and customary segregation, see Bertram Wilbur Doyle, *The Etiquette of Race Relations: A Study in Social Control* (1937; reprint, New York: Schocken Books, 1971). For legal issues, see Gilbert Thomas Stephenson, *Race Distinctions in American Law* (New York: D. Appleton and Company, 1910); Franklin Johnson, *The Development of State Legislation Concerning the*

Free Negro (New York: Arbor Press, 1919); Bruce Beezer, "North Carolina's Rationale for Mandating Separate Schools: A Legal History," *Journal of Negro Education*, 52 (Summer 1983): 213–26; Stephen J. Riegel, "The Persistent Career of Jim Crow: Lower Federal Courts and the 'Separate But Equal' Doctrine," *American Journal of Legal History*, 28 (January 1984): 17–40; Herbert Hovenkamp, "Social Science and Segregation Before *Brown*," *Duke Law Journal*, 1985 (June–September 1985): 624–72; and John Braeman, *Before the Civil Rights Revolution: The Old Court and Individual Rights* (Westport, Conn.: Greenwood Press, 1988). On Justice John Marshall Harlan's opinion on the *Civil Rights Cases* and *Plessy v. Ferguson*, see Linda Przybyszewski, *The Republic According to John Marshall Harlan* (Chapel Hill: University of North Carolina Press, 1999). On the role of Albion W. Tourgée in the *Plessy* case, see Mark Elliott, "Race, Color Blindness, and the Democratic Public: Albion W. Tourgée's Radical Principles in *Plessy v. Ferguson*," *Journal of Southern History*, 67 (May 2001): 287–330. On Jim Crow in the broader context of space and modern state formation, see Barbara Y. Welke, "Beyond *Plessy:* Space, Status, and Race in the Era of Jim Crow," *Utah Law Review*, 2000 (2000): 267–99.

Recent state and local studies on segregation include Barry D. Crouch and L. J. Schultz, "Crisis of Color: Racial Separation in Texas during Reconstruction," *Civil War History*, 16 (March 1970): 37–49; Herbert A. Thomas, Jr., "Victims of Circumstance: Negroes in a Southern Town, 1865–1880," *Register of the Kentucky Historical Society*, 71 (July 1973): 253–71; John Kellog, "The Formation of Black Residential Areas in Lexington, Kentucky, 1865–1887," *Journal of American History*, 48 (February 1982): 21–52; Wali Rashash Kharif, "The Refinement of Racial Segregation in Florida after the Civil War" (Ph.D. diss., University of Florida, 1983); James M. Smallwood, "The Woodward Thesis Revisited: Race Relations and the Development of Social Segregation in Reconstruction Texas, A Brief Essay," *Negro History Bulletin*, 47 (July–December 1984): 6–9; Ira C. Colby, "The Freedmen's Bureau: From Social Welfare to Segregation," *Phylon*, 46 (September 1985): 219–30; John R. Wennersten, "A Cycle of Race Relations on Maryland's Eastern Shore: Somerset County, 1850–1917," *Maryland Historical Magazine*, 80 (Winter 1985): 377–82; Jennifer Roback, "The Political Economy of Segregation: The Case of Segregated Streetcars," *Journal of Economic History*, 46 (December 1986): 893–917; John William Graves, "Jim Crow in Arkansas: A Reconsideration of Urban Race Relations in the Post-Reconstruction South," *Journal of Southern History*, 55 (August 1989): 421–48; Thomas C. Battle, "Behind the Marble Mask," *Wilson Quarterly*, 13 (New Year's 1989): 84–88; Jean Preer, " 'Just and Equitable Division': Jim Crow and the 1890 Land-Grant College Act," *Prologue*, 22 (Winter 1990): 323–37; Gregg D. Kimball, "The Working People of Richmond: Life and Labor in an Industrial City, 1865–1920," *Labor's Heritage*, 3 (April 1991): 42–65; Nupur Chaudhuri, " 'We All Seem Like Brothers and Sisters': The African-American Community in Manhattan, Kansas, 1865– 1940," *Kansas History*, 14 (Winter 1991): 270–88; Lawrence L. Hartzell, "The Exploration of Freedom in Black Petersburg, Virginia, 1865–1902," in Edward L. Ayers and John C. Willis, eds., *The Edge of the South: Life in Nineteenth-Century Virginia* (Charlottesville: University Press of Virginia, 1991), 134–56; Glenn T. Eskew, "Black Elitism and the Failure of Paternalism in Postbellum Georgia," in John C. Inscoe, ed., *Georgia in Black and White: Explorations in the Race Relations of a Southern State, 1865–1950* (Athens: University of Georgia Press, 1991), 141–72; Nan Elizabeth Woodruff, "African-American Struggles for Citizenship in the Arkansas and Mississippi Delta in the Age of Jim Crow," *Radical History Review*, 55 (1993): 33–51; Randal M. Jelks, "Making Opportunity: The Struggle Against Jim Crow in Grand Rapids, Michigan, 1890–1927," *Michigan Historical Review*, 19 (Fall 1993): 23–48; David Wright and David Zoby, "Ignoring Jim Crow: The Turbulent Appointment of Richard Etheridge and the Pea Island Lifesavers," *Journal of Negro History*, 80 (Spring 1995): 66–80; William D. Green, "Race and Segregation in St. Paul's Public Schools, 1846–69," *Minnesota History*, 55 (Winter 1996–1997): 138–49; Thomas H. Cox, "From Centerpiece to Center Stage: Kelly Ingram Park, Segregation, and Civil Rights in Birmingham, Alabama," *Southern Historian*, 18 (1997): 5–28; and Adam Fairclough, " 'Being in the Field of Education and Also Being a Negro . . . Seems . . . Tragic': Black Teachers in the Jim Crow South," *Journal of American History*, 87 (June 2000): 65–91.

For a comparative study of the rise of segregation in four southern cities, see Don H. Doyle, *New Men, New Cities, New South: Atlanta, Nashville, Charleston, Mobile, 1860–1910* (Chapel Hill: University of North Carolina Press, 1992). W. Fitzhugh Brundage examines the concomitant rise of racial violence, white supremacy, and segregation in *Lynching in the New South: Georgia and Virginia, 1880–1930* (Urbana: University of Illinois Press, 1993), and ed., *Under Sentence of Death: Lynching in the South* (Chapel Hill: University of North Carolina Press, 1997). On lynching, see James Allen, Hilton Als, John Lewis, and Leon F. Litwack, *Without Sanctuary: Lynching Photography in America* (Santa Fe, N.M.: Twin Palms, 2000).

Several monographs chronicle the relationship between Jim Crow–era racial violence and race riots. See Elliott Rudwick, *Race Riot at East St. Louis, July 2, 1917* (Carbondale: Southern Illinois University Press, 1964); William M. Tuttle, Jr., *Race Riot: Chicago in the Red Summer of 1919* (New York: Atheneum, 1970); John D. Weaver, *The Brownsville Raid* (New York: W. W. Norton, 1973); Robert V. Haynes, *A Night of Violence: The Houston Riot of 1917* (Baton Rouge: Louisiana State University Press, 1976); William

Ivy Hair, *Carnival of Fury: Robert Charles and the New Orleans Race Riot of 1900* (Baton Rouge: Louisiana State University Press, 1976); Scott Ellsworth, *Death in a Promised Land: The Tulsa Race Riot of 1921* (Baton Rouge: Louisiana State University Press, 1982); H. Leon Prather, *We Have Taken a City: Wilmington Racial Massacre and Coup of 1898* (Rutherford, N.J.: Fairleigh Dickinson University Press, 1984); Richard C. Cortner, *A Mob Intent on Death: The NAACP and the Arkansas Riot Cases* (Middletown, Conn.: Wesleyan University Press, 1988); Stewart E. Tolnay and E. M. Beck, *A Festival of Violence: An Analysis of Southern Lynchings, 1882–1930* (Urbana: University of Illinois Press, 1995); and James G. Hollandsworth, Jr., *An Absolute Massacre: The New Orleans Race Riot of July 30, 1866* (Baton Rouge: Louisiana State University Press, 2001). The overthrow of biracial democracy and the triumph of Jim Crow in Wilmington, North Carolina, is analyzed in David S. Cecelski and Timothy B. Tyson, eds., *Democracy Betrayed: The Wilmington Race Riot of 1898 and Its Legacy* (Chapel Hill: University of North Carolina Press, 1998); Melton A. McLaurin, "Commemorating Wilmington's Racial Violence in 1898: From Individual to Collective Memory," *Southern Cultures,* 6 (Winter 2000): 35–57; and Walter Hölbling and Justine Tally, "The 1898 Wilmington Massacre in History and Literature: An Essay on the Discourse of Power," in Fritz Gysin and Christopher Mulvey, eds., *Black Liberation in the Americas* (Münster: Lit Verlag, 2001), 71–93.

On the intersection of race and gender, see Mary Frances Berry, "Judging Morality: Sexual Behavior and Legal Consequences in the Late Nineteenth-Century South," *Journal of American History,* 78 (December 1991): 835–56; Robin D. G. Kelley, " 'We Are Not What We Seem': Rethinking Black Working-Class Opposition in the Jim Crow South," *Journal of American History,* 80 (June 1993): 75–112; Jane Dailey, "Deference and Violence in the Postbellum Urban South: Manners and Massacres in Danville, Virginia," *Journal of Southern History,* 63 (August 1997): 553–90; Tera W. Hunter, *To 'Joy My Freedom: Southern Black Women's Lives and Labors after the Civil War* (Cambridge, Mass.: Harvard University Press, 1997); Karin L. Zipf, " 'The Whites shall rule the land or die': Gender, Race, and Class in North Carolina Reconstruction Politics," *Journal of Southern History,* 65 (August 1999): 499–534; Joan Marie Johnson, " 'Drill into us . . . the Rebel tradition': The Contest over Southern Identity in Black and White Women's Clubs, South Carolina, 1898–1930," *Journal of Southern History,* 66 (August 2000): 525–62; and Laura F. Edwards, *Scarlett Doesn't Live Here Anymore: Southern Women in the Civil War Era* (Urbana: University of Illinois Press, 2000).

Students will want to consult several edited collections of primary sources that document segregation from the perspective of various participants. In *The Development of Segregationist Thought* (Homewood, Ill.: Dorsey

Press, 1968), Idus A. Newby presents the writings of various segregationists and white supremacists. Otto H. Olsen's *The Negro Question: From Slavery to Caste, 1863–1910* (New York: Pitman Publishing, 1971) reprints the opinions of blacks and mostly white racial moderates. *In the Cage: Eyewitness Accounts of the Freed Negro in Southern Society, 1877–1929* (Chicago: Quadrangle Books, 1971), edited by Alton Hornsby, Jr., records the impressions of a broad range of racist and hostile observers. John David Smith's *Anti-Black Thought, 1863–1925: "The Negro Problem,"* 11 vols. (New York: Garland Publishing, 1993), includes texts that represent the full range of white supremacist ideology, including paternalism, colonization, exclusion, and segregation.

In 1908 the reform journalist Ray Stannard Baker compiled one of the most valuable firsthand accounts of life in the age of Jim Crow. His *Following the Color Line: An Account of Negro Citizenship in the American Democracy* (New York: Doubleday, Page) was based both on careful observation and interviews with members of both races. Baker concluded that the race "problem," north and south, stemmed from "lack of understanding and sympathy between man and man." Its solution, he insisted, lay in "a gradual substitution of understanding and sympathy for blind repulsion and hatred" (p. 301). As its long and complex history suggests, the riddle of Jim Crow proved easier to diagnose than to solve.